# *Wind and Wings*: the History of Soaring in San Diego

by

Gary Fogel

To Bob Anderson –
Looking forward to spending more
time with you in the air – perhaps
with some PSI profiles at Torrey.
Gary Fogel

Rock Reef Publishing House
and Gary Fogel

First published in the United States of America, 2000
by Rock Reef Publishing House
4530 Pauling Avenue
San Diego, California, 92122-2722



Second Printing, April 2001.



Library of Congress Cataloging-in-Publication Data

Fogel, Gary, 1968-
Wind and Wings: the History of Soaring in San Diego / by Gary Fogel.
p. cm.
Includes bibliographical references and index.
ISBN 0-9670339-5-0 (hardcover : alk. paper)
1. Gliding and soaring--California--San Diego County--History. I. Title.
TL760.4.U6 F64 2000
797.5'5'0979498--dc21
00-009879

 All quotes in this book remain unedited to reflect their historical accuracy except for minor changes in brackets.

ISBN 0-9670339-5-0

To my father, Larry,

and to the memory of

Richard H. Benbough

# CONTENTS

# Preface

As "Air Capital of the West," San Diego's contribution to American aviation is well documented. San Diego's contribution to American gliding and soaring has, however, generally been overlooked in its importance. This history has never been described completely in one manuscript. San Diego County is filled with historic soaring sites: many of the pilots who trained in San Diego made soaring history locally, nationally...even internationally. In that regard, the book focuses not only on gliding events that occurred in San Diego County, but also on the achievements of San Diegans at other locations in the United States.

At the time of this writing, many of soaring's early pioneers have already passed. With every new year, early American soaring history becomes ever more difficult to record accurately. I have gone to great lengths to personally interview those pilots who made this history possible. Many of them have read and reread portions of this manuscript. Other links to the past were found in books, newspapers, magazines, and photos through libraries and glider associations. Although I am thankful for these links to the past, it was common for newspaper columnists to take liberties with the truth in the quest for a better story. Despite my efforts to the contrary, I am confident this bias remains in various locations in this book. More attention should be directed at recording and preserving the true history of soaring in America before it disappears along with our pioneers.

I began writing this book in 1991 as part of the documentation required for recognizing the Torrey Pines Gliderport as a National Soaring Landmark, a designation that was granted by the National Soaring Museum in 1992. Following this designation, a more extensive historical documentation was required by the City of San Diego to establish Torrey Pines as San Diego City Historical Site #315, a designation that was celebrated in 1993. Since then, the entire Torrey Pines Gliderport has been listed on the State Register of Historic Sites and National Register of Historic Places (the first gliderport to receive such designations). The importance of Torrey Pines to American aviation is established.

Despite this historical value, the "non-soaring" public has little preparation for understanding the rich history associated with Torrey Pines. I hope that this book might help to change this situation. I also hope that the Torrey Pines Gliderport has been adequately preserved for future generations to enjoy and generate their own new history in motorless flight. Similar efforts should be directed towards the preservation of other gliderports in America as we face increasing pressure from urban growth.

I would have enjoyed including more information on the history of gliding in Los Angeles, San Francisco, Hawaii, and other areas in the west, but in an effort to generate the book in a reasonable time, many details on events in these others regions were not included. I apologize for this because so much of what happened in San Diego was tied to events in other areas of the nation. I have made my best effort to be complete, but I am quite confident this book just scratches the surface. I have also focused on events that happened prior to 1950. Further research is required before a detailed account of more recent events can be included. This is not meant to suggest that post-1950 events were in some regard less important than those pre-1950...it is just that I did not have adequate time for the research prior to the publication of this book.

The book would not have been written without the aid and constant support of many individuals. These include: Rick and Alicia Benbough, Ruth Bowlus, Woody Brown, Blair Burkhardt, Bill Buyer, Jeff Byard, Frank Cooper, Dr. Bard C. Cosman, Jackie Daegling, Helen Dick, Mrs. Alan R. Essery, Bob Fronius, Doug Fronius, Albert Gabbs, Marcus Hill, David and Maya Jebb, Howard Jope, Lennart Johnsson, Steve and Henrietta Kesckes, the La Jolla High School Alumni Association, Bob Marshall, Dr. Paul MacCready, Len Moore, Bud Perl, John Pierce, Cliff Robertson, John Robinson, Alcide Santilli, Victor Saudek, Ernie Shattuck, Martin Simons, Apollo and Elisabeth Smith, Lloyd Standley, George Uvegas, Bob, Bill, and Helen Van Dusen, Spencer Wilson, and June Wiberg. Also helpful were: Dr. F. Lewis Orrell, Jr. for assistance with the history of U.S. Army Camp Callan, Frank Allen, Ed Leiser, Dr. Mary Scott, and the staff at the San Diego Aerospace Museum, Jim Frost, Steve Pachura, John Peterson, Ed Slater, and the members of the Associated Glider Clubs of Southern California, Pat Schaelchlin of the La Jolla Historical Society, Alice Bartley of the Escondido Historical Society, Kristi Hawthorne of the Oceanside Historical Society, Gloria Snyder of the Redondo Beach Historical Society, the staff of the microfiche libraries at U.C. Los Angeles and U.C. San Diego, Mark Hirsch and Mark Gatlin at the Smithsonian Institution, Raul Blacksten and the Vintage Sailplane Association, Larry Sanderson of the Soaring Society of America and James Swinnich and William Gallagher at the National Soaring Museum. Some portions of this book are reprinted with permission from the editors of *Sailplane and Electric Modeler*, *Bungee Cord*, *Gull Wings*, *The Towline*, and *Wind and Wings*. I thank the editors for making this material available for reprint. I especially thank Wil Byers and Gregory Vasgerdsian of *Sailplane and Electric Modeler* magazine for giving me the opportunity to hone my writing skills in the pages of their publication. I would like to make it clear that the title of this book was chosen specifically to honor the long tradition of *Wind and Wings*, the newsletter of the Associated Glider Clubs of Southern California.

Special acknowledgment is reserved for Richard Benbough, without whom this book could not have been researched and written, David Sanders for his assistance with the various three-view drawings, Sara Oellers for editorial skills, and Dan Barth for publishing the resulting manuscript. I am indebted to their assistance and dedication to historical preservation. Indeed, I will especially miss Richard Benbough's guidance and friendship. Special thanks go to Vonn-Marie May and State Historical Preservation Officer Maryln Lortie for their invaluable direction. Without their assistance, I doubt that soaring at Torrey Pines would have continued into the 2000s.

I would be remiss if I did not thank my sister-in-law Jacquelyn Fogel for getting me started on a list of possible newspaper articles to search and my brother David for his encouragement to get the job done. My mother, Eva, continues to be the "glue" that keeps everyone headed in the right direction, and I appreciate the Lee family for their interest in learning from history and transferring that knowledge to future generations. Most of all I would like to thank my wife Joanne for her unending patience during all of the late nights that I stayed up typing on the computer. I could not have finished this book without her support as well as through the excellent technical advice of Kumar Chellapilla. And of course, I must thank my father Larry Fogel, for being an inspiration and for showing me my first thermal. Thank you, dad.

A certain distinction between "gliding" and "soaring" exists in the pages of this book. "Gliding" refers to the use of gravity to maintain airspeed while continuously losing altitude in the process. Early attempts at gliding generally started at the top of a hill and ended only a short distance below the point of takeoff. "Soaring" refers to the use of atmospheric conditions suitable for maintaining or even gaining altitude in a motorless aircraft. In the past, "hang gliders" or "primary gliders" were used for gliding, whereas higher performance "secondary gliders" or "sailplanes" were used for soaring. I have chosen to maintain a serious distinction between gliders and sailplanes to emphasize their difference when placed in the proper historical context.

When you read this book, every now and then think of how barren the area around San Diego must have been in the early 1900s, how odd it must have felt to be the first in your city to fly in an aeroplane (especially one without a motor), or how difficult it was to afford a desire for flight during the Great Depression. Only in this light can the history in the pages of this book truly come alive.

A key element of this book is the recognition of individuals who, as Dr. Paul MacCready once suggested, "worked with nature rather than against it"...individuals who found new and innovative ways to extract energy from the atmosphere rather than focus on developing "better," more artificial means to propel themselves through the sky. There are few sports as environmentally friendly as soaring, whether it be with a sailplane, hang glider, paraglider, or radio-controlled model sailplane. Those who have already experienced the thrill of silent flight understand what it means to be a true master of the sky.

*Gary Fogel*
*La Jolla, California*

# *Introduction*

Before you start reading you might assume this book is merely a recitation of soaring events that took place long ago in one local area. However, Gary Fogel has brought the events to life. As you read about aviation pioneers, and flights even before 1900, the characters emerge as real people - and you are there. Gary also illustrates how soaring in this area served as an incubator for talents, technology, and visions that have had important consequences for our present world and will be yielding dividends in our future.

There was a spirit of change, of opportunity, in Southern California at the turn of the century. The locale was perfect for early aviation experimenters. Good weather, hills, open spaces, and regular sea breezes all contributed to making the area ideal for gliding. Teenagers could assemble readily available sticks and cloth into a glider and make short flights. Some moved on to powered flying while others carried gliding to a more advanced stage.

The first of the talented and daring innovators was John Montgomery. The evidence for him flying briefly in *Gull Glider* in 1883 is good but not as definitive as the reports of the early experiments of Lilienthal or the Wright Brothers. Montgomery's position as a true aeronautical pioneer is more firmly established by the wide media coverage of the 1905 flight when his tandem-wing glider was lofted by balloons 4,000 feet above ground, released, and then flown down by pilot Daniel Mahoney. A flight accident killed Mahoney later that year and Montgomery died in 1911 from a crash while testing a new design - among the first of many who subsequently lost their lives as the infant development materialized into safe vehicles and training.

In the 1920s glider records for duration were set by various pilots, then broken, and broken again - attracting wide media interest. Aviation was taking hold; people were hearing about it. Two remarkable young men made 1930 a special year for soaring in San Diego. One was Hawley Bowlus, who for years had demonstrated a passion and skill for developing and flying gliders, and the other was Charles A. Lindbergh. In 1927 he selected Ryan Aircraft in San Diego to create the *Spirit of St. Louis*. Bowlus served as production manager and the two became close friends. In 1930 Bowlus set duration records then lured Charles Lindbergh into soaring at Point Loma and in the lift at Torrey Pines. Soon after, Anne Morrow Lindbergh became the first woman to earn a first-class glider license. Needless to say, the media was enthralled with the record flights and the flights of the Lindberghs, then probably the world's most famous couple.

Charles Lindbergh's first flight was more than just a boost for San Diego soaring: it fired his enthusiasm. He was delighted to find that he could actually talk to people on the ground as he soared low overhead. From other flights in Southern California he found what others keep realizing: the spirit of silent soaring, of the mingling of technology and nature, never leaves you. Hawley Bowlus moved glider building and flying to higher priority when in 1933 he and Richard DuPont became partners in Soaring Ventures. In 1938 the ad with pictures for the kit for his beautiful Bowlus Baby Albatross sailplane was in national magazines. I was a young teenage model airplane builder then and the image lodged deep into my mind and has never left.

Charles Lindbergh, a rather private person, was kept continually on the world stage until well after the end of World War II. On a trip to Africa he escaped the intrusive reporters. There he was able to relax on a hillside watching a soaring bird circling overhead. He found himself wondering what he would choose if the choices were either a world with aircraft but without birds or one with birds with no aircraft. He realized he would choose the latter and he subsequently devoted the last third of his life to the vital mission of seeking a balance between nature and science/technology. After his death the Lindbergh Foundation was created to carry on his dedication to balance. I have had the good fortune to become friends of the legendary founders, including Jimmy Doolittle, Neil Armstrong, Anne Morrow Lindbergh and their daughter Reeve, Charles' best friend, James Newton, and others who shared his vision. We will never know how much Lindbergh's vision and the ensuing Foundation owed to his glider flights in Southern California. I would bet that those soaring experiences greatly expanded his thinking. As a recipient of the 1982 annual Lindbergh Award, and as a director of the Foundation, I am dedicated to search for the balance that he initiated. I know that soaring certainly had a major affect on my perspectives about nature and technology.

I started soaring in 1946. After a little flying at Elmira, New York and Texas, I brought the *Orlik* sailplane to California and in 1948 experienced the beauty of flight at Torrey Pines. In 1948 I participated in the Torrey Pines "competitions" (actually more of a wonderful, warm get-together of soaring enthusiasts than a tough competitive event). After World War II, as many veteran pilots took up soaring and surplus sailplanes augmented the old home-built ones, the Torrey Pines Gliderport became widely used. The annual contest brought in pilots and planes from around the Southwest. The beauty of the site, the regular sea breeze providing lift, the beach below for landing if the breeze failed, the chance to fly while, as Lindbergh found, you could easily communicate with friends on the ground, all made for magical experiences. I participated in 1949 as well as 1948 (and winning) and still have memories of every wonderful flight.

There have been strong pressures to take over the beautiful and unique Torrey Pines glider site. Fortunately Gary Fogel and his father, Larry, were successful in leading the move to have the Torrey Pines glider port formally designated a "National Soaring Monument" in 1992. It is now a wonderful location for radio controlled model sailplanes, for hang gliders and paragliders and for the occasional sailplane event. And it is a treasure for the whole San Diego area. There are many locations for condominiums and tennis courts but only one unspoiled Torrey Pines glider site atop the cliffs overlooking the Pacific. It is a site treasured not only throughout the San Diego area but by aviation pioneers throughout the world. In summary, the glider port played an important part in the development of soaring sailplanes and the associated persons and culture that have fueled much of Southern California's aerospace industry.

Soaring inevitably instills in the pilot, who is utilizing nature's atmospheric energy for staying aloft, a dedication to efficiency of the vehicle and the way it is used. My flights at Torrey Pines, in the high altitude waves at Bishop, California, and at national contests in the United States and international championships in Europe, certainly stoked my interest in efficiency and doing more with less. The result, for me and my teams at AeroVironment, has included a series of vehicles for land and air that operate on the small power of human muscles, solar cells, or small batteries. Subsequent to the 1977 human powered *Gossamer Condor*, we had found ourselves deeply involved in full cells, photovoltaic cell systems, battery and hybrid powered cars, electric airplanes (from video-equipped tiny flyers of just 6 inch wingspan to the giant 247 foot span *Helios* for month-long flights in the stratosphere), and many other areas that fit the philosophy of efficiency, low power, and renewal energy sources that are features of soaring for both birds and sailplanes. Soaring and observing nature's many flying creatures are fun but also valuable.

So here is a fascinating story of people and events in the development of soaring, told by a gifted author who is more than an historian. Gary has established close connections to the pioneers of soaring in the San Diego area. His broad insights let him perceive the way these aircraft, flights, and locations affected people and events near and far and how they will continue to have impact on our future.

*Paul MacCready*
*Monrovia, California*

# CHAPTER 1

# 1883-1927
# The Glider Pioneers

## John J. Montgomery

John J. Montgomery was born on February 15th, 1858 in Yuba City, California and was noted to be interested in bird flight early in childhood. He attended school at Santa Clara College (1874-1875) and St. Ignatius College (1875-1880) where he received his bachelor of science and master of science degrees in physics. Shortly after his graduation, the family moved south to San Diego, living at the "Fruitland Ranch" near Otay Mesa. At the ranch, Montgomery set up a workshop in a barn for constructing a flying machine. He began his studies of flight with investigations of seagull and vulture wing design with three objectives in mind: equilibrium, complete control, and long continued or soaring flight. He was interested specifically in studying the importance of wing curvature as a means to generate lift.

During the period from 1882 to 1883, John constructed his first flying machine, the *Gull Glider*, from ash and unbleached muslin with the help of his sister Jane E. Montgomery. The aircraft had a wingspan of 20 feet and total wing area of 90 square feet. In the early morning of August 28th, 1883, John and his brother, James Montgomery, loaded the *Gull Glider* onto a hay wagon and rode from the ranch to the rim of the mesa, from where John expected to launch. Some accounts note that the brothers "drove off holding rifles as if to suggest they were going rabbit hunting" to avoid the ridicule of the local neighbors towards the flying machine. The brothers set up the glider on the rim of Otay Mesa facing west towards the Pacific Ocean and the prevailing wind. The earliest accounts of the flight state that James used a rope to pull John into the air as he ran down the hill into a steady breeze. After the launch, Montgomery wrote:

*John J. Montgomery.*

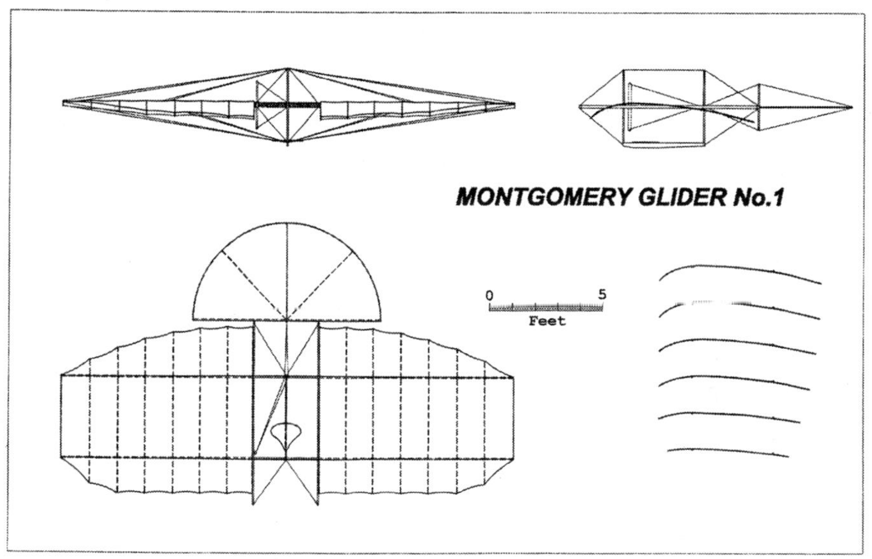


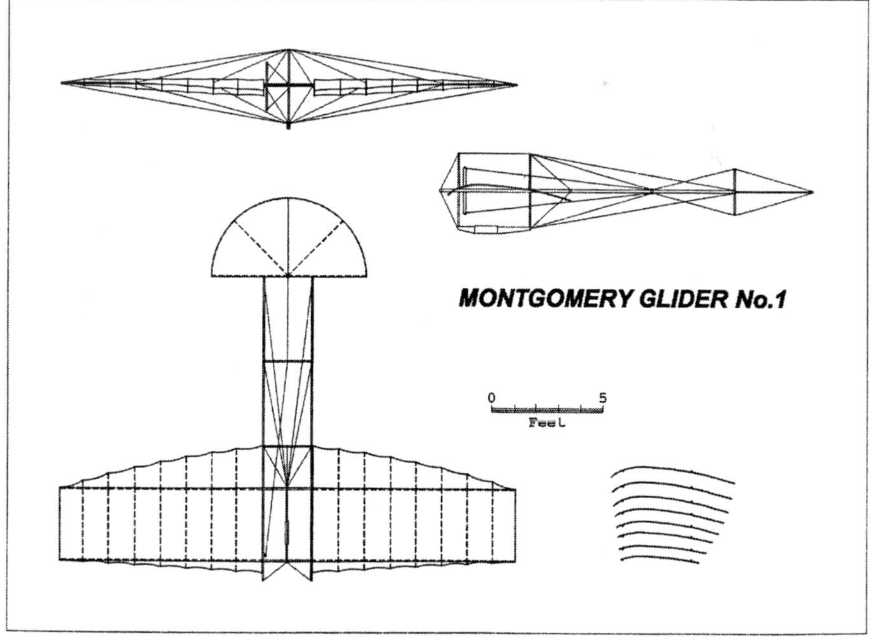


*Two drawings of the Montgomery "Gull Glider" including that of Victor Lougheed's book Vehicles of the Air (top) and that of Herb Kelley from W.W.I. Aero magazine (bottom), the latter based on drawings signed by John J. Montgomery.*

> *...I found myself launched into the air...I proceeded against the wind, gliding downhill for a distance of about 600 feet. In this experience, I was able to direct my course at will. A peculiar sensation came over me, the fact that I was placing myself at the mercy of the wind and immediately after, came a feeling of security when I realized the solid support given by the wing surfaces. This support was of a very peculiar nature because there was a cushiony softness about it, yet it was firm. When I found that the machine would follow my movements in the seat for balancing, I felt I was self buoyant...*

After this initial flight, it has been written that John Montgomery made several other flights in the *Gull Glider* that day. However, it has also been suggested that when the glider was carried back up the hill and readied for a second flight, either James tripped on the launching rope, sending the glider crashing to one side, or that the wind picked up the glider and toppled it over. Significant damage to the glider prohibited subsequent flights.

According to Arthur Dunning Spearman (who wrote a comprehensive biography of John J. Montgomery in 1967), Montgomery constructed two other gliders while in San Diego; one used a flat wing and the other that used a gull shaped curve to the wing from the root to the tip. These were constructed with the help of Charles Burroughs in 1884. According to Montgomery's reports, neither of these gliders ever flew and were experiments in wing design. After these failed attempts, Montgomery spent the period of 1884-1885 at the family ranch carrying out experiments on the ground to test the importance of airfoils in generating lift.

Montgomery presented his theories and experiments at the International Aeronautical Congress at Chicago, Illinois, August 1st through 4th, 1893. After his presentation, Montgomery settled in Northern California to teach at the College of Mount Saint Joseph, in Roherville (near Alton). There, Montgomery experimented with a successful tandem wing free-flight model glider named *The Pink Maiden*.

Between 1895 and 1903, Montgomery continued to test glider designs in the Aptos and San Jose areas, constructing several successful gliders. In 1904, he designed and built *The Santa Clara*, a tandem wing glider that was launched by balloon on April 29th, 1905, with stunt man Daniel Maloney at the controls. At a height of approximately 4,000 feet, Maloney cut himself free from the unmanned balloon and started a 20 minute gliding decent to a safe landing at a predetermined location. This achievement received national publicity in newspapers as the first high-altitude controlled flight by a manned aircraft anywhere on Earth.

On May 21st, 1905, Maloney was once again ready at the controls of *The Santa Clara*, but at 150 feet, the plane separated from the balloon by accident, and after a short glide down, Maloney was ready for another attempt in an alternate glider, *The California*. As Maloney was rising in the glider, however, he noticed that someone had loosened several stove-bolts on his controls. Maloney tried without success to retighten the bolts and it became too dangerous to separate the glider from the balloon. The balloon, the glider, and Maloney landed still attached some 30 miles away

*Above: (l-r) Associate Justice W. G. Lorigan, Frank Hamilton, John J.* Montgomery, *and Daniel Maloney beside The Santa Clara glider in 1905.*

*Right: Daniel Maloney ascending in The Santa Clara attached to a balloon on May 21st, 1905.*

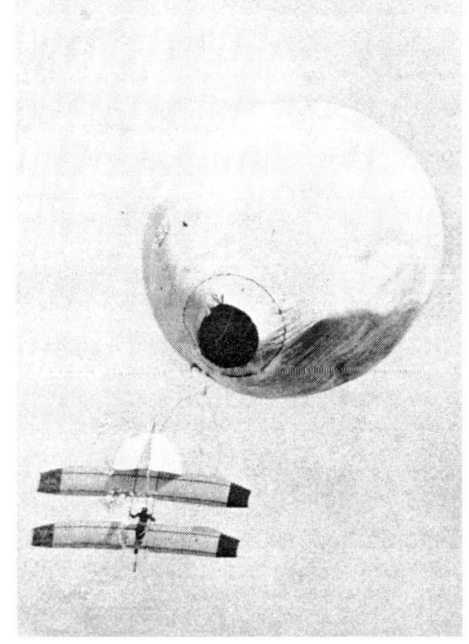

in Gilroy, much to the disappointment of the large crowd that had gathered in anticipation of the performance.

On July 18th, 1905, Daniel Maloney rose above the crowds in *The Santa Clara* attached to a balloon. During the separation at 4,000 feet, the glider became tangled with a balloon guide wire sending the frail craft plummeting to the ground. Soon thereafter, Daniel Maloney became the first American to die in a glider accident.

Montgomery received United States Patent Number 831,173 for *The Santa Clara* tandem wing glider on September 18th, 1906. Later, he constructed *The Evergreen* glider, which he flew repeatedly in the San Jose area. On October 31st, 1911, during one flight in *The Evergreen*, he reportedly lost control as his glider was hit by a sudden wind gust and crashed. He died as a result of injuries suffered in the crash before doctors arrived at the scene.

Montgomery's earliest flight(s) of 1883 at Otay Mesa are still a matter of controversy among some aviation historians. In his attempt for secrecy, John had only one witness to his initial flight (his brother James), and no photographs are known of the *Gull Glider* in flight or otherwise. As Montgomery historian Arthur Spearman commented, "Montgomery's over-sensitivity, coupled with his self-imposed secrecy and excited ambition were real handicaps to him." Others have noted that the distance of the initial glide increased in the literature from 100 feet in 1894 to as much as 603 feet in later reports. In January, 1916, after heavy winter rains came to the San Diego area, the Sweetwater Dam burst, sending water down the Otay River and causing the Lower Otay Dam to break open. A massive flood rushed through Otay Valley destroying much of the Fruitland Ranch, including the remains of the *Gull Glider* and the two other early Montgomery machines.

Although there were no regularly published weather accounts in San Diego newspapers at the time, the recorded weather for Los Angeles that day in 1883, as published in the *Los Angeles Daily Times*, stated that "at 12:15 p.m., the temperature was 92° F and the wind was from the west at sixteen miles per hour." With a similar geography and climate to San Diego, perhaps this suggests that a good seabreeze might have been available to Montgomery on the day he made his first glider flight.

In 1894, Octave Chanute wrote the influential book *Progress in Flying Machines*. This historic book was used by the Wright brothers and other aviation pioneers as a guide in the development of early aircraft. Living near Chicago, Illinois, Chanute corresponded directly with a large number of pioneering glider pilots from around the world. Chanute had a sincere desire to publish accurate accounts of all the flights described in his manuscript:

> *The foregoing pages comprise all the experiments, the result of which has been published, which the writer has been able to collate, and which he has considered of sufficient importance to be described in this account of 'Progress in Flying Machines.'...The writer has gathered from the newspapers, accounts of some other experiments, but these seem to be so erroneously or vaguely described that no instruction could be obtained by*

*republishing them. It has been the aim of the writer throughout to gather all the information possible, but only to publish that which was reliable and instructive.*

Considering his flight reliable and instructive, Octave Chanute mentioned John J. Montgomery's 1883 flight in *Progress in Flying Machines.* According to this account, the *Gull Glider* had a 20-foot wingspan with an average chord of 4 1/2 feet. A horizontal tail was controlled by a set of pulleys and the apparatus weighed 40 pounds without a pilot. Chanute's account reported that Montgomery launched into a sea breeze blowing steadily from 8 to 12 miles per hour and jumped into the wind without any previous running. The total distance of the glide was 100 feet. Following this attempt:

*Mr. Montgomery carried his machine back to the top of the hill and prepared to repeat the experiment, but as soon as he got into position the apparatus began to sway and to twist about in the wind; one side dipped downward, caught on a small shrub, and, as quick as a flash, the operator was tossed some 8 or 10 ft. into the air, overturned, and thrown down headlong. He fortunately fell without serious injury, and found, as soon as he recovered himself, that one side of this machine was smashed past mending.*

Chanute considered the San Diego vicinity to be well suited to the testing of early flying machines. In 1894, Chanute visited San Diego, a small town with a total population of 16,000. Following his visit, he wrote:

*It would be desirable to select the vicinity of some projecting tongue of land or of some isthmus where captive preliminary tests [of airplane designs] may be made, and also that there should be a cliff in the neighborhood whence models and perhaps the apparatus itself might be floated off. There are many such spots to be found within the proximity of machine shops in the Mediterranean, in the Gulf of Mexico, and on the coast of Southern California, and the attention of designers of flying machines, who may want to test the merits of their devices upon a really adequate scale, is particularly directed to the vicinity of San Diego, Cal., where all the circumstances which have been alluded to are to be found combined...*

As his interest in Montgomery's gliders grew, Octave Chanute wrote to Montgomery and asked him to return to San Diego to meet and conduct experiments together. Chanute wrote on March 30th, 1894:

*I would like to...test some ideas on the subject [of flight] which my study of the failures which I have been passing in review have suggested. Please let me know whether it is probable that you could join me, should I conclude to do this at San Diego.*

Montgomery was, however, bound to his teaching position in Northern California and declined the opportunity to experiment with Chanute in San Diego. Later, in an essay written in 1896, Octave Chanute noted that his personal aerodynamic "studies were based on observing sea gulls at San Diego." On May 17th, 1900, in a letter to Wilbur Wright, Chanute wrote:

*The two most suitable locations for winter experiments which I know of are near San Diego, California, and St. James City (Pine Island), Florida, on account of the steady sea breezes which I have found to blow there.*

Chanute helped to increase early interest in San Diego as a premiere location for the development and testing of both powered and motorless aircraft.

Through a push by local San Diego politicians and members of the aviation industry in the 1940s and 1950s, Montgomery became a celebrated hero in San Diego's aviation history. In 1946, Columbia Pictures produced the movie "Gallant Journey," a biography of John J. Montgomery starring Glenn Ford and Janet Blair. The movie debuted in San Diego and was well received. In 1949, a section of the Interstate 5 freeway, from the Mexican border to downtown San Diego (a distance of 11 miles), was dedicated as the Montgomery Freeway. On May 20th, 1950, 2,000 pieces of souvenir glider mail, with an orange sticker cachet of Montgomery and the 1883 *Gull Glider*, were distributed to the crowd when Gibbs Field in Kearney Mesa was officially dedicated as Montgomery Field in honor of the "first American to fly." Several members of the Montgomery family were in attendance, including James Montgomery, who took a ride in a Schweizer TG-2, a sailplane then owned by the John J. Montgomery Soaring Club of San Diego. On May 21st, 1950, a wing-shaped monument was dedicated to John J. Montgomery at Otay, California, and remains as a part of the Montgomery-Waller Park. This monument was established as part of California State Historical Landmark #711, the "Montgomery Memorial." An elementary school in the same area was later named after John J. Montgomery.

At Santa Clara on April 29th, 1946, a granite monument was placed where Daniel Maloney was launched 31 years previously on the campus of Santa Clara University. On March 15th, 1961, a California State Senate Memorial Resolution was passed to honor John J. Montgomery. Montgomery was inducted into the Aviation Hall of Fame in Dayton, Ohio, on December 17th, 1964, and on October 31st, 1967, 56 years after his death, "Montgomery Hill" near San Jose was dedicated as California State Historical Landmark #813. In May, 1996, Montgomery's *Gull Glider* was designated as an International Historic Mechanical Engineering Landmark by the American Society of Mechanical Engineers. Montgomery is recognized by the National Air and Space Museum of the Smithsonian Institution as the first American to build and fly a man-carrying glider. Congressman Norman Y. Mineta of California remarked on the history of Montgomery in the Congressional Record on April 29, 1975. Montgomery's original *Evergreen* glider is on loan from the Smithsonian Insitition to the San Diego Aerospace Museum where it is currently on display.

## *Donald H. Gordon*

In 1903 and 1904, at the age of twenty, Donald H. Gordon constructed gliders with his brother at the family ranch in Bostonia near El Cajon. His early gliders were made of bamboo and bed sheets and had an unsuccessful, short career. Experiments continued nonetheless, and Gordon built several flying model gliders in 1906.

Between 1907 and 1908, Gordon designed and constructed a glider patterned after the famous *Wright Flyer*. The first flight of this aircraft occurred in November or December, 1908, when Gordon was 25 years old. The biplane glider used a controllable biplane elevator in front as a canard. Dihedral in the wing served as the sole source of lateral stability as there was no rudder on the glider. Unlike most hang gliders of the time, Gordon sat on top of the lower wing rather than hang from beneath the aircraft. The aircraft's wingspan was 28 feet, chord was 4 feet wide, and the glider had a total length of 18 feet.

Gordon's glider was launched from the top of a small hill on the family ranch. Since the glider used skids for landing, a unique launching apparatus was constructed. The glider was placed on a wheeled undercarriage (a "dolly") and sent down the hill on a small ramp. When the glider reached a sufficient flight speed, it could rise off the dolly and continue airborne down the slope.

Approximately 50 successful glides were made of 150 yards, although his highest altitude attained was only 20 feet, in winds of about 15 miles per hour. After these early initial gliding experiments, Gordon continued on with powered flight and constructed several of the earliest powered aircraft in San Diego.

## *Waldo D. Waterman*

In April of 1909, *Popular Mechanics* magazine published an article on the construction of a Chanute-type hang glider. After reading this article, Waldo D. Waterman constructed his *White Swan No. 1* biplane glider in the backyard garage of his parent's home near the intersection of Hawthorn and Albatross Streets in San Diego. As a high school freshman and student in a machine shop class, Waterman cut spars and ribs for the 20-foot wingspan glider at Barth's Machine Shop and then transported them home for assembly.

By mid-June, the glider was ready for flight. On June 30th, 1909, with the help of classmate Hansel Schnoover, they borrowed the Schnoover family Stoddard-Dayton

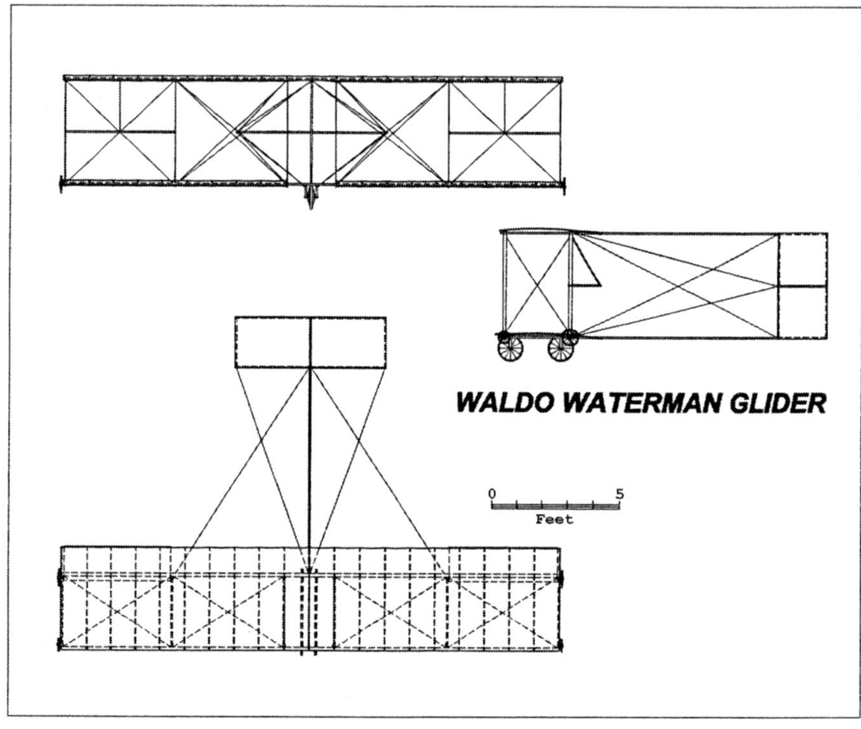


*The 1909 Waldo Waterman glider "White Swan No. 1." This hang glider design was the result of plans published in Popular Mechanics. Wheels under the center section and outer tips of the wings as well as outboard Curtiss-type ailerons set between the two wings were added later by Waterman. The aircraft had a wingspan of 20 feet, wing area of 160 square feet, length of 13.1 feet and was constructed of wood and fabric.*

and drove the glider to a hill at the intersection of Juniper and Albatross Streets. After a few unsuccessful attempts with the *White Swan No. 1*, they realized that the hillside was not steep enough for sufficient airspeed. Moving higher up the hill on Laurel Street, the boys tried again but achieved similar results. A required steeper slope was found at the intersection of Albatross and Maple Streets. The area was cleared of overgrown brush and the boys planned to return the next morning to fly the glider.

Just after dawn on July 1st, 1909, Schnoover and Waterman set up the glider atop the steep cliff at the end of Maple Street. Waterman later recollected:

> *There was a slight breeze blowing in from the bay when I lifted the glider and positioned myself. Then, with a short run climaxed by as high a jump as I could make, I propelled the glider off the crest of the hill. There was the slightest of hesitations, and then I found myself airborne. I was flying!*

By the end of the morning, Waterman successfully piloted the glider to the bottom of the ravine, a distance of approximately 125 feet. At the age of 15, Waldo Waterman became the first pilot to fly a glider within the city limits of San Diego.

After this initial success, Waterman experimented with other means of launching the glider. Wheels were attached to the lower wingtips and ailerons were added to provide increased control. A wooden catapult rail was constructed, measuring 20 feet by 2 inches by 8 inches, with a roller at one end. A rope was passed from the front of the glider over the roller and back to the car, which acted as a winch. With this arrangement, however, the two boys were unsuccessful in attaining sufficient airspeed and ended up damaging the aircraft more than flying it.

After extensive repairs, early one morning in late July, 1909 Schnoover and Waterman once again loaded the glider into the Stoddard-Dayton and parked at the intersection of Sixth Avenue and Maple Street. With a 50-foot rope between the glider and the car, Hansel started driving south on Sixth Avenue with the glider in tow. Waterman recalled:

> *But after about three swoops to the left, the glider veered way off and struck a newly planted palm tree beside the road. That ended the flight and smashed up the wing enough to cause us to head for home. We did stop to prop up that tree...it was leaning a bit...you can still spot that tree today, a leaning runt in a line of 100-foot-tall palms!*

After learning of this incident, Waldo's mother put an end to all flights with the glider. Undaunted, Waterman embarked on a very successful career in aviation, designing and building the world's first *Flying Auto* among many other aircraft. Three of his planes have become part of the collection of the Smithsonian's National Air and Space Museum. His original *White Swan No. 1* biplane glider was displayed for many years in the San Diego Aerospace Museum, but was destroyed in a fire that consumed the museum in 1978. On July 1st, 1959, 50 years after his first flight from Albatross

Street in San Diego, the Early Birds, a national group of pilots who flew before 1912, marked the spot with a plaque honoring Waldo Waterman. The plaque reads:

*Commemorating*

*Establishing a record of fifty years as an active pilot and for his many contributions to the science of flight, The Early Birds in cooperation with the San Diego Historical Society dedicate this plaque to Waldo Waterman on the fiftieth anniversary of his first flight from this spot.*

*Dedicated July 1, 1959*

## *Frazier Curtis*

In 1910, the first glider took to the skies over La Jolla. Several articles suggesting that Chanute-type hang gliders were an easy way to learn the principles of flight were published in the early 1900s in *Aeronautics*, *Scientific American*, *Aviation*, and *Popular Mechanics*. Advertisements for mail-order glider kits from a variety of sources could also be found in these journals.

After placing an order for a glider, a Chanute-type hang glider kit arrived at the home of Frazier and Diana Curtis of La Jolla on July 1st, 1910. After construction, the glider was taken up the northwest slopes of Mount Soledad near Pepita Street (now known as Pepita Way) and flown in a series of short successful hops on July 28th, 1910. Frazier Curtis, Ralph Kline, Dick Borrowdaile, and Nathan Rannells (the La Jolla Postmaster at the time), flew the glider in the afternoon. Diana Curtis recalled:

*Frazier tried the machine in the morning. He took it up Soledad. He, Ralph Kline and Nathan Rannells flew in the afternoon. Dick Borrodaile broke a strut in falling. I went to a sewing bee at Hardy's...*

*You could guide the glider by swinging your legs or at least that is what it said in the advertisement. As I remember, none of the men who went up in it were ever calm enough to keep their feet together and they'd takeoff and they'd still be running in the air.*

*Two of us would take a rope and run down hill into the wind, pulling the glider after us. It was very much like flying a kite. Frazier would go up 50 feet or so, flutter along for a 100 feet and come down into a cactus bush. Then we'd carry the glider home and mend it, and Frazier would spend the rest of the day picking out cactus spikes.*

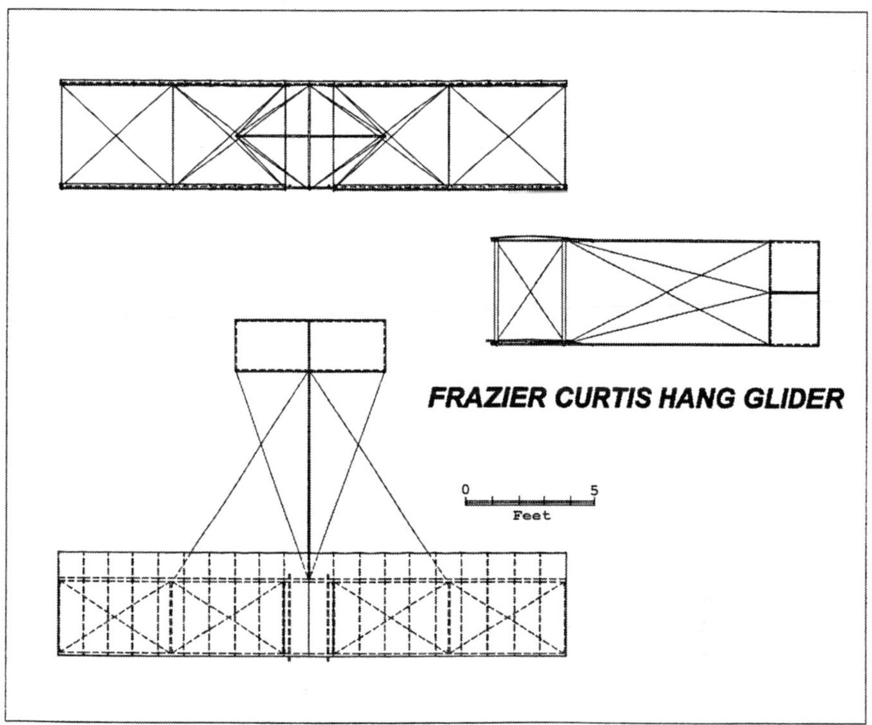


*The Chanute-type hang glider built by Frazier Curtis was the first glider to fly in the skies over La Jolla. The aircraft had a wingspan of 20 feet, wing area of 160 square feet, length of 13.1 feet and was constructed of wood and fabric.*

Nathan Rannells commented:

> *They wanted me to try it because I was light. Fortunately, I lit in one of those big mahogany bushes. If we'd just had a little larger wing sweep and known a little more about it, I think we'd have gotten up all right. Whether we would have gotten down or not, I don't know.*

Rannells' horse was used to pull the glider back to the launching spot on the top of the hill. On at least one occasion, attempts were made to pull the glider up into the air using single horsepower instead of multiple manpower.

Prior to leaving La Jolla in 1911, the Curtises gave the glider to Roy Rutherford, a young boy in La Jolla. Roy's father was horrified at the thought of his son flying in a glider and immediately began instructing his son in golf instead. The whereabouts of the glider after this period are unknown.

A small poem was written later by John L. Morgan to honor the pioneer gliding activities of the Curtises in La Jolla:

*Diana Curtis lived here then*
*So did her husband Frazier.*
*They both for flying had a yen*
*Gliding was their pleasure.*

*Diana pulled the towing rope*
*While running like a deer.*
*To soar aloft Frazier would hope,*
*The branch he'd barely clear.*

*Twas Nathan Rannells with his horse*
*And lasso of some length*
*That pulled the glider on its course*
*And saved Diana's strength.*

## *Halfway to Oz on a Magic Umbrella*

In 1904-1905, fiction author L. Frank Baum visited La Jolla while wintering at Coronado. Baum is perhaps best known for *The Wonderful Wizard of Oz* and other Oz related stories. Dr. Bard C. Cosman noted that three of his novels, *The Sea Fairies* (1911), *Sky Island* (1912), and *The Scarecrow of Oz* (1915) were all written with La Jolla in mind.

Baum's *Sky Island* was particularly prophetic because of its connection with fictional motorless flight. The story begins at a cottage located on a high bluff overlooking the Pacific. Two of the main characters (Trot and Button-Bright) take a ride under a magic umbrella on a swing seat built by Cap'n Bill.

> *Button-Bright and Trot both thought Cap'n Bill's invention very clever. The sailor placed the board upon the ground while they sat in their places, Button-Bright at the right of Trot, and then the boy hooked the rope loop to the handle of the umbrella, which he spread wide open. 'I want to go to the town over yonder,' he said, pointing with his finger to the roofs of the houses that showed around the bend in the cliff [presumably the town of La Jolla as viewed from the bluffs above Black's Beach].*
>
> *At once the umbrella rose into the air; slowly, at first, but quickly gathering speed. Trot and Button-Bright held fast to the ropes and were carried along very easily and comfortably. It seemed scarcely a minute before they were in the town, and when the umbrella set them down just in front of the store--for it seemed to know just where they wanted to go--a wondering crowd gathered around them. Trot ran in and changed the yarn, while Button-Bright stayed outside and stared at the people who stared at him. They asked questions, too, wanting to know what sort of an aeroplane this was, and where his power was stored, and lots of other things; but the boy answered not a word. When the little girl came back and took her seat Button-Bright said: 'I want to go to Trot's house.'*
>
> *The simple villagers could not understand how the umbrella suddenly lifted the two children into the air and carried them away. They had read of airships, but here was something wholly beyond their comprehension.*
>
> *Cap'n Bill had stood in front of the house, watching with a feeling akin to bewilderment the flight of the Magic Umbrella. He could follow its course until it descended in the village and he was so amazed and absorbed that his pipe went out. He had not moved from his position when the umbrella started back. The sailor's big blue eyes watched it draw near and settle down with its passengers upon just the spot it had started from.*
>
> *Trot was joyously and greatly excited.*
>
> *'Oh, Cap'n, it's gal-lor-ious!' she cried in ecstasy. 'It beats ridin' in a boat or--or--in anything else. You feel so light an' free an'--an'--glad! I'm sorry the trip didn't last longer, though. Only trouble is, you go too fast.'*
>
> *Button-bright was smiling contentedly. He had proved to both Trot and Cap'n Bill that he had told the truth about the Magic Umbrella, however marvelous the tale had seemed to them...*

*...They walked to the high bluff overlooking the sea, where a gigantic acacia tree stood on the very edge...They put the broad double seat on the ground and then the boy and girl sat in their places and Button-Bright spread open the Magic Umbrella. Cap'n Bill sat in his seat just in front of them, all being upon the ground.*

*'Don't we look funny?' said Trot, with a chuckle of glee. 'But hold fast the ropes, Cap'n an' take care of your wooden leg.'*

*Button-Bright addressed the umbrella, speaking to it very respectfully, for it was a thing to inspire awe.*

*'I want to go as far as Smuggler's Cove, and then turn around in the air and come back here,' he said.*

*At once the umbrella rose into the air, lifting after it, first the seat in which the children sat, and then Cap'n Bill's seat.*

*'Don't kick your heels, Trot!' cried the sailor in a voice that proved he was excited by his novel experience; 'you might bump me in the nose.'*

*'All right,' she called back; 'I'll be careful.'*

*It was really a wonderful, exhilarating ride, and Cap'n Bill wasn't long making up his mind he liked the sensation. When about fifty feet above the ground the umbrella began moving along the coast toward Smuggler's Cove...*

It is interesting to note that although this story was written in 1912, the activities with the Magic Umbrella are uncannily similar to modern gliding activities along the cliffs at the Torrey Pines Gliderport in La Jolla.

## *A. Clare Rand*

On July 13th, 1907, A. Clare Rand was born in Escondido and grew up on the family hay farm. His first encounter with aviation occurred at the annual "Grape Day Festival" held in Escondido. By the age of 13, Rand was already interested in building his own glider:

*In the fall of 1920, when in the 7th grade, my friend, Dick Hershey, and I became interested in the plans of a glider I had discovered in the Popular*

*Mechanics magazine. This machine was a biplane of quite sturdy design, and I believe it would have been a practical design for our purposes, if we had been able to construct it. However, Dick's mother refused to finance his half of the cost, and I was unable to finance the total cost, so the glider was not built.*

*In the spring of 1922, I started, in the school woodshop, the construction of my first glider, a monoplane of 27 foot wingspan. The plans which I obtained from Popular Mechanics, had not called for ailerons, but I decided to include ailerons in the wings, as the method of lateral control advocated by the designer, George White, I did not feel was a practical method (he expected the pilot to maintain lateral control by violently swinging his legs from side to side).*

Construction on the glider was interrupted when the Rand family made a trip to Venice, California, near Los Angeles. Here, Clare Rand visited the Venice Airport and learned more about aviation. After returning to Escondido in the fall of 1922:

*I continued the building of my first glider, a monoplane, and tried it out in the latter part of August, 1922, by running with it, down Washington Avenue into the west wind. I held up the tail and several boys of the neighborhood held the wing tips and pulled on a rope in front. With one in the machine, it wouldn't takeoff and fly easily, provided we had a tailwind of at least 12 miles per hour a ground speed of about nine or ten miles per hour. I did not attempt to fly this glider, as I had no flexible control cable for the ailerons and I could not work the ailerons with the stiff clothesline cable I was using. Also, I had never been in the air, and it is no doubt a good thing I did not fly it.*

*During the Spring and Summer of 1924, I had been constructing a biplane glider of my own design and a few days after Grape Day 1924, with the help of Dick Hershey and Art Hopkins, I assembled it on my Grandfather's lawn (455 W. Washington) and the next day we towed it out to Hubbard's Hill, northeast of town, and I made two very short 'test flights' on the west slope. A strong west wind was blowing. The glider was rocking in the wind as I climbed onto the seat, for the first hop. Dick Hershey and Hilbert Park, who lived near by, were ready to pull on a rope out ahead, and Tommy Hostetler was on a lower wing and Art Haskins was steadying the other wing tip. I said 'Lets go' and everybody ran in to the wind with the machine. It lifted quickly and the wheels were about 3 feet off the ground for several seconds. This was my first glider flight. However the machine was not balanced right and was very tail heavy. I could not keep the 'nose' down, and the glider soon stalled and dropped, striking on the wheels with a heavy thud, and breaking a rear landing gear strut.*

*In the latter part of July, 1925, I latched the front of the double landing skids of the biplane glider (glider No.2) to the rear of my 'T' Ford car, and had Horace Church (Dr. Church, dentist, of Escondido) drive the Ford "bug" car. The glider would lift about 3 feet and trail steady behind, with me as pilot, keeping the wings steady, with the old Curtiss type ailerons which were hinged to the wing struts between the wings. On the afternoon of August 9, 1925, I decided to make a flight on the end of a tow line. Robert Cook, driving his 'T' Ford 'cut down bug' towed me this time, with Herbert Hall, Escondido auto mechanic, riding backward beside him. Hall put on a pair of leather gloves so that he could keep the slack out of the steel tow cable as I glided down, as I did not cut loose from the tow line on this flight. The scene of these operations was a large triangular hay field between Metcalf Ave. and the Santa Fe tracks which later became the location of the large Sunkist Orange Packing House and refrigeration plant. We pushed the glider into the extreme southeast end of the field, next to Washington Ave., hooked up the tow line, and looked over the wires and fittings on the glider to be sure nothing had jarred loose. I had not had time to build a seat on the glider, so I just sat on a lower wing spar and held on to a strut with my left hand and the "joy stick" with my right hand. 'Bob' Cook gave the Ford 'the gun' and away we went into about a 15 mile per hour northwest wind. Due to the glider's extremely light wing loading (1.6 lbs. per sq. ft.) it lifted quickly. The machine was tail heavy and I soon found myself over 50 feet above the ground in some very rough air. There I was, 50 feet up, with only 15 minutes previous flying experience (in powered aircraft) to my credit, and that acquired a year previously. So needless to say, I was a little 'rusty' with the controls to say the least!*

*The glider drifted dangerously close to a power line on the left, at the same time pitching violently. I managed to keep it away from the wires as 'Bob' Cook started slowing down. As the Ford slowed, down I came, down in a series of short dives and glides, like steps in a stairway. Every time the tow line went slack, Herb Hall pulled in on the cable, keeping it tight. When I saw the ground about 10 feet below me, I started easing down the tail. By the time I was skimming the ground, everything was ideal for a good landing, and the glider settled down easily and rolled along through the stubble and stopped. The whole landing operation had been so gentle, and perfect, that I could hardly believe we had accomplished it. As I walked around the wings and toward the tail, several people crowded around. Some slapped me on the back. Someone shouted 'Lets see you fly her again.' So, although reluctant to fly it again that afternoon, as I wanted to make some changes in the tail surfaces to improve control, I took off again, to satisfy the crowd, after changing the leverage between the joy stick and the elevator (horizontal rudder). I did not allow the machine to climb so steeply as before and leveled off at about 30 feet and flew along, very much smoother than before. I was getting used to the controls and it made a big difference. I landed the second time as gently as the first, thanks to the expert assistance of Hall and Cook and we towed the glider home, highly satisfied with the afternoon's operations.*

*Four days later, on Aug. 13, 1925, Bob Cook towed me again to two flights, on the same field. The wind was even stronger than on the 9th. I decided to cut loose this time and try a landing free of the tow line. I climbed the glider to about 30 feet and cut loose. I pushed ahead on the control stick and the next thing I knew, I had struck the ground, damaging a lower wing and the landing gear. We patched up the glider and I took off again. This time I decided to climb to 50 feet and cut loose. I climbed too steeply. The tow line parted, suddenly, leaving me in a stall from which I was unable to recover, nearly 50 feet about 'terra firma'! The glider hung in the stall an instant, then slipped tail first into the ground! I found myself lying on the ground amidst a tangled mass of broken wooden ribs and struts and torn wreckage, just as Bob Cook, with my brother Ferris beside him, came tearing back, dragging the tow line behind the 'T' Ford. As I looked myself over, I discovered no injuries, whatever, excepting a very small scratch on the back of my left hand!*

In January of 1927, Rand repaired the glider for some additional flights:

*With the help of my friends Hollis E. Watrous and Art Haskins, I had managed to get the old glider assembled and towed to a hayfield just west of Quince Street and south of W. Washington Ave. This was about 4:00 p.m. Watrous drove my father's 1920 Buick as a tow car. The field was very soft, due to recent rains and the Buick in 2nd gear could only get up to 25 miles per hour. We towed the glider down the field 3 times without getting it off the ground. The on a fourth trip down the field, I managed to get her off about two feet and fly a short distance. The absence of wind and the speed registered on the tow car's speedometer gave me the exact minimum flying speed of the glider--25 miles per hour. This was the old machine's last flight.*

The old glider had a wingspan of 26 feet, wing chord of 4 feet, wing loading of 1.6 pounds per square foot, and empty weight of 80 pounds. Clare Rand continued with an interest in aviation and helped construct the *Spirit of St. Louis* at the Ryan Aeronautical Company in 1927. In the late 1920s, the Escondido Glider Club was formed and had 25 members. Each took turns flying their "kite-like" glider on the weekends. Members of the club included Fred Beven and Clare Rand's brother, Ferris Rand.

# *CHAPTER 2*

# *1928-1929*
# *Glider Fever in San Diego*

## *Max Shemer and Maury Tombler*

In late 1927 and early 1928, a biplane hang glider was built by Max Shemer and Maury Tombler at Point Loma. The hang glider was unusual in that it had an elevator mounted on top of the fin in a T-tail configuration. By February 6th, 1928, the glider was ready for flight tests. It was launched as a kite with strings from a hill at Cañon Street with Shemer at the controls. With a general lack of steering, it is believed that the glider and pilot quickly found their way into a hillside and crashed. No other information on this glider is known.

## *Elmore E. Shoudy*

By the end of the 1920s, San Diego was known as the "Air Capital of the West." Public interest in aviation increased following Lindbergh's successful crossing of the Atlantic in the famous *Spirit of St. Louis*, an aircraft built in San Diego by the Ryan Aeronautical Company. Elmore E. Shoudy and Russel Winterrowd constructed a 36-foot wingspan primary glider at 824 41st Street in San Diego, with the financial help of Richard M. Allen and H. Grafton Chapman. The glider had ailerons, a tricycle landing gear with support struts from the wings, and a framework fuselage. The wings were fashioned to look like a webbed "bat wing" at the tips.

A successful maiden flight was made on Friday, October 26th, 1928, on a hill at 56th and Market Streets east of downtown San Diego. After a launch of 400 feet by tow rope, Shoudy slowly glided down over a reported period of approximately 5 min-

*Max Shemer and Maury Tombler's T-tail hang glider on Point Loma in 1928.*

utes. Later, he stated to the press that he was "very well satisfied with the stability of this craft." Shoudy was eager to enter his glider in the San Diego Chamber of Commerce glider meet planned for the Spring of 1929.

On Saturday, December 1st, 1928, Shoudy notified the aviation department of the San Diego Chamber of Commerce that he would make public glider flights at Bonita starting at 1 p.m. Sunday, December 2nd. It was billed as the first public glider exhibition in San Diego. After several successful test flights for the press, 27-year-old Shoudy was ready for a public demonstration. The exhibition was advertised in the *San Diego Union* and a large crowd gathered at the scene, including Shoudy's wife and two children. The launching site was on a hill approximately 450-feet high, located a half-mile south of the Ella B. Allen School in Bonita.

Shoudy made at least one glider flight for the crowd between 1:00 p.m. and 3:00 p.m. With a desire to "try for more altitude," Shoudy substituted a larger tail to his glider. At about 3:00 p.m., with one end of a 200-foot tow rope attached to his glider and the other end attached to a car driven by H. Grafton Chapman, Shoudy was launched skyward into a northwest wind. The takeoff was perfect, but the newly attached tail came loose and he lost control of the aircraft, falling rapidly to Earth. He was transported from the crash scene with broken legs and severe internal injuries. He died *en route* to the Paradise Valley Sanitarium, becoming the first glider-related fatality in San Diego County.

Following Shoudy's crash, on December 5th, 1928, it was announced by the Aviation Department of the San Diego Chamber of Commerce that San Diego would be the first city in the United States to formulate rules and regulations for the operation of gliders. These laws would be enforced in accordance with municipal air laws. William Van Dusen, Mr. J. J. Harrigan, and James A. Moore, members of the San Diego Board of Air Control were placed in charge of drafting the proposed rules and submitting them to the City Council. At the time, no regulations in the United States covered glider flying, although the Federal air laws applied to every other type of aircraft.

In an article of November 29th, 1959, *San Diego Union* columnist Larry Freeman suggested that a memorial should be placed at the site of this first public glider exhibition in local history. In his words, the plaque should read:

*On this spot*
*E. E. Shoudy an unsung pioneer of the air age*
*died on Dec. 2, 1928*
*in what was the first public glider exhibition*
*in San Diego history*

## *William Hawley Bowlus*

One can easily make the case that the single most important individual in the early development of motorless aviation in San Diego was William Hawley Bowlus. In 1930, when documenting Bowlus' contribution to motorless flight, Edwin Way Teale wrote:

> *Bowlus was born at Ohio, Illinois, on May 8, 1896. He spent his early boyhood in the Middle West. When he was thirteen, his parents moved to California. The next year, 1910, he saw Curtiss, Latham, Paulhan, and other pioneer birdmen fly at the Los Angeles Aviation Meet, one of the first held in America. From then on, his chief interest has been flying.*
>
> *In the fall of the same year he won a prize at a kite meet in Los Angeles and then began the construction of his first glider on his father's chicken ranch near San Fernando. The machine was a monoplane "hang" glider. It was wrecked after a 250-foot hop in 1911. But it flew.*
>
> *His next glider was a biplane, almost exactly the same size and design as the one the Wright Brothers had used at Kitty Hawk. It flew splendidly, with Bowlus lying prone upon the lower wing and operating the front elevator and the rear rudder by means of controls. Several flights of 1,000 feet were accomplished in 1912.*

*During the time he was attending high school, he spent his evenings working on new gliders and building models to try out original ideas. At the same time he made a collection of stuffed soaring birds to study the shapes and curves of their wings. Several buzzards and hawks were preserved in the exact attitude of flight, with their wings outstretched. Bowlus experimented by launching them from hillsides in calm air in attempts to make them soar. One of his stuffed buzzards, with a wingspread of several feet, sailed for a considerable distance down the slope before losing its balance.*

*Another experiment which Bowlus made about this time was a towed flight, with the glider hitched to "Old Cap," his father's racehorse. The motorless biplane, of the "hang" variety, was tied tightly to the back of a two-wheeled sulky with a long rope. When everything was ready the driver in the sulky clucked and 'Old Cap' started to walk, then broke into a run. Bowlus, coming behind, holding up the glider, lengthened his stride until he was making hops like a jackrabbit. Just as he tilted up the forward edge of the glider and the machine reared into the air, 'Old Cap' looked around over his shoulder. Seeing the huge white wings behind him, he made a wild jump. The rope broke, Bowlus let go, the glider slid backward and hitting the ground folded up in a heap.*

*When America entered the World War (World War I), Bowlus enlisted as a mechanic in the Army Air Service. He spent fourteen and a half months in the United States, England and France. In each place he continued his glider experiments, gaining permission to use odds and ends in constructing motorless machines during his spare time. He built one glider in France and two in England.*

*For two and a half years after the war he was Chief Flight Test Inspector at McCook Field (now Wright Field), Dayton, Ohio. He had to inspect all the planes twice a day, sometimes going over 150 machines morning and afternoon. While there, he built two more gliders.*

*In the fall of 1922 he returned to San Fernando, worked as an automobile mechanic, experimented with hundreds of model gliders and with a number of full sized experimental machines. Two years later, he became "the first and only employee" of the Ryan Flying School at San Diego, starting on a salary of twenty-one dollars a week. With the owner of the company he designed a "parasol" monoplane for mail-carrying. It was this plane, known as the Ryan M-1 that attracted the attention of Charles A. Lindbergh when he was "pushing mail" to Chicago and planning to fly the Atlantic. The Ryan M-1 was the direct ancestor of "The Spirit of St. Louis," the most modern plane in the world.*

*Bowlus was holding the position of plant superintendent at the Ryan factory when the famous telegram arrived: 'CAN YOU BUILD A PLANE TO CROSS ATLANTIC STOP SINGLE ENGINE STOP SINGLE PILOT STOP QUOTE PRICE." It was signed by the then unknown air-mail pilot Charles A. Lindbergh. As a result, "The Spirit of St. Louis' was built, Bowlus and the other members of the organization working day and night to complete the craft within the specified sixty days. Bowlus was in charge of the actual building of the machine and several of the original features of the plane were his ideas.*

*He remained with the Ryan company until 1929 before joining the Airtech Flying School, the only school operating at Lindbergh Field, San Diego. While still with Ryan, he began the construction of his first soaring craft, the sixteenth motorless machine he had built.*

## *Bowlus Sailplane #16 (493)*

Construction of Bowlus' sixteenth motorless aircraft began in late 1928, at the Bowlus residence on Point Loma in San Diego. Working as Chief of the Technical Training Division for the San Diego Air Service Corporation, William Hawley Bowlus completed construction on serial S-16 (his first true sailplane) by New Year's Day, 1929. The aircraft had a wing chord of 4.1 feet, overall wingspan of 44 feet, and length of 25 feet. Built with a light overall weight in mind, the weight of the empty airframe (160 pounds) was thirty pounds lighter than that of the useful load (190 pounds), giving a gross weight of 350 pounds. Of particular interest was the use of craft paper in the construction of the ribs. Ribs were constructed by cutting a web of craft paper and then gluing 1/8-by-1/16-inch cap strips on each side. The resulting rib was exceptionally light, easy to construct, and very strong. Later, this Bowlus model S.P.-1 became known as the "Paperwing" because of this unusual construction. The aspect ratio of 11:1 coupled with the USA 35A airfoil gave the sailplane an advantage over previous hang glider and primary glider designs.

First flights of sailplane "Number 16" were made by auto tow at Lindbergh Field in early January, 1929, with a landing gear attached to the aircraft. Application for an aircraft licence was filed by Bowlus on January 28th, 1929. By February 5th, 1929, the United States Department of Commerce sent a telegram reading "SP1 PLANE NOT ELIGIBLE FOR LICENSE STOP UNLICENSED IDENTIFICATION MARK FOUR NINE THREE ASSIGNED SP1 PLANE NUMBER SIXTEEN." At the time, sailplanes were not approved for aircraft licensing. In fact, a subsequent letter from the United States Department of Commerce to Bowlus stated "...your identification mark assignment cannot be issued until you have advised this Department the type

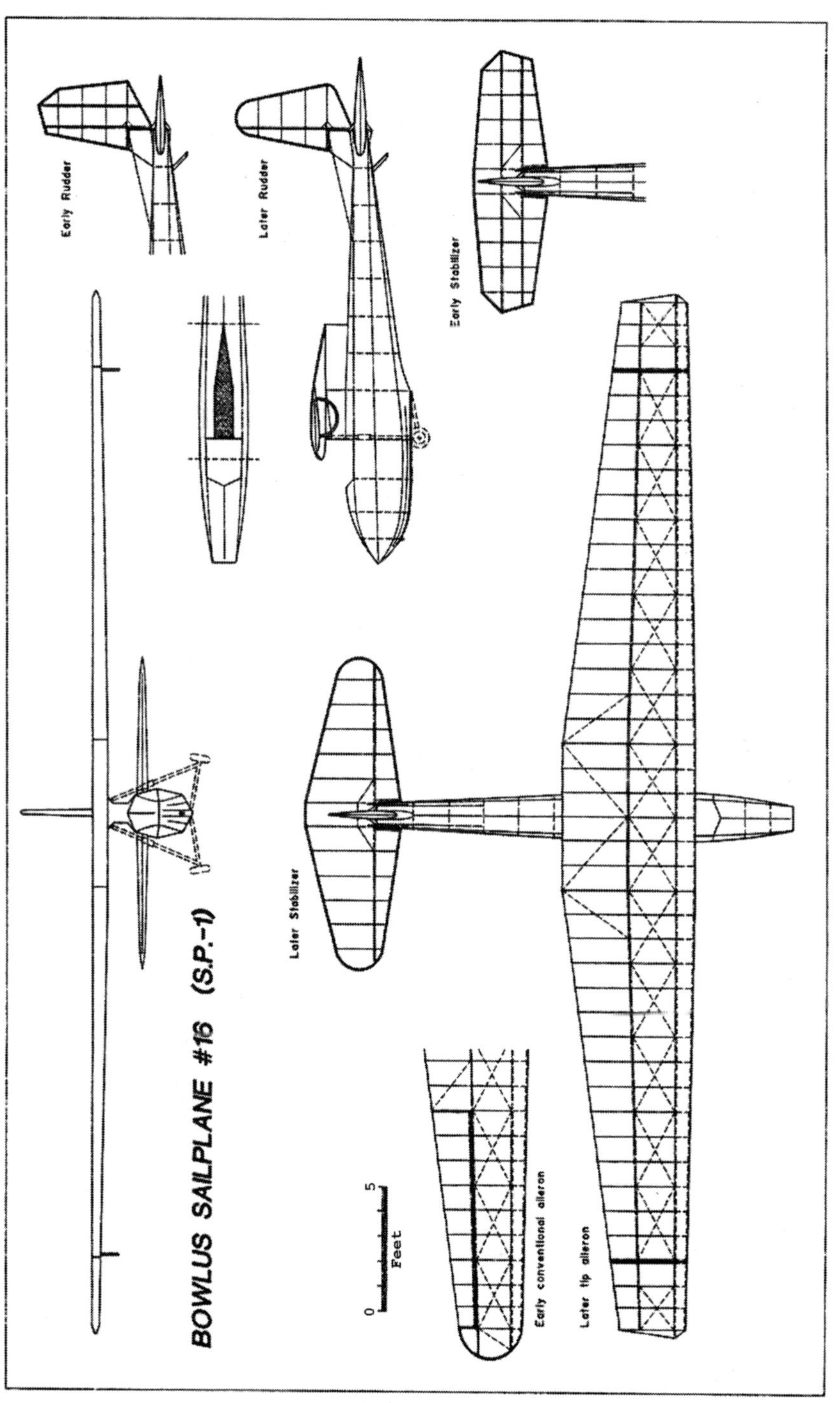
BOWLUS SAILPLANE #16 (S.P.-1)
Early Rudder
Later Rudder
Early Stabilizer
Later Stabilizer
0
5
Feet
Early conventional aileron
Later tip aileron

*Bowlus Sailplane #16 (493) gliding on a test flight at Lindbergh Field in January, 1929 following auto tow. Two wheels were mounted below the aircraft for landing on the dirt runway. The first building at Lindbergh Field, the San Diego Air Service hangar stood near the southeast corner of the airport.*

and number of the motor which has been installed in the plane." In early 1929, the United States Department of Commerce was not well versed in motorless aircraft.

Test flights of 493 were made from the hills at Bonita Heights near the Sweetwater Valley in April, 1929, in a series of many long glides. Wingtip ailerons later replaced the conventional ailerons for more effective lateral control. Piloted by Bowlus in early glider contests and at endurance record flights, 493 became one of America's most famous sailplanes. Following an accident with Peaches Wallace at the controls on May 17th, 1930, Bowlus intended to salvage what remained of the aircraft. On May 22nd, 1930, the identification mark 493 was officially canceled. However, records indicate that the sailplane (or what remained of the sailplane) was sold on September 30th, 1930, to the Booth Company of Los Angeles for the lofty sum of $1.00. A flurry of correspondence from the United States Department of Commerce soon followed, suggesting that both S.P.-1 and Bowlus' 17th motorless aircraft S.P.D. (identification mark 599M) shared the identification mark 493 for part of 1930. By

*William Hawley Bowlus kneeling in front of Bowlus Sailplane #16 outside the San Diego Air Service hangar at Lindbergh Field. The small windsock attached to the nose of the aircraft was used as a yaw indicator.*

January 9th, 1931, identification mark 493 was once again officially canceled because the Booth Company had failed to submit a proper bill of sale to the government.

## *Bowlus Sailplane #17 (599M)*

On August 27th, 1929, Bowlus wrote to the United States Department of Commerce in order to obtain an experimental airplane license for his model "S.P.-D" sailplane. Serial S-17 had an overall wingspan of 52 feet, length of 25 feet, wing chord of 5 feet, 6 inches, and empty weight of only 180 pounds. On September 11th, a letter was returned stating that the unlicensed identification mark 599M was granted to the sailplane due to the fact that gliders were not eligible for any other type of distinction. It is believed S-17 was used by Bowlus for instructional purposes through March of

*Bowlus in the #16 sailplane on a test glide at Lindbergh Field. The Bowlus sailplane #16 is considered by many to be the first sailplane designed and built in America.*

1930. According to official paperwork, following a crash in July, 1930, the sailplane was sold to Bud Perl, William Beuby, and William Smilie for $40.00. It was completely reworked by Bud Perl and William Beuby. Repairs included a new right wing panel, new center section, and new fuselage. Following confusion over transfer and reassignment of ownership of the aircraft from Bowlus to the new owners, 599M was officially canceled on January 24th, 1931. However, the aircraft was relicensed as G599M on February 6th, 1931, with ownership granted to Perl, Beuby, and Smilie. The glider was inspected on June 23rd, 1931, and approved for re-licensing in mid-July. However, due to a lack of correspondence, the identification mark expired on July 1st, 1932.

## *Dale Drake*

Dale Drake made the first successful aerotow in America by flying 250 miles from Reedley, California to Long Beach, California on February 28th, 1929. At the time, it was believed to be the longest aerotow flight of its kind in the world. On April 6th and 7th, 1929, at a location just north of the San Diego County line in San Clemente, Dale Drake attempted to break the existing endurance record for gliders. Arrangements for the attempt were made by Drake and his manager, H. M. Willis, Jr., who helped finance and build Drake's glider at Reedley, California.

On April 6th, Drake set a Pacific Coast endurance record by keeping his glider aloft for 7 minutes and 30 seconds, breaking his previous duration mark of 5 minutes, 5.8 seconds set at Reedley. At San Clemente, Drake's glider was shock cord launched from a 1,500-foot high mountain near the coast. He glided down a valley and landed at the north edge of town. Members of the Long Beach Glider Club were on hand to officiate the record attempt.

On April 7th, he broke his endurance record twice with flights of 8 minutes, 18.2 seconds, and 8 minutes and 14 seconds, respectively. On his second attempt, Drake had a perfect takeoff and glided south down the coast. After gliding out over the ocean, he encountered headwinds that increased his descent. In trying to make a suitable approach for landing, he encountered cross-winds and made a hard landing on the beach near the San Diego County line. The glider was not irreparable and Drake was uninjured. Repairs were completed just in time for Drake to attend a glider meet held at the Long Beach Municipal Airport May 4th and 5th, 1929, where he took top honors for distance and time aloft. As an eyewitness to Drake's flights near the San Diego County line, John Pierce wrote:

> *The first glider flight off a hill which I witnessed was made by Dale Drake in his secondary type machine at the hills of San Clemente. On arriving at the hill, I found Mr. Drake about to takeoff. He was on a high point, almost a thousand feet above the sea. The hill sloped down to a sandy beach, which*

*Dale Drake preparing to launch from a hill at San Clemente in April, 1929.*

*afforded a good landing place. One had to fly over the town of San Clemente, however, to get to the beach. There was no intermediate place to land, as the hill itself offered no opportunities, and the town, as usual, was a network of electric lines, even in open districts. For this reason it was dangerous to try to hang too long over the hill and perhaps lose one's chance of passing over the town. In addition, the cliffs along the beach extended only to the south, and as the wind was blowing a little north of west, one had to go somewhat with the wind in order to soar along them.*

*The first time Drake took off, he headed directly for the ocean, testing the performance of his machine. He landed on the beach below easily, and soon had his machine back on the hill top for a second trial. This time, after he took off, he angled slightly to the left, passing diagonally over the town, and gaining much altitude as he passed over the hillside, for there was a stiff breeze blowing. Then he came to the cliffs and started to soar along the edge, as one sometimes sees a sea gull doing; going, as I said was necessary, partly with the wind and traveling at a great rate of speed. About that time an airplane, traveling along the coast, decided to investigate. The pilot swooped down to see Drake's machine. Drake said that the propeller wash made wind conditions no better. He found himself too near the beach to turn into the wind, and had to land with it, going at a high rate of speed. Fortu-*

*nately he made a successful landing about three miles down the coast from San Clemente. The flight had lasted over eight minutes according to the nearest estimate. It was some time before the timers located him. Although Drake failed to break the record for an American machine, flown by an American, established in early days by the Wright Brothers, he certainly made a flight worth seeing, and all who witnessed it went away enthusiastic about gliders.*

Dale Drake's secondary glider used wheels as a landing gear with a one-piece wing. The wing spars were solid and the wooden ribs were built in two separate pieces, the rear portion of built-up construction. The tail surfaces were rounded, thin, and small. Both the fuselage and tail assembly were made of steel construction. The wing spanned 35 feet, with a chord of five feet. A Clark Y airfoil was used and the glider had an overall weight of 190 pounds.

## *The Meysenburg Sailplane (3051)*

By April 20th, 1929, Richard Meysenburg of La Jolla finished construction on his glider. This ship had a length of 18 feet, wing chord of 4 feet, and wingspan of 44 feet, and was suggested to be a "sailplane" on official correspondence of the United States Department of Commerce. The sailplane was stationed at the San Diego Air Service hangar at the east end of Lindbergh Field.

Meysenburg sold the sailplane (identification number 3051) to George Faria of Pittsburgh, California in the San Francisco Bay area for the sum of $53.00 on February 18th, 1930. The aircraft was damaged badly during shipping and was repaired by George Faria. On December 21st, 1932, the United States Department of Commerce requested a license renewal inspection for the ship, and canceled the identification mark on June 17th, 1932, when correspondence was not returned. The fate of the Meysenburg sailplane remains unknown.

## *The Pacific Beach Glider Meets*

The first glider meet in San Diego, the "Pacific Coast Glider Contest," was held in Pacific Beach on July 4th and 5th, 1929. Arranged by the Pacific Beach Business Men's Association and the San Diego Chamber of Commerce, the meet was a highlight of the Pacific Beach Midsummer Flower Show, which ran from July 3rd through the 7th. The launching site was located on a 350-foot hill located on the south slope of Mount Soledad in the vicinity of Castle Hills Drive, Windsor, and Monmouth Streets. Gliders were launched by a shock cord towards the empty fields of Pacific Beach to

*Above: A primary glider from the Riverside Polytechnic High School being launched by shock cord at the July, 1929 Pacific Beach Glider Meet.*

*Left: An unscheduled landing of the Riverside primary glider shortly after a poor shock cord launch.*

*Above and Right: Hawley Bowlus and the Bowlus Sailplane #16 towards the undeveloped flats of Pacific Beach below at the July, 1929 glider meet. Tip ailerons were used as replacements to earlier conventional ailerons.*

the southwest. In the late 1920s, the general public rarely ever saw a glider, and was fascinated to learn of the prospect of motorless flight. A large crowd turned out to witness this public glider exhibition.

Three classifications were used in the contest: primary training gliders, secondary training gliders, and "soarers" (sailplanes). Officials from the National Aeronautic Association and Fédération Aéronautique Internationale were on hand in the event that any glider records were broken. Representing the Airtech School of Aviation, Hawley Bowlus entered his series S-16 sailplane in the contest. Seven or eight youths from the Riverside Polytechnic High School brought a primary glider to the meet. Out of this group, Irven "Irv" Culver (age 17), H. B. Collins, and William "Bill" Atwood (age 18), had several successful flights with the Riverside primary.

Bowlus won the duration and distance categories with a flight of 58 seconds on July 4th and a flight of 1 minute, 45 seconds on July 5th. Bowlus' longest distance traveled was three quarters of a mile. Culver won the altitude portion of the contest with an altitude of 300 feet above launch. Atwood landed his primary glider within nine feet of the marker, giving him first place in the "accuracy" category. There were no accidents at the meet and a large holiday crowd enjoyed the modern spectacle of silent flight. Baron Koenig Warthausen (age 23), a German aviator on an excursion around the world with his powered plane, remained in San Diego specifically to view the contest. Warthausen participated in gliding while at college in Berlin, Germany. Photos from the first glider meet were used in brochures enticing tourists to visit sunny San Diego.

This first glider meet was so popular that Pacific Beach was selected as the site for a second meet in 1929. The "Pacific Coast Glider Meet" took place on September 1st and 2nd, on two hills near the intersection of Fanuel and Agate Streets in north Pacific Beach. The lower hill was about 300 feet, and the upper hill 400 feet above sea level. The meet was once again sponsored by the Pacific Beach Business Men's Association. Four Southern Californian cities were represented: San Diego, Riverside, Long Beach, and Glendale. With a growing interest in gliders in San Diego, there were a number of local entrants, including Hawley Bowlus, Alan "Dick" Essery, I. N. Lawson, Jr., and Adolf R. "Bud" Perl. At the time, Letain Kittredge was helping a number of San Diego Senior High School students construct primary gliders, and several of these were entered in the meet. Student Albert Gabbs had one flight in a primary glider at the event. Thousands of spectators were reported to have watched the events.

On the first day of the meet, Bowlus had a hard landing, but succeeded in establishing the best duration mark of the day by staying in the air for 1 minute, 17.6 seconds. Although contest records suggest that Bowlus entered his S-17 sailplane (identification mark 599M), photographs from the meet suggest that his S-16 sailplane (identification mark 493) was used instead, perhaps as a replacement for S-17 during the contest. Lawson's primary glider ground-looped on takeoff, damaging the wing, stabilizer, and fuselage enough to remove him from the remainder of the competition. Dick Essery made two flights on the first day, and then decided to "tighten-up his ship" for the following day.

Two categories of aircraft, primary (gliders) and secondary (sailplanes), were judged at the meet. John Pierce, a competitor from Long Beach, was skilled enough to enter a primary glider in the secondary class, and nearly equaled Bowlus' duration mark for the meet. Pierce took top honors for spot landing on the first day, stopping his glider 8 feet and 2 inches from the mark. Apollo Milton Olin (A.M.O.) Smith, also of Long Beach, secured first place in the primary class with a duration of 46.2 seconds. According to John Pierce:

> *We flew better poised on the skid that jutted out ahead of all else. Aloft so, we could see nothing but our feet and the scene below. We had a sense of truly flying, and boundless ambition for more. Clearly, we were ready for a glider meet. The meet was held a hundred miles away, in San Diego. We put the wings of our glider on the roof of the Packard, the fuselage on a trailer behind, and off we went. When we had arrived at the top of the hill and assembled our glider, we took off toward the plain below and flew over a real live news cameraman, wondering whether or not we would clear him. There was something wonderful about our glider which was missing in copies. Apollo and I have wondered what it could have been. It was of no use to copy the shapes of the ribs or the wings, for they were far apart and the cloth sagged between them, touching the spars. In some way, we had hit by accident on a most suitable wing profile, and the glider flew like a charm.*

On the second day, the competitors from Long Beach captured all the awards in the primary class and might have captured the secondary class as well, had it not been for an exceptional flight by Bowlus in the S-16 sailplane. Following a launch, Bowlus traversed the sky like a bird, flying a circuitous route to a landing in the empty fields below.

> *Bowlus provided the spectators with the most extended flight, staying in the air more than a minute and a half and performing evolutions over part of the crowd that thronged the fields on the south side of Soledad. He traveled an airline distance of 2,925 feet, but altogether must have traveled almost twice that distance as he made several complete circles and dipped and soared over the plain below the takeoff hill.*

Flying the Long Beach primary, Apollo Smith captured the secondary class altitude mark with a height of 72 feet. According to newspaper accounts, Smith was launched so fast that his hands left the control stick on takeoff and placed him in a sharp stall approximately 70 to 75 feet above the ground. Spectators recalled hearing Smith utter a startled "gosh" as he reached for the control stick in order to regain control of the aircraft. With barely enough altitude to pull out of the ensuing dive, he

*A photo from the camera installed under the left wing of the Bowlus sailplane #16 just moments prior to takeoff.*

managed to make a quick touch-and-go, then stayed aloft for one additional minute, much to the enjoyment of the crowd.

After a hard landing on the second day of competition, Dick Essery withdrew his ship from the meet. The Riverside entries also did not fare well. Irv Culver landed the Riverside primary in a clump of thick sagebrush with such a force that the right wing was damaged severely. Culver escaped the accident without injury. But a young man running to Culver's aid sustained the first and only injury of the meet when he ran straight into a cactus bush. The Riverside Aero Club primary glider flown at the Pacific Beach meet had a wingspan of 33 feet and chord of 5 feet, 8 inches. A Göttingen 398 airfoil was used. Although the primary was never weighed, John Pierce of the Long Beach Glider Club later referred to the glider as being much too heavy.

Bowlus captured the overall distance (2,925 feet) and duration awards (1 minute, 42.8 seconds). It is of interest to note that on one of his flights, Bowlus flew with a Sept 35mm camera under his left wing and took motion pictures of the meet from the air. This camera was mounted by Hawley and his brother, Glenn. It was one of the earliest recorded accounts of a motion picture camera carried aloft in a sailplane in the United States. With regards to the Bowlus sailplane that flew at the Labor Day meet, John Pierce recalled:

*In the air aboard the Bowlus sailplane #16 over Pacific Beach in 1929.*

*The flight of the sail-plane entered by Mr. Bowlus was certainly beautiful. It seemed to fairly float along. Over the lower hill, in spite of the lack of wind, it rose gracefully up to a considerable height, circled, and glided in curves out over the flat land below, making banks and turns in order that it might reach the thousands of cars parked to see the meet.*

*After the second day of the meet, we went to see the sail-plane being constructed by Mr. Bowlus, a marvel of lightness and strength. How clumsy previous craft seemed in comparison.*

## *Contestants at the Pacific Beach Glider Meets*

At the age of 14, Irv Culver built and flew his first glider, a replica of the Chanute hang glider. At age 17, he helped construct the primary glider used in the 1929 Pacific Beach glider meet with the members of the Riverside Aero Club. With the help of other local glider enthusiasts, Culver was instrumental in the formation of the Crown City Glider Club near Los Angeles, where they built and flew a total of five gliders, including the *Dingbat*, *Dingbat 44*, and the *Screamin' Weiner.* In 1938, he joined

Lockheed Aircraft Corporation and helped design the P-38 *Lightning* as well as the *Constellation.* He was later picked to design the fuselage and engine for the F-80. During the very secretive F-80 project, Culver once answered the phone "Skunk Works, Inside Man Culver" and the Skunk Works name stuck. His very successful career continued, with emphasis on the X-7 ramjet, U-2 spyplane, and many other projects.

At age 15, Bill Atwood built his first aircraft, a 20-foot hang glider fashioned after the Wright Brothers' *Wright Flyer.* This hang glider was Atwood's first introduction to gliding. Soon thereafter, he joined the Riverside Aero Club and began flying the club primary glider, including flights at the Pacific Beach Glider Meets in 1929. By 1930, he had limited flight instruction in Curtiss Jenny biplanes. Over a period of 16 months, he completed a sailplane with a 60-foot wingspan and tip ailerons. This sailplane was flown at various locations in the "Inland Empire" near Riverside, including the Shandin Hills (Little Mountain). While still a youngster, Atwood became interested in small gas-powered model boat racing, and after studying several engine castings purchased by his machinist friend, Bert Cundiff, Atwood started designing and building his own model engines. From the 1930s to the 1970s, he built model engines for model boats, cars, and airplanes, making several engines that were used on championship models of all types, including some models that ended up in the collection of the National Air and Space Museum of the Smithsonian Institution. By the 1960s and 1970s, his engine designs propelled Cox model aircraft flown around the world.

Apollo Smith graduated from the California Institute of Technology in 1938, and joined the El Segundo Division of the Douglas Aircraft Company as Assistant Chief Aerodynamicist. He worked on aerodynamic design of the A-20, DB-7, and B-26 aircraft, among others. In October of 1942, he went to Aerojet Engineering Corporation as their first Chief Engineer. His early work at Aerojet led to what would become the foundation for the Jet Propulsion Laboratory (JPL). Smith was commemorated with six other founders on a bronze plaque at the entrance to JPL. Smith was also involved with the development of the jet-assisted takeoff (JATO) unit, for which he received the Robert H. Goddard Memorial Award of the American Rocket Society in 1954. In later years, his studies culminated in the design of the F4D-1 *Skyray.*

In September 1928, James Caruso and Ray D. Chesley of Long Beach learned about the formation of the Long Beach Glider Club. Caruso and Chesley finished their first primary glider (identification mark 2887) on Easter Sunday, 1929. The glider was test flown by Dale Drake at Crawford's Airport in Seal Beach. Over May 4th and 5th, 1929, Caruso won the cup for primary gliders at the Pacific Coast Glider Contest held at the Long Beach Airport with a distance of 385 feet. Chesley won in the primary glider endurance category, with a flight of 12.6 seconds. Others that attended the contest included Ed Gettins, Apollo Smith, John Pierce, Dale Drake, Maurice Collins, and Glen Harvey. Prior to the meet, Caruso and Chesley had 11 flights in the primary glider and no instruction. Primary glider #2887 was entered in the Pacific Coast Glider Meet held in September, 1929, in Pacific Beach. Eventually,

Caruso and Chesley sold the primary glider to Fred Comer. Comer's boss, Wayne Fisher paid $90.00 for the glider. With Comer as the pilot, the primary glider was flown at the 1929 Los Angeles Glider Meet at the intersection of Pico Boulevard and Robertson Boulevard in west Los Angeles, and took first place. At the meet, W. E. Thomas of Pacific Aeromotive wrecked the glider. The primary glider was made of Oregon pine, except for the landing skid, which was made of hickory. It had a 32 foot wingspan with a wing chord of 5 feet and Göttingen 387 airfoil. The overall weight of the aircraft was 210 pounds. Long, narrow tail surfaces were used.

## *The Evans Prize*

Edward S. Evans, chairman of the aircraft bureau of the Detroit Board of Commerce and a pioneer in American commercial aviation, noted the importance of the motorless flight in America to other board members. Gliding was viewed as an inexpensive means for the training of new pilots. Evans helped finance the organization of a gliding association, the Evans Glider Clubs of America. Following a name change, this association became known as the National Glider Association in 1929. Evans posted a $2,000 reward to the first American pilot to fly in a glider for ten hours, with an additional $100 for each hour thereafter. During a time when money was scarce, this large cash award helped to stimulate interest in American endurance soaring.

## *Bowlus Establishes United States Glider Records*

After determining that Point Loma was a suitable site for ridge soaring, Hawley Bowlus embarked on a series of flights to increase the United States and world sailplane endurance records. On October 5th, 1929, Bowlus was launched from the top of Point Loma by shock cord in his S-16 sailplane. His flight was the first in a motorless aircraft from that location. By soaring along the bluffs in the prevailing westerly sea breeze between the Bennington Monument (a 60-foot gray obelisk marker at Fort Roscrans National Cemetery) and the old Point Loma Lighthouse, Bowlus stayed aloft for 14 minutes and 10 seconds. D. W. Campbell of the National Aeronautic Association and Ed White of the San Diego Chamber of Commerce officially timed Bowlus' flight.

> *After a start gained by being jerked into the air by a shock cord, Bowlus slowly glided in great circles over the group of people on the ground below. At times he was out over the cliffs that rise out of the sea and make Point Loma. On these flights over the water Bowlus estimated that he was 770 feet above the dashing waves below.*

The launch was made at 2:54:30 p.m., and landing occurred at 3:08:40 p.m., 450 feet from the point of takeoff. The event was carried by the local and national press and represented the first time that a sailplane of American design and construction had bested the Wright Brothers' glider endurance mark of 9 minutes, 45 seconds set in 1911. On July 29th, 1928, German Peter Hesselbach soared in the German-built D-17 *Darmstadt I* sailplane for 4 hours and 5 minutes over the slopes at Cape Cod, Massachusetts. In August, 1929, American Ralph Barnaby made a soaring flight of 15 minutes in a German *Prufling* secondary glider at Cape Cod, achieving the first "C" glider license in America. Bowlus' flight, however, was the first time that the Wright's endurance record was broken by an American in an American aircraft.

On October 19th, five days prior to Black Thursday and the crash of the stock market, Bowlus set up his S-16 sailplane once again on the road halfway between the old Point Loma Lighthouse and the Bennington Monument. Officials from the National Aeronautical Association were on hand as timers for the event. Bowlus was catapulted by shock cord into the air shortly after noon. This was part of the welcome demonstration arranged for the return of the local Russell Parachute Company plane, which was then on a national tour. The majority of Bowlus' 1 hour and 21 minute soaring flight exceeded an altitude of 750 feet above the ocean. It was the first soaring flight over one hour duration in the United States. Among many others, Merle Huster and Dr. H. K. W. Kumm witnessed the event.

Shortly after this record attempt, William Van Dusen (San Diego Air Control Board member and local National Aeronautical Association representative) and Donald Walker (manager of the National Glider Association) learned that Bowlus' flight could not be recognized "officially" by the Fédération Aéronautique Internationale. Fédération Aéronautique Internationale rules required that a circle be completed during the record attempt, prior to landing. Bowlus had made no such circle, although had he known of this requirement ahead of time, he could have easily completed many circles during the flight. Typically, Bowlus flew a standard "figure eight" course along the ridge, always turning away from the slope on each pass. Although the 1 hour, 21 minute flight was not recognized by the Fédération Aéronautique Internationale, the National Council of the National Glider Association did officially recognized the flight. Bowlus was awarded with a Citation for Distinguished Service in the cause of the American Glider Movement in November, 1929, specifically for this 1 hour, 21 minute flight. Similar citations were awarded to Wallace B. Franklin and Lt. Ralph Barnaby for their contributions for soaring.

The October, 1929, issue of *Popular Mechanics* featured an article entitled "Gliding on the Wings of the Wind." The review on gliding and soaring focused on its rapidly increasing popularity in America. A portion of this article focused on Hawley Bowlus' achievements in soaring at San Diego, including various photos of Bowlus' S-16 sailplane in flight and on the ground. A detailed account of the 1 hour, 21 minute flight was later described by Bowlus:

*Hawley Bowlus soaring over Point Loma in the Bowlus Sailplane #16 during one of several record flights.*

*At my signal, the shock cord crew ran directly into the wind. As they reached the brow of the hill and disappeared down its side, the cords gradually tightened until they became stretched to their limit... Contrary to the usual way of launching, the plane was not held back by a device. It merely rested on the ground.*

*At the moment the cord reached its elastic limit the plane began to move forward. Within three feet it took to the air, and, by the time it reached the launching crew, had risen thirty feet. As I had planned, the ship sailed into an upward moving current at the end of 100 feet and immediately I was lifted 300 feet above the crown of the point.*

*Due to the mild breeze, I had expected to turn immediately after taking off and land on the cliffs. Instead, during the first circle [circuit] I rose nearly 400 feet and decided conditions warranted an attempt to remain up at least an hour.*

*While I was occupied during the first few minutes seeking updrafts which would send me up high enough to glide into my takeoff point in case the breeze failed me, I could hear the ground crew discussing the takeoff. Communication between a glider pilot and persons on the ground can be carried on without any difficulty. Voices reached me with the clarity one would expect in casual conversation.*

*During the first forty-five minutes I sailed about in sweeping circles, free from any annoyances sometimes experienced in the air, easily maintaining an altitude of about 800 feet. Before another two minutes had passed, however, the air became very bumpy. Little wisps of fog blowing in from the ocean cast shadows on the surface of the water and on the hills. These cooled the air beneath. Where the shadows came in contact with sunny spots, rather sharp updraft-downdraft lines were formed, and soon I would find myself rising gently in the sunshine, only to be bumped sharply downward as I sailed into a shadow.*

## Stocks Fall While Gliders Soar

October 24th, 1929, changed the lives of many Americans, and had a lasting negative effect on the development of gliding in San Diego. The stock market tumbled drastically, following previous tumbles in May and November of 1928. Money was tight, and gliding represented a less expensive means to take to the skies than powered flight. It was a difficult year for everyone except for, perhaps, Babe Ruth, who accepted a two-year contract worth $160,000 to play for the New York Yankees. The contract was more than President Hoover earned at the time. In agreeing to the contract, the Babe explained that he had a better year than the President.

## Training New Glider Pilots

By November, 1929, Claude T. Burns of the San Diego City Playground Department was drafting plans for a glider camp to be established at Mount Palomar to the northeast of San Diego. Bowlus, who was Chief of the Technical Training Department of the Airtech School of Aviation, was listed as chief instructor for the proposed glider camp. At least 150 boys were expected to attend the camp between October, 1929, and January 2nd, 1930, but no other information about this camp is available.

November 5th, 1929, was a remarkable day in San Diego gliding history. Following instruction by Hawley Bowlus, ten pilots were awarded their third-class glider license during flights witnessed by William Van Dusen on behalf of the National

*The first graduating class of the Bowlus Glider School. Standing left to right: I.N. Lawson, Jr., Wm. Hawley Bowlus, Fred Rohr, Roy Pemberton, William Van Dusen, Doug Kelley, Earl Mitchell; kneeling, left to right: Arnot Cole, Jack Barstow, George M. McLeod, Al Lacey, Jr., and Rufus Spalding.*

Aeronautic Association. Pilots included John C. "Jack" Barstow, Arnot Cole, Doug Kelley, Al Lacey, Jr., I.N. Lawson, Jr., George M. McLeod, Earl Mitchell, Fred Rohr, Rufus Spalding, Jr., and Roy Temberton. This first class of glider enthusiasts was the result of a glider school operated by Bowlus in combination with the Airtech School of Aviation at Lindbergh Field. In addition to these 10 students, 20 more pilots were reported to be enrolled in the school for glider instruction. Bowlus and William Van Dusen planned for a National Glider Meet proposed for February 22nd, 1930 to be held at Pacific Beach. Hopes for the success of the glider meet were high...more than 12 glider clubs and over two dozen gliders were expected to be in attendance.

Seven primary gliders were under construction at San Diego Senior High School under the supervision of woodshop instructor Letain Kittredge. At the time, Bowlus already had several new sailplanes under construction at his new factory located at the southeast corner of Lindbergh Field.

San Diego's ten newest glider pilots met on subsequent weekends for practice at a field in the hills near Bonita. The pilots would routinely spend all day Saturday flying primary gliders, camp overnight at the site, and continue practice all day Sunday.

Glider licenses in the United States were issued by the United States Department of Commerce and signed by Orville Wright. Two types of licenses were issued: Sporting licenses, governed by the rules of the Fédération Aéronautique Internationale, and Federal licenses, issued by the United States Department of Commerce. Under the rules of the Fédération Aéronautique Internationale, first, second, and third-class sporting licenses were issued. The requirements for each of these licenses were as follows: for a third-class license, a pilot was required to make a flight of 30 seconds, followed by a normal landing. This was usually accomplished following a takeoff from the top of a long, sloping hillside as witnessed by official timers. To obtain a second-class license, a pilot was required to make a flight of one-minute duration, perform two "S" turns in flight, followed by a normal landing. Before this official test for the second-class license, the pilot was required to have made two flights of 45 seconds duration each. For a first-class license, the pilot was required to takeoff and fly for five minutes at an altitude greater than that of the spot from which the aircraft was launched.

When taking a license test, prior arrangements would typically be made so that if a flight qualified the pilot for a higher license than the one he was taking tests to obtain, the pilot could apply for both licenses at once, basing the applications on the same flight. Airplane pilots who held United States Department of Commerce licenses were allowed to try for first-class sporting glider licenses without first obtaining the third- and second-class licenses.

The United States Department of Commerce offered three types of glider pilot licenses: student, noncommercial, and commercial. Student permits authorized the holder to receive instruction and to fly solo in licensed gliders while under the jurisdiction of a licensed glider pilot. A noncommercial license served club members and those engaged in motorless flying for sport. Pilots were required to pass a test consisting of a minimum of three glider flights with moderate turns in either direction. A commercial glider license was issued to pilots who passed the same kind of physical examination that is required for a private airplane pilots license. No written examination was required. In addition to normal takeoffs and landings in the glider, a series of moderate turns and complete circles in the air was required, as well as precision landings. An arrangement between the National Aeronautic Association and the National Glider Association permitted the latter organization to issue third- and second-class sporting licenses and to supervise tests for first-class sporting licenses.

*William F. Crawford at Lindbergh Field on November 28th, 1929 following a flight from Seal Beach, California.*

## *William F. Crawford's Motorglider*

To the north of San Diego at Seal Beach, William F. Crawford completed construction on a series of motorgliders. These aircraft were essentially primary gliders with an open framework fuselage. The pilot sat in a bucket seat with a 40-horsepower Szekely engine mounted directly in front of him. Three motorgliders of this type were constructed by Crawford (identification marks 604N, N10, and 878N) between 1929 and 1930. Local aviator Clyde Schlieper (age 16) successfully landed one of the powered motorgliders on top of a speeding motorboat at 45 miles per hour near Long Beach. Pilots used to discuss the day's events over seafood at the nearby Glider'er Inn restaurant, which remains in business in Seal Beach.

On November 28th, 1929, Crawford, piloted a motorglider on a flight from Seal Beach to Lindbergh Field in San Diego. The 400-pound aircraft was flown at heights between 6,000 and 10,000 feet, and arrived in San Diego in the late morning. The

*Oceanside Blade-Tribune* reported that residents in Oceanside could catch a glimpse of this "spectacular flying demonstration" as Crawford flew over Oceanside on his way to San Diego. Quite a sensation was created when the motorglider arrived at Lindbergh Field.

## *Cimmino and Leonard Primary Glider (593V)*

Frank Cimmino and Robert Leonard of San Diego completed their primary glider in December, 1929. Application for an identification mark was not filed until March 6th, 1930, and identification mark 593V was granted March 21st. Very little is known about this primary glider, other than what was conveyed by Alice Cimmino (wife of Frank Cimmino) to the United States Department of Commerce in December of 1933. She wrote:

> *My husband has been out of the city for some time and the glider was not used nor bothered with for about two years. It was broken quite a good deal, and in fact was what I thought to be absolutely useless. With my husband's consent I gave it away to a boy with the understanding that it would never be used to fly in, nor try to fly in, and that he could cut up the wood in same and make little toy gliders or some such thing. This boy has had the glider for about a year now and I know it is not being used for anything but the wood.*

Identification mark 593V was canceled officially on March 8th, 1933.

## *McLean Northrup Primary Glider (594V)*

In December of 1929, John Walter McLean of San Diego finished construction on a standard Northrup primary training glider. The *McLean Glider* had a wing chord of 5 feet, 4 inches, wingspan of 32 feet, and overall length of 18 feet. It was initially inspected and approved for license on January 11th, 1930, but due to a clerical error, an identification mark (594V) was not issued by the United States Department of Commerce until March 15th, 1930. Number 594V, serial number P-T-1 (Primary-Trainer #1), was sold to Robert W. Leonard on July 3rd, 1930, after one wing was remodeled. In October, 1930, the identification mark was altered to G594V to reflect its status as a glider. By July 23rd, 1931, the United States Department of Commerce wrote to Mr. Leonard requesting renewal paperwork on the aircraft. When no correspondence was returned, the license was canceled on October 1st, 1931. There are no available photos of this aircraft.

## *Pacific Beach Glider Club*

The Pacific Beach Glider Club was run by five high school boys who had been attracted to gliders by local La Jolla Junior-Senior High School woodshop class instructor, Mr. Heckleman. Members included Blair Rogers, Dick Ward, Jack Ryan, Stanley Saville, and Lloyd Standley. All of the boys attended the La Jolla Junior-Senior High School but lived in Pacific Beach.

The club's first glider was completed in December, 1929, and was flown unlicensed at several locations in Pacific Beach through January and February, 1930. On March 10th, 1930, the primary glider was sold to Edgar Rosenow and John Kelder of Los Angeles. Rosenow and Kelder filed paperwork to obtain an identification mark. On March 21st, 1930, identification mark 596V was granted. The glider was moved to the Hollywood Riviera Gliderport near Redondo Beach. On April 5th, 1930, the glider was "cracked up completely" according to official United States Department of Commerce paperwork, and the identification mark was canceled on May 28th, 1930.

The second primary glider of the Pacific Beach Glider Club was completed on January 15th, 1930. The first flight of this glider occurred on January 26th at "Crane Hill" in Pacific Beach near the intersection of Kendall and Thomas Streets. Launches were made by shock cord. This Northrup primary glider was flown unlicensed and sold on March 4th to Harry H. Haw, O. E. Heckleman, Owen Thamer, E. G. Bigelow, and James J. Kass of La Jolla. It was inspected on March 16th at La Jolla, and an application for identification mark was filed on April 3rd, 1930. Identification mark 367W was officially granted on April 11th, 1930. The glider was flown for the majority of 1930. However, by December of 1932, the glider was donated to the La Jolla Junior-Senior High School manual training department for load testing and educational purposes. The aircraft was dismantled in the process. The identification mark was canceled officially on April 10th, 1933.

## *The Redondo Beach Glider Meet*

The Redondo Beach Glider Club sponsored a large glider meet at the Hollywood Riviera Gliderport on December 1st, 1929. This coastal gliderport was located just east of the Pacific Coast Highway between Torrance and Redondo Beach. Judges for the event included Rufus Pilcher, W. P. Bolderson, Fred Worthy and W. E. Thomas, officials of the National Aeronautic Association

*Hawley Bowlus soaring at the 1929 glider meet at Redondo Beach.*

An estimated 25,000 to 30,000 people witnessed the glider activities. A lack of wind was a disappointment, however, especially for the pilots interested in breaking Bowlus' duration record. Entrants included Jay Buxton, Dale Drake, Guy Rowell and 12 year old Betty Leekley as well as San Diegans Jack Barstow, W. H. Bowlus, Bud Perl, and William Van Dusen. Three sailplanes were entered by Bowlus, three Evans all-steel gliders from Vic Evans Glider Company of Los Angeles, two gliders from the Long Beach Glider Club, and one glider each from the Redondo, Torrance, and Bell Glider Clubs. Charles Crawford of Seal Beach entered the meet with his Szekely-powered motorglider, and made several successful flights for the crowd. Jack

Barstow won the soaring duration contest with a time of 2 minutes and 2.2 seconds in a Bowlus sailplane.

## *Bowlus Sailplane #18 (586V)*

Bowlus sailplane model "A", serial S-18, was completed in 1929. It was the first in a progression of "standard" Bowlus sailplanes to be completed by the Bowlus factory. The model "A" 60-foot wing was divided into three sections: two 18-foot outer panels with 5-foot tip-ailerons and one 14-foot center section. When empty, the sailplane weighed only 175 pounds. Total length of the fuselage was 19 feet and the aircraft had an aspect ratio of approximately 18:1 using the same USA 35A airfoil that was found on the S-16. The light wing loading of 1.67 pounds per square foot allowed the pilot to land at roughly 18 miles per hour.

On December 3rd, 1929, Bowlus set up the S-18 sailplane (later granted identification mark 586V) for a soaring flight at Point Loma. William Van Dusen, Dr. H. K. W. Kumm, and James A. Moore officiated for the National Aeronautic Association. During the afternoon, Bowlus remained aloft for 1 hour, 26 minutes, and 25.7 seconds and landed within 100 feet of the takeoff location on top of the ridge. The flight satisfied all requirements as a new United States soaring endurance record.

On December 10th, 1929, Bowlus broke his own duration record by soaring for 2 hours, 47 minutes, and 13.5 seconds above the slopes of Point Loma in the S-18 sailplane. This was his third official duration record within two months. A favorable wind aided him during the flight, which was observed by local officials of the National Aeronautic Association, including Dr. H. K. W. Kumm, James A. Moore, and William Van Dusen.

*Bowlus took off in a brisk west wind and skimmed above Point Loma in long easy loops taking advantage of the wind at each turn, until the breeze died down and darkness had settled over the point. When he landed, he received an ovation from the crowd which had watched him.*

*In landing, Bowlus demonstrated his mastery in handling the ship that he had kept in the air longer than any other American, without power. Night had fallen when Bowlus called to the watchers below that the wind had died down. As the crowd frantically ran to automobiles in an effort to maneuver them so the head lights would illuminate the point of takeoff, Bowlus glided out of the darkness and set his ship down less than 100 yards from the point of takeoff.*

Five Bowlus sailplanes were nearing completion at the sailplane factory and orders were received for more gliders from all over the country.

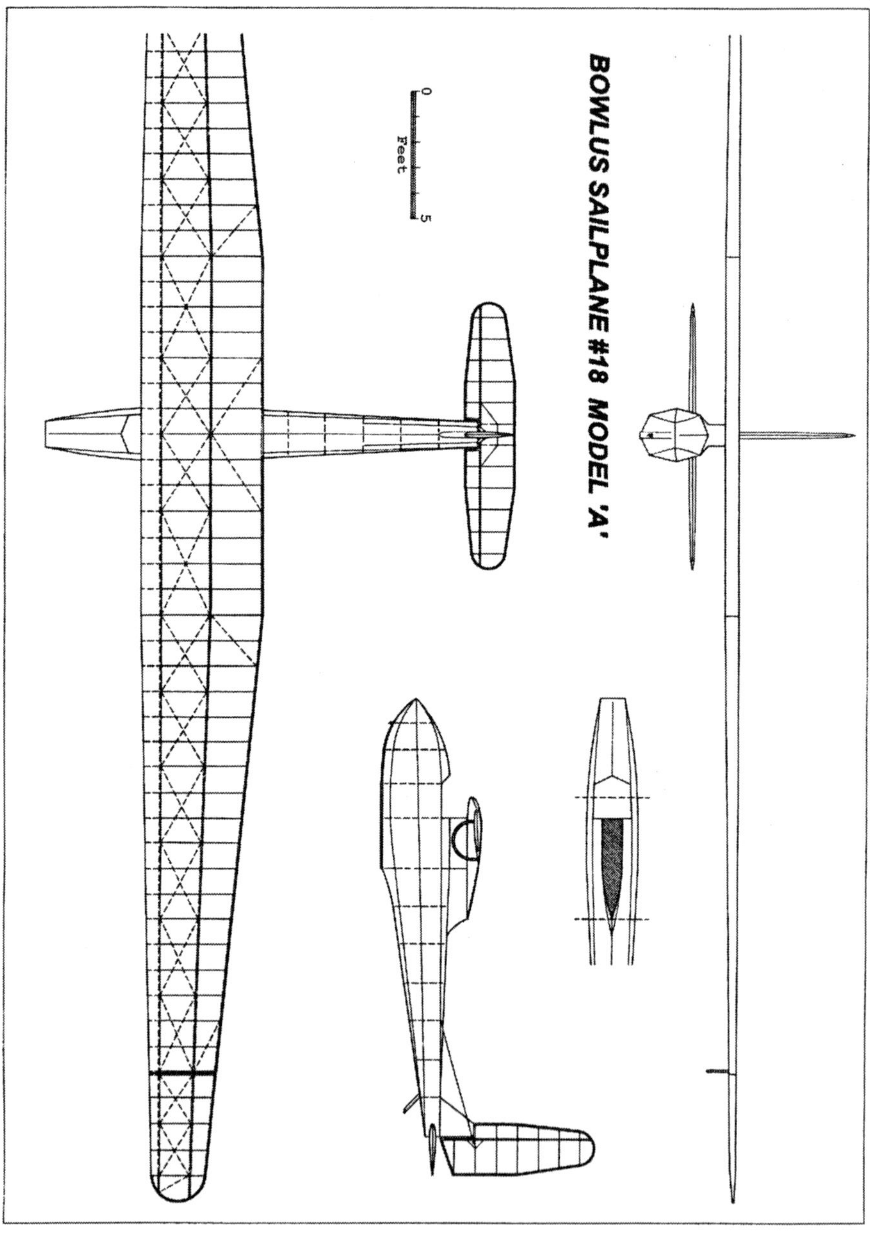
BOWLUS SAILPLANE #18 MODEL 'A'
0
Feet
5

## *Western Flyers Primary Glider (372V)*

Dick Essery, Joe Thurston, and William Dickenson finished construction on their third primary glider on December 28th, 1929. The glider had a wingspan of 35 feet, length of 17 feet, and wing chord of 5 feet, 3 inches. Application for an identification mark was sent on January 15th, 1930. Identification mark 372V was granted on February 19, 1930 and was relicensed as G-372V on July 18, 1930. A requested inspection for renewal of the aircraft license was not completed after this time, and the identification mark was canceled on August 1st, 1931.

## *Robert Goebel Primary Glider (39W)*

On December 29th, 1929, Robert Goebel of San Diego finished construction of a primary glider (serial 2000). New elevators and “flying fittings” were incorporated on December 30th. Application for licensing of the glider did not take place until March 5th, 1930, and identification mark 39W was granted on March 22nd, 1930. Goebel, however, did not keep the ship long; rather, he sold it to the Y.M.C.A. “Y-Triangle” Glider Club on April 1st, 1930 for the training of young pilots in San Diego. By December, 1932, the aircraft was permanently dismantled or salvaged, and the identification mark officially expired on January 12th, 1933.

# *CHAPTER 3*

# *1930*
# *The Golden Year of Soaring*

## *Soaring Records for Bowlus*

On January 6th, 1930, Bowlus set another unofficial American sailplane endurance record, this one lasting 5 hours, 27 minutes, 1.6 seconds on a flight at Point Loma. The flight was not considered "official" as Bowlus did not carry a sealed barograph and did not takeoff and land from the same location. When the winds subsided rapidly, he was forced to land at 1:31 p.m. along the sagebrush-covered flats below the old Point Loma lighthouse. On this attempt, Bowlus soared in his S-18 sailplane (identification mark 568V) and Jack Barstow, a student at the Bowlus Glider School, joined him in the air with a second, newly completed, Bowlus sailplane. Both pilots were forced to land below at a paired duration of 2 hours and 30 minutes. Bowlus' unofficial record was suggested to be one hour greater than the duration record set by the German, Peter Hasselbach, at Cape Cod in 1929. William Van Dusen, of the National Aeronautic Association and Fédération Aéronautique Internationale, officiated at the flight, while James A. Moore, and Roy Campbell, Jr. were witnesses. The flight occurred between the old Point Loma Lighthouse and the Bennington Monument in the prevailing westerly sea-breeze.

On January 12th, 1930, Bowlus took off in his sailplane S-18 from Point Loma at 1:17 a.m. into the early morning darkness with a sealed barograph on board. A barograph had been ordered by Bowlus from the East Coast, but it had failed to arrive in time for this flight. Luckily, he managed to borrow a barograph from the Los Angeles chapter of the National Aeronautic Association for the attempt. Overnight, Bowlus negotiated a strong westerly seabreeze to set a new official American endurance record of 6 hours, 19 minutes, and 3 seconds. Around 4:00 a.m., the wind ebbed to 8 miles per hour, just barely enough to keep the aircraft aloft. The few spectators that had gathered on the top of the ridge huddled around a campfire while Bowlus worked the ridge back and forth, sometimes only a mere 10 feet above their heads. He was forced to land when the wind died completely at 7:39 a.m.

A very happy, but exhausted Bowlus assured those spectators who had stayed throughout the night that he would make another attempt for the coveted Edward S. Evans Prize in the near future. Officials of the National Aeronautic Association and Fédération Aéronautique Internationale, including William Van Dusen, Jack Kicklin, Dr. H. K. W. Kumm, and James A. Moore, suggested the possibility that Bowlus also set a new American altitude record, surpassing the official record of 400 feet. New records were coming in so fast that the editors of the *San Diego Sun* suggested:

> *Unless W. Hawley Bowlus sets a glider record and sticks to it, officials of the National Aeronautic Assn. are going to have to hire a flock of office help to keep up with their work.*

On January 13th, the Bowlus Sailplane Company was officially incorporated, and demand for Bowlus gliders and sailplanes increased. Certified articles of incorporation for the Bowlus Sailplane Co., Ltd. were filed with J. B. McLees, the San Diego County Clerk. The company was located at 1200 W. Juniper Street, at the southeast corner of Lindbergh Field. This was in the same building used for the construction of the *Spirit of St. Louis* by the Ryan Aeronautical Company (a building currently occupied by Solar Turbines). This famous building was a former tuna fish cannery prior to the construction of Lindbergh Field.

On January 13th, Bowlus was the guest of honor at a banquet sponsored by the Aero Club of San Diego. The banquet was held in the Green Hat Room of the Waldorf Cafe and was billed as "glider night" by the local press. Dr. H. K. W. Kumm, President of the newly formed Associated Glider Clubs of Southern California, spoke on Southern California's leading role in gliding; James A. Moore, head of the local board of air control discussed regulations on gliding; and Roy Campbell, Jr. spoke on the commercial aspects of gliding. W. A. Huggins delivered a comic account of his gliding instruction; San Diego Mayor Harry Clark related the importance of Bowlus' flights to San Diego; and Letain Kittredge discussed his San Diego Senior High School woodshop glider construction class. T. C. MacAulay acted as toast master for the event and a motion picture of glider activities was shown. Following the banquet, Bowlus recalled to the audience that shortly after takeoff on his latest record flight, an apple rolled from out of his lunch box and jammed itself near the base of the control stick. Upon realizing this (and with a certain degree of urgency) Bowlus pried the apple loose and threw his "breakfast and lunch" overboard.

Hawley Bowlus was once again honored for his accomplishments in aviation. On January 14th, 1930, he was the guest speaker for a meeting of the Los Angeles Chapter of the National Aeronautic Association held at the Hotel Alexandria (in Los Angeles). His presentation included several glider films. During the second week of

January, 1930, Bowlus lectured to the aviation class of the Oceanside-Carlsbad Union High School. This was an attempt to educate young students on the virtues of soaring.

## *Bowlus Sailplane #20 (584V)*

Bowlus sailplane model "A," serial S-20, was granted identification mark 584V on March 15th, 1930. By July 21st, 1930, ownership of 584V had been transferred to the Anne Lindbergh Gliders Club of San Diego. Errors in paperwork were cleared by January 26th, 1931 when it was formally disclosed that the Bowlus Sailplane Company, Ltd. had sold the aircraft to the Anne Lindbergh Gliders Club for $10.00. In 1932, sailplane 584V was placed on display in the War Memorial building in Balboa Park. Prior to a large exhibition in Balboa Park in 1935, the sailplane was housed in another park building. The San Diego City School Visual Education department helped display the ship from the ceiling. During the 1935 exhibition, the sailplane was exhibited in the Ford Building (the same building that would eventually become home of the San Diego Aerospace Museum). William Beuby took care of 584V following the exhibition until he left San Diego. Beuby left the sailplane in the care of his father-in-law, C. J. Mortz of San Diego, while local glider enthusiasts attempted to place the ship in a museum. In December, 1939, two persons representing themselves as members of the Anne Lindbergh Gliders Club called at Mortz's home and left with the sailplane. Following this, the whereabouts of 584V remain a mystery.

## *Several Clubs Join to Form the Associated Glider Clubs of Southern California*

With the assistance of Dr. H. K. W. Kumm and an advisory panel, the Associated Glider Clubs of Southern California was an association of the following clubs: The Bowlus Glider Club (45 members), the Anne Lindbergh Gliders Club (25 members), San Diego Glider Squadron (San Diego Senior High School's woodshop club), Y.M.C.A. "Y-Trangle" Glider Club (30 members), Pacific Beach Glider Club, Solar Aircraft Club, Soledad Glider Club of La Jolla, Western Flyers Glider Club, Escondido Glider Club, Oceanside Glider Club, Riverside Glider Club, San Bernardino Glider Club, Long Beach Glider Club, Redondo Glider Club, Fullerton Glider Club, Hollywood Glider Club, Marvel Crosson Glider Club, Los Angeles Glider Club, Pacific Glider Club, Grasshopper Club, Aerotruss Club, and the Pelican Glider Club. It was hoped that the Associated Glider Clubs of Southern California could serve to increase communication between these clubs and act as a unified political voice representing glider activities throughout the region.

## *Charles Lindbergh Soars at Point Loma*

On Sunday, January 19th, Colonel Charles Lindbergh had his first try at soaring with a flight in a Bowlus sailplane along the ridge at Point Loma. While serving as superintendent at the Ryan Aeronautical Company during the construction of the *Spirit of St. Louis*, Bowlus had become well acquainted with Lindbergh. At 27 years of age, Lindbergh had very limited prior experience with gliding and had not tried his hand at soaring. Lindbergh visited Bowlus' sailplane factory in 1930 and soon enough, Lindbergh was interested in soaring at Point Loma.

> *When Lindy first arrived at Point Loma, he questioned Bowlus, 'You don't fly here do you? Where do you land?' Bowlus explained that with the light weight and wing loading of the Bowlus sailplanes, landings could either be made on the road on top of the ridge or below in the brush near the low cliffs.*

Using the S-18 sailplane, Bowlus gave a short 15-minute demonstration of soaring flight for both Lindbergh and the crowd that had gathered to witness the event at Point Loma. Then it was Lindbergh's turn while his wife, Anne, Hawley Bowlus, Forrest Hieatt and others watched with the crowd. It was Anne Lindbergh's first visit to San Diego. San Diego Senior High School student Albert Gabbs proudly held Lindbergh's wingtip during the launch. Gabbs recalled:

> *The big day...Charles Lindbergh was to takeoff in a Bowlus sailplane with a 60-foot wingspan...the crew of 10 persons pulling the shock cord. At 16 years of age, I was designated to hold the wing level for take off. The call was given, the crew ran out, the shock cord stretched, the man at the glider's stern let go and I too felt the wing leaving me. The great Charles Lindbergh was shot into the air...what a thrill for a 16 year old!*

Lindbergh was launched near the entrance to what is now the Cabrillo National Monument. Takeoff occurred at 2:46 p.m. and he soared for 31 minutes along the coastal ridge, landing almost exactly at the starting location. Reporters noted his course:

> *At first the Colonel contented himself with flying in short circles over the heads of those below, going from the old Spanish lighthouse to the Bennington cemetery. Then he essayed a cruise out over the Pacific and swung out almost half a mile before he pointed the nose of the glider shoreward again. Then came a long swing toward the mainland. Passing over the Theosophical Institute, he went as far as Sunset Cliffs before turning to come back.*

*Above: Charles Lindbergh (l) and Hawley Bowlus (r) posing for the cameras during Lindbergh's introduction to soaring.*

*Left: A happy Charles Lindbergh in the cockpit of Bowlus Sailplane S-18 following a successful flight at Point Loma.*

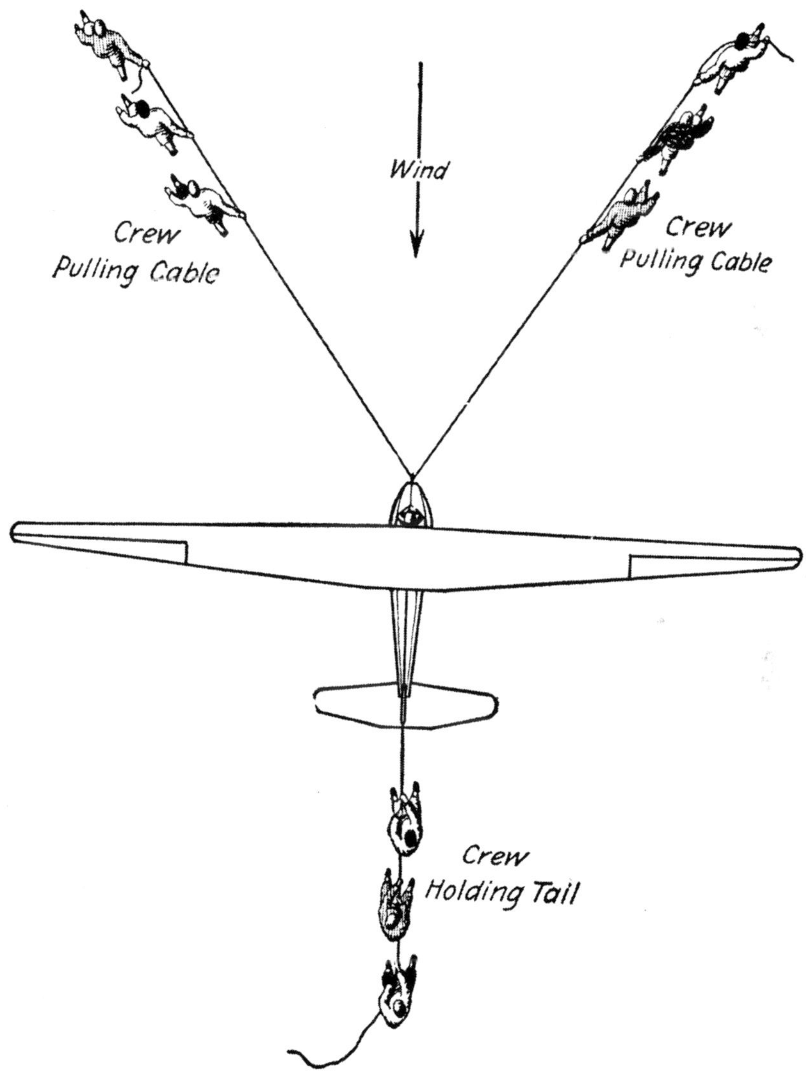


*An example of the typical shock cord launch. A crew in front of the sailplane pulls the shock cord in a "V" formation. A crew behind the sailplane pulls on a rope serving as a temporary anchor. The resulting tension in the shock cord is released by the crew holding the tail, resulting in a catapult of the sailplane into the prevailing wind.*

Local National Aeronautic Association representatives William Van Dusen and Dr. H. K. W. Kumm, were official observers for Lindbergh's flight. Occasionally during the flight, wind speed and direction were shouted above to Lindbergh: Van Dusen shouting "The wind velocity is twenty-one miles" with Charles replying, "That's fine, thanks. Let me know if it goes down suddenly." After his necessary five-minute soaring flight to attain his first class glider license, Van Dusen shouted:

> *Congratulations, Charlie, you have earned your 'gliding spurs,' and are the ninth in the United States to get a first class license. Now you may come down any time you feel so inclined. Lindbergh answered: 'Many thanks. I don't care to come down yet.'*

The crowd greeted Lindbergh's reply with loud cheers. Bowlus later remarked:

> *Colonel Lindbergh's exhibition of remaining in the air thirty-one minutes in this first attempt, and to maneuver it sufficiently, was a considerable tribute to his ability as a pilot.*

Upon landing, Lindbergh commented:

> *It was great sport. All you need is a hill and some wind. This was my first flight in a sailplane but it certainly was great sport. It also was the first time I have ever carried on a two-way conversation from plane to ground [without radio, only by voice].*
>
> *Gliding not only offers a flying medium of safety because of a landing speed of ten miles an hour, but it is much cheaper to learn to pilot a glider than a powered plane. The principle of flight is the same in glider and power planes, with standard airplane controls in both. A glider student learns the feel of a ship, how it banks, turns, and lands and he does it at a ridiculously low price as compared with power plane instruction. There is a thrill, too, to gliding. It is a superlative sport which appeals to Americans, young and old. A few can band together and buy a good glider. I see a great future for gliding in America. It will sweep the country during 1930 and I expect to see a million glider pilots within the next three years.*

Lindbergh's first soaring flights were extensively covered by the media, and several articles appeared in local and nationally distributed publications. A very thorough account of these activities was published in *Popular Mechanics Magazine*. With his first soaring flight, Lindbergh qualified for a first-class glider license, the 9th such license awarded in the United States by the National Glider Association. He was also awarded his second- and third- class glider licenses for the same flight. Local cameraman, Howard Jope, captured Lindbergh's flight on motion picture film. On January

21st, Bowlus addressed members of the local Kiwanis Club at a luncheon held at the Cabrillo Cafe located in the El Cortez Hotel. He was quoted as saying:

> *Did you ever lie on your back on a straw stack when you were a boy and watch a bird sail gracefully through the air? I have, and that is where I had my boyhood dreams about flying without an engine. I wanted to sail through the air like a bird. I began building my first glider in 1911, and two years later I built a glider that would carry my weight. My first glider was fastened together with wire and I used all of mother's spare bed sheets. That ship was demolished, but I never gave up. I knew it could be done, and that Point Loma was the best place in California to do it.*

On Friday, January 24th, Lindbergh and Bowlus left San Diego for an aerial survey of new potential glider sites in Southern California. At the time, the media was unaware of the purpose of this expedition and was somewhat mystified by their excursion. Two days later, Bowlus returned quietly to San Diego from Los Angeles by train. The importance of this journey will become evident later in this book.

## *Bowlus Primary Glider G-1 (598M)*

Primary glider G-1 (as designated by I. N. Lawson, Jr., an associate of Bowlus) was issued identification mark 598M on September 11th, 1929. This was the first of a series of Bowlus primary gliders. Title to G-1 was transferred to the Pacific Coast Gliders, Ltd., a franchise Bowlus system for glider and sailplane flight instruction. Similar Bowlus primary gliders using the Lawson design were given the Bowlus model designation G-100 and manufactured for private purchase.

The standard G-100 model primary glider had a 20-foot long framework for a fuselage made of welded steel tubes. Its height at the wing was 5 feet, 6 inches. The gross weight of the glider was 220 pounds, with an estimated 10:1 best gliding angle. The aircraft was offered for $550 with the choice of either a bungee cord or tow rope.

Primary glider 598M became the official training glider at the Bowlus Glider School. Typical equipment for the Bowlus system of glider instruction called for a "small roadster, one quick release attachment, and a 3-foot megaphone." Forrest Hieatt's Studebaker sedan was typically used at the Bowlus school at Lindbergh Field, with the instructor pointed rearward toward the glider as it was towed behind the car. A letter to the United States Department of Commerce Aeronautics Branch was sent requesting permission for the towing of gliders at Lindbergh Field. A reply was returned, "Granted. Use proper length of rope." The primary was towed behind a car traveling at low speeds down the dirt runway at Lindbergh Field to give the student the feeling of glider flight. The speed of the car was gradually increased until the pilot was confident enough to try a Bowlus sailplane.

*Charles Lindbergh (left) and William Van Dusen (right) review Lindbergh's soaring flight at Point Loma.*

Students of the Anne Lindbergh Gliders Club nicknamed the 598M primary glider *Tillie the Toiler*, or *Tillie* for short (named after the leading lady in a Sunday comic strip common to newspapers of the period). Glider students at the Bowlus school, and the affiliated Airtech Flying Service used *Tillie* at Lindbergh Field on a daily basis. Qualified airplane pilots, as well as students, were checked out in *Tillie* before they were introduced to soaring. Seven of the first twelve pilots who were awarded United States first class glider licenses flew in *Tillie* during their glider instruction.

High school student Al Gabbs traded his time as *Tillie*'s official "mechanic" for a few flights at the end of the day, and it was in *Tillie* that Gabbs took his first flight. Gabbs recalled:

> *My eagerness to fly had finally gotten to Bowlus Instructor Forrest Hieatt, so finally they let me take the first flight where you run along the field keeping the tail level. I had practiced for a week in my chair with my feet and*

*imagining a flight...I could almost feel the controls. Now I had the actual controls! It did feel somewhat familiar. The car started and being about 3 feet from the ground, the speed was almost frightening! I held the tail up and was instructed to do so, but somehow the glider kept rising off the ground. Now I was 12 feet up, scared, and then 30 feet and I could see the scared looks on the guys in the towing car. The wind blew by my ears and the tow car was way down there. Now Hieatt had to make a decision...there was a plowed field at the end of the dirt runway at Lindbergh Field and he could not take the car over the much rougher ploughed area. He decided to cut me loose. Here was a 15 year old kid up about 30 feet in the air on this first flight! I came down and made a perfect landing in the plowed end of Lindbergh Field. I was then a hero and was proclaimed the mechanic of Tillie the Toiler.*

Despite such success, *Tillie's* career was short lived. Student pilot Max Miller later confessed in the *San Diego Union* that during July, 1930, he crashed *Tillie* beyond repair following a stall of the aircraft at Lindbergh Field. The primary glider was swiftly transformed into a collection of parts stacked behind the back wall of the Airtech hangar. Miller was uninjured in the mishap.

## *Bowlus Primary Glider T-2 (365V)*

On January 19th, 1930, Bowlus primary glider serial number T-2 was completed at Lindbergh Field. An application for identification mark was filed on January 31st and the glider was to be used for "primary student training." Identification mark 365V was issued on February 10th. By September, 1931, the training glider was sold to former Bowlus student and employee Albert E. Hastings for use in glider instruction at Mines Field (now the site of the Los Angeles International Airport). Hastings had trained at the Bowlus school in 1930 and became the winner of the First and Second National Glider Contests at Elmira, New York. Identification mark 365V was canceled in November of 1931, due to a lack of correspondence.

## *Peaches Wallace*

While Bowlus was scouting for glider sites, Miss Peaches Wallace, a 20-year-old San Diegan aviatrix, became the second woman in the United States to qualify for a third class glider license. Launched by an 8-man shock cord team on January 26th, 1930, Wallace made a 36 second flight in a Bowlus sailplane. The flight was made on a hillside near Morena (Bay Park), facing Mission Bay at a location about one mile east of

*The young aviatrix Peaches Wallace in the cockpit of a Bowlus sailplane. Wallace became the second woman in the United States to earn a third class glider license. Her flights in powered and non-powered aircraft in San Diego were the subject of widespread publicity as women became more interested in aviation.*

the highway, midway between Old Town and Pacific Beach. Although there was no prevailing wind at the time, her launch was of sufficient height such that the required 30 second duration was easily attained in the glide. Her flight followed three hours of instruction at the Bowlus Gliding School at Lindbergh Field, under the supervision of Forrest Hieatt. Miss Wallace already held a United States private pilot license at the time. Representing the National Aeronautic Association, William Van Dusen and Phillip de Mandel officiated her flight.

## Mount Soledad

As a direct result of Bowlus' and Lindbergh's flights, soaring received increased attention in the local press. Dr. H. K. W. Kumm, first president of the Associated Glider Clubs of Southern California, surveyed the Mount Soledad region on January 19th, 1930, in the hopes of finding a suitable launching site. Captain W. C. Crandall, Mr. Vandergriff, Major D. C. Rumsey, and Lieutenant George W. Pardy accompanied Dr. Kumm through the region. The tour party requested that Mount Soledad be the site of a proposed "Southern California Glider Meet" to be held February 22nd-23rd, 1930. It was their unanimous opinion that "Mount Soledad and the surrounding region [would] prove [to be] the outstanding glider base for the entire United States." The idea of a large glider meet was a carry over from Bowlus' idea of a National Glider Meet to be held in the San Diego area in the spring of 1930. At the January 24th meeting of the Associated Glider Clubs of Southern California, the glider meet was postponed to April 25th-28th to coincide with Easter vacation in the hopes that this would attract more publicity and participants to the events. The January 23rd, 1930, edition of the *La Jolla Journal* headlined, "Mount Soledad Selected as Location for Glider Base."

## Anne Morrow Lindbergh

On the morning of Wednesday, January 29th, Anne Lindbergh completed a short course in basic primary glider instruction at the Bowlus Glider School. She was already quite familiar with powered flight. Her glider instruction was carried out using the Bowlus primary glider *Tillie the Toiler* (identification mark 598M).

That same afternoon, Anne Lindbergh became the first woman in the United States to qualify for a first class glider license. Her qualifying flight of six minutes duration was made from the top of Mount Soledad to a landing at the north end of La Jolla Shores, near the foot of the Biological Grade. The flight was officially timed by William Van Dusen and J. L. Hicklin while Charles Lindbergh, Jack Maddux, and a large contingent from the news media looked on. Bud Perl helped serve in the ground crew for the flight. Her flight, satisfying the licensing requirement, was described in the *San Francisco Chronicle* and other newspapers and magazines across the country.

> *Mrs. Lindbergh's takeoff was as good as though it had been done by the Colonel himself. From the flat mountain top she sailed directly west toward the ocean, the glider resembling a great bird in flight. After flying about three minutes directly west she manipulated a 90° right angle bank and headed north, only to make another 90° bank to the left and then run southward...Within a few seconds she made a perfect landing in a field beside the State highway.*

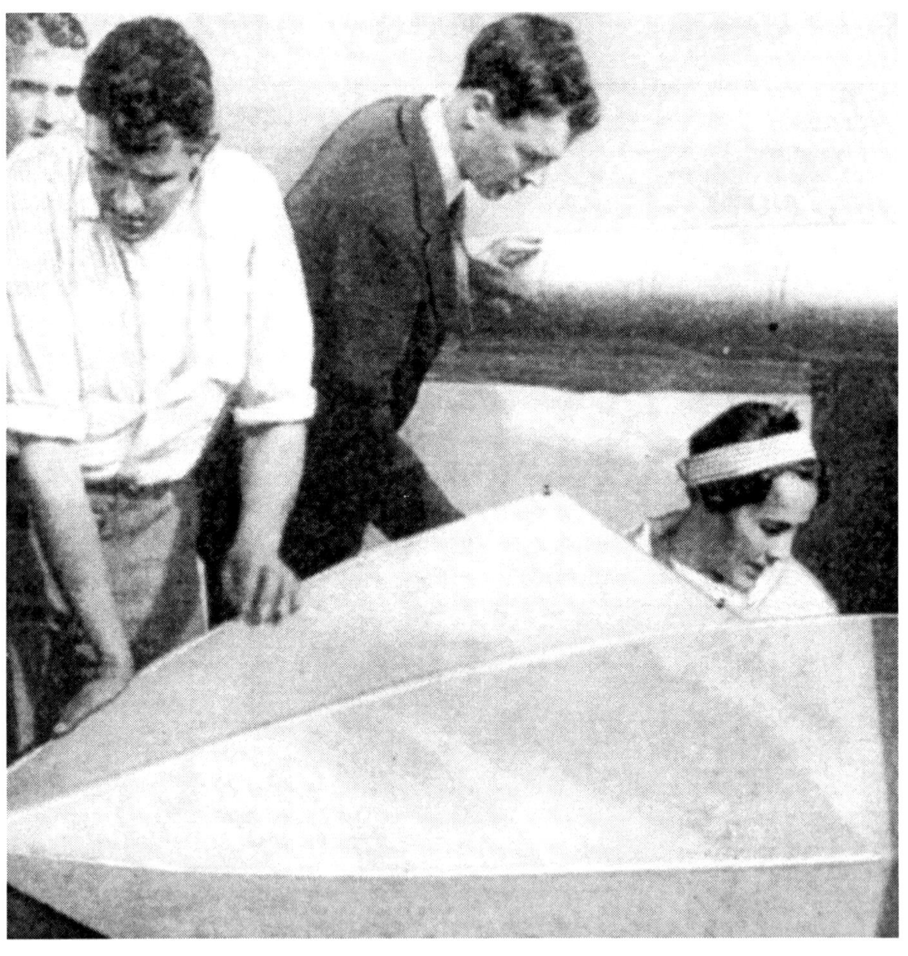

*Left: Anne Morrow Lindbergh in the cockpit of a Bowlus Sailplane while Hawley Bowlus (l) and Charles Lindbergh (r) assist in the preparation for takeoff from the top of Mount Soledad. Previous to this launch, Anne Lindbergh had received glider instruction in the primary glider Tillie the Toiler at Lindbergh Field.*

*Above: The shock cord launch of Anne Lindbergh in a Bowlus sailplane. Charles Lindbergh witnessed the flight (standing, bottom right). With this flight, Anne Lindbergh became the first woman in the United States to qualify for a first class glider license.*

Anne published a description of her sailplane adventure in the book *Hour of Gold, Hour of Lead*:

> *...when I got into the cockpit and all the people stood around and C. [Charles] said 'All set?' and Hawley said 'All set?' to the men on the ropes, I felt like a lamb about to be sacrificed (right on the top of a mountain, too!)...Then the men started running, pulling the rope. I heard the keel scrape and I was off! In a second...I did very little soaring because I felt rather timid about getting too near the sides of hills. I didn't want to experiment this first time. But I felt the ship go up to currents in each crevasse in the hillside. When I was quite near the [landing] field, I heard a bird singing. Then I turned around the field to face it the long way and skimmed along the ground and it stopped, without any jolt, like a sled plowing into snow with a slight crust. Then I jumped out, lifted up the tail to see if the scraping had hurt anything (it's very light), and looked at the road. Cars were stopping and people (a few) came up. 'We've been watching you. We wondered what you were doing so close to this field. We thought you were a plane.' They stood around grinning. 'Where did you come from?' I, in my white overalls, pointed up to the mountain that looked in the clouds. One excited lady called over and over, 'She's all right! She's all right! This little girl came all the way down from that mountain, and she's all right!'*

For this flight, Anne was awarded her first, second and third class glider licenses. Later, she suggested that it was the first glider flight from the top of Mount Soledad, a location personally chosen by Charles Lindbergh for Anne's flight. The launching site was at the crest of the mountain top and the sailplane was launched towards La Jolla Hermosa to the northwest. Members of the Associated Glider Clubs of Southern California were so thrilled by Anne's flight that they filed a request with the San Diego City Council petitioning that the point near which Anne landed the glider be named "Anne Point" in her honor.

## *The Anne Lindbergh Gliders Club*

After securing her third class glider license, Peaches Wallace announced that she would help set up an all women's glider club "to foster interest in the handling of powerless craft." By Sunday, January 30th, the "Anne Lindbergh Gliders Club" was born, with Anne Lindbergh serving as the club's Honorary President. Three women with private pilot's licenses were inducted as Charter Members: Ruth Alexander, Peaches Wallace, and Guinivere Kotter. With the help and leadership of Dr. H. K. W.

*Above: Members of the Anne Lindbergh Gliders Club pose for the cameras ready to shock cord a Bowlus sailplane at Lindbergh Field.*

*Middle: Anne Lindbergh Gliders Club ready for instruction at the Bowlus Gliding School.*

*Right: Official certification of the Anne Lindbergh Gliders Club as an affiliate of the National Glider Association.*

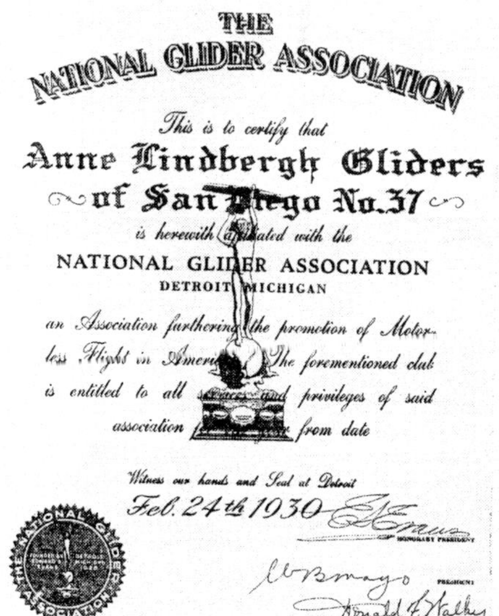

THE
NATIONAL GLIDER ASSOCIATION

This is to certify that
Anne Lindbergh Gliders
of San Diego No. 37
is herewith affiliated with the
NATIONAL GLIDER ASSOCIATION
DETROIT MICHIGAN
an Association furthering the promotion of Motorless Flight in America. The forementioned club is entitled to all services and privileges of said association [illegible] from date

Witness our hands and Seal at Detroit
Feb. 24th 1930

HONORARY PRESIDENT

PRESIDENT

Donald F. Walker
SECRETARY

*Hawley Bowlus (r) giving glider instruction to a member of the Anne Lindbergh Gliders Club (l).*

Kumm, on Friday, February 14th, San Diego became the official home of the club. Their affiliation with the National Glider Association certified them as the 37th glider club in America.

To raise enough money to buy their own Bowlus sailplane, the girls held a dance at the U.S. Grant Hotel on February 20th. Motion pictures of glider activities were shown, especially those of Mrs. Lindbergh's flight from Mount Soledad. Over 20 women signed up for the club making it one of the largest glider clubs in the country at that time. The sailplane they hoped to purchase was nearing completion at the Bowlus factory and had already been christened *The Good Ship Anne* by the glider club. Club members included Ruth Alexander, Gwen Bacon, Jean Barnes, Margaret Burnett, Claire Cesmat, Anne Dunn, Kay Fiedeke, Mary Jane Freeman, Suzanne Garvin, Alice Sue Hardin, Hazel Kelley, Laura Lindley, Kathleen Mitchell, Doreen

Moore, Margaret Neyenesch, Florence Rainwater, Deloris Rauner, Helen Twisleton, Julia Twisleton, Helen Van Dusen, Etta Mae Wallace, Peaches Wallace, and Verna Wallace.

The successful avaitrix Ruth Alexander had previously set several United States altitude records for women in powered aircraft. Her first two tries were made from Ryan Field in a Great Lakes airplane. Later, she made altitude attempts from Lindbergh Field using a NB-1 Barling aircraft. By March 3rd, Helen Van Dusen was taking lessons at the Bowlus Glider School in the primary glider *Tillie the Toiler* under the instruction of Forrest Hieatt.

Ellen Guinivere "Gwen" Kotter received her bachelor's degree in 1925 from Utah State Agricultural College and began teaching in Brigham City. She later attended Columbia and Stanford Universities and accepted a position at San Diego State University in 1928. That year, she learned to fly at Lindbergh Field and, in 1929, she became the first woman from Utah to receive both private and commercial pilot's licenses. She taught education for more than 40 years at San Diego State University and retired in 1969 as an associate professor.

In the afternoon of February 17th, 1930, Mrs. Kotter qualified for her third class glider license with a flight of 58 seconds at La Jolla. She followed with a flight of more than a minute, qualifying her for a second class glider license. Dr. H. K. W. Kumm officially observed both flights. At the time of the flights, conditions were less than adequate for soaring. To ensure safety, the flights were made only after Jack Barstow took responsibility on behalf of the Bowlus Glider School.

On February 11th, 1930, an Evans primary glider was purchased by the Anne Lindbergh Gliders Club from Richard D. Ferguson of San Diego. This glider was manufactured February 1st, 1930 by the Evans Glider Company. Miss Julia Twisleton handled all paperwork as club Secretary. On March 15th, the club filed for an identification mark with the United States Department of Commerce with a bit of urgency; they were not allowed to fly the glider unlicensed. Following two telegrams to speed up the paperwork, identification mark 26W was granted on March 21st.

After flying the primary for much of 1930, the glider fell into disrepair by October. The glider was overhauled at the Chula Vista Airport by Dick Williams, and repairs included refinishing of metal parts and control wires and a recovering of the airframe. Following restoration, the glider identification mark was changed from 26W to G-26W, to note its use as a glider.

The glider was sold to the "Y"-Triangle club of San Diego on September 22nd, 1931, to be used for the training of high school boys. On November 20th, 1931, the glider license was canceled when the aircraft was not inspected for relicensing. It is unknown what happened to this glider after this time.

*Above: William Van Dusen (kneeling) and two unknown persons preparing Charles Lindbergh (cockpit) for a shock cord launch at Lebec, California.*

*Below: Charles Lindbergh attaching a tip-aileron to the wing of a Bowlus sailplane.*

# *Glider Operations at Lebec, California*

On February 2nd, 1930, Hawley Bowlus and several of his glider friends left San Diego for Lebec, California with an auto towed trailer carrying a Bowlus sailplane. A potential soaring site near Lebec was spotted by Lindbergh and Bowlus on their previous reconnaissance flight. Bowlus met Charles and Anne Lindbergh at Lebec in the hopes that Charles might set a few new soaring records.

A glider camp was set up between the towns of Sandberg and Lebec in a secluded area covered with trees. A large contingent from the press followed them, including five movietone newsreel companies and reporters from 12 regional newspapers. After his famous transatlantic crossing, Lindbergh was constantly hounded by the media. The glider camp was far removed from the quiet seclusion that the pilots had sought.

On February 3rd, Lindbergh was launched by shock cord in the Bowlus sailplane S-18. A few seconds after takeoff, one of the ailerons on the tip of the wing came off in mid-flight. Undaunted, and with independent tip-aileron control from the cockpit, Lindbergh soared nearly a mile over several hills and landed without incident. The story was carried immediately by the national press. The *Los Angeles Times* headlined "Flying Ace Cheats Death in Motorless Craft." William Van Dusen recollected:

> *We began a week of thrills, successes and disappointments. And our most exciting moments occurred the first day the sailplane was flown. Hawley Bowlus made two short flights. Then Colonel Lindbergh took his place in the cockpit and was shot into the air. When he attained a height of forty feet, one of the ailerons broke off--to our horror. Ailerons of this particular type of sailplane are on the extreme tip of the wing. Some of us knew that an airplane would fly with one aileron gone, but the effect of its loss upon the flight of a glider was unknown...frantically, we shouted. Looking back, Colonel Lindbergh saw what had happened, but the course of his flight did not falter. Following a gently winding valley, he glided along above its growth of trees...we had been paralyzed--now we rushed into action. Several press men immediately drove madly away to find the nearest telephone and notify their offices that Colonel Lindbergh had been injured in a glider crash. I leaped into a car and dashed down the rolling mountain side, into valleys and over ridges, miles and miles it seemed, although later estimates placed the distance at four or five miles. Soon a barbed wire fence blocked the path. Other rescue cars were racing behind...leaving the car, I jumped the fence and ran on, shouting to the others to cut it and drive through. Soon I reached a vantage point and just below saw the sailplane sweep to a perfect landing and Lindbergh step safely out. A motor car roared by me. Hawley Bowlus, with the trailer tagging crazily behind, drove precariously down an unbelievably steep bank and soon reached the Colonel... We rushed up breathlessly only to find a calm young man, who was far less excited than any of us... 'The metal*

*tubing in the aileron must have become crystallized,' he commented, 'but there was practically no difference in the control.'*

The glider group celebrated Charles Lindbergh's 28th birthday on February 4th, with a picnic after a new set of tip-ailerons were ordered from San Diego. By the following day, the ship had been repaired with the assistance of Jack Barstow and Philip De Mandel. Lindbergh took the first test hop in the sailplane. Without a strong prevailing wind, ridge soaring was not possible. Even in poor soaring conditions, Lindbergh managed to glide a distance of about 4 miles, landing approximately 500 feet lower than the point of takeoff.

Glider enthusiasts from Bakersfield drove south to witness the activities, including Don and Ross Cardiff. San Diegans William Van Dusen and Lt. S. C. W. Kingsbury were in attendance to officiate for any possible record attempts. Bowlus proposed the idea of a continuous soaring flight from Los Angeles to San Diego by night at an undisclosed later date. However, by February 7th, the glider experiments at Lebec ended, and Bowlus returned to San Diego due to lack of suitable prevailing winds.

Others that attended flight operations at Lebec were Howard Jope (cameraman) and A. R. "Bud" Perl, who at the age of 17 was already training on Bowlus sailplanes. In 1988, Bud Perl recollected:

*Charles and Anne had a house in Los Angeles, so they would spend the night there and drive up very early in the morning [to the glider camp at Lebec]. Well, one morning, Charles and Anne got up real early and arrived at the camp at 4 a.m. Charles turned off the engine and the lights (he was driving a Franklin then) and drifted close up to the tents. About 10 feet from the tents, he blasted his two air horns. It was pandemonium in the tent!*

## *The Barr-Batzloff Sailplane (58W)*

By February 19th, 1930, Harold Barr and Wilbur Batzloff of San Diego Senior High School finished the construction of a sailplane with a wingspan of 47 feet and length of 18 feet. The plane was patterned after the Bowlus sailplanes and used a very similar fuselage, tapered wing, and wingtip ailerons. Identification mark 58W was granted by the United States Department of Commerce on March 28th, 1930. The sailplane was later damaged in a minor crash on July 10th, 1930, and was not repaired. All metal fittings were salvaged and the rest of the aircraft was used in experimental load testing. The identification mark was canceled on March 8th, 1933.

*Pacific Beach Glider Club sailplane G80W soaring at Morena, east of Mission Bay near the present-day community of Bay Park.*

## *Gliders in La Jolla*

Members of the newly formed Soledad Glider Club announced that Hawley Bowlus was to speak February 7th, 1930, at 7:30 p.m. at the American Legion Hall in La Jolla. Letain Kittredge, however, substituted for the then-exhausted Bowlus. George Pardy also gave a few remarks on the upcoming Southern California Glider Meet. Several glider movies were shown including the well-publicized soaring flights by the Lindberghs in San Diego.

Three of the Pacific Beach Glider Club boys qualified for their third class glider licenses in their primary glider at Morena on February 15th, 1930. Letain Kittredge and Ruth Alexander qualified for their second class glider licenses in the same primary glider with flights at Mount Soledad on February 16th.

On February 21st, 1930, Dr. H. K. W. Kumm, president of the Associated Glider Clubs of Southern California, wrote a letter to W. H. Moore, owner of the property on the top of Mount Soledad, with the request that he grant permission for a hangar to be constructed for the storage of gliders. On the evening of February 22nd, Bowlus gave a lecture on gliding at the American Legion Hall in La Jolla at 8:00 p.m. Local papers noted that:

> *...during the past few weeks a large group of La Jollans have shown a decided interest in the new found sport of sailing the air in motorless planes. The American Legion Post has offered to construct a hangar at the top of Soledad and much activity is promised this district in the near future.*

On Sunday, February 23rd, Ruth Alexander crashed in her attempt for a first class glider license. The misguided takeoff occurred at Mount Soledad. A crowd of approximately 300 onlookers witnessed the crash, including William Van Dusen who officiated at the license trials. A sudden downdraft struck the glider shortly after takeoff and forced Alexander to land on the mountainside. Her only injuries were a scratch on her nose, several bruises, and the fact that she fainted when the plane struck the Earth. Damage to the ship was confined to one wing and the cockpit.

At this time, local boys were constructing a glider in the woodshop of La Jolla Junior-Senior High School, under the supervision of Mr. Heckleman (perhaps a sailplane, identification mark G80W, or a primary glider constructed by the Falcons Glider Club of the La Jolla Junior-Senior High School, identification mark 303W). This sailplane was patterned after the large 60-foot wingspan Bowlus sailplane design. The April 15th edition of the *La Jolla Light* suggested that the high school division of the Mount Soledad Glider Club was in the process of constructing a glider. Falcons member Spencer Wilson helped in the construction. The Mount Soledad Glider Club was also busy reconditioning a glider and was almost finished. Construction of gliders at the high school woodshop was taking so much room that excess glider construction was moved to the building formerly occupied by the Arcade Garage in La Jolla. This building was donated for this purpose by a local realtor, Robert Hill.

## *Bowlus Sets Another Record and Charles Lindbergh Soars on the Lift at Torrey Pines*

Fresh from his lecture at the American Legion Hall in La Jolla the previous evening, Bowlus headed out on the morning of Sunday, February 23rd, 1930, to Mount Soledad and set up his record-setting S-18 sailplane. Bowlus' intent on this day was to once again break the United States or world sailplane endurance records. In the early afternoon, Bowlus was launched by shock cord from the top of the mountain and enjoyed a 45-minute soaring flight that ended at the foot of the Biological Grade near the buildings of the Scripps Institution of Oceanography. After bringing the sailplane back to the top of the mountain, Bowlus launched again, resulting in a similar "short" hop. Bowlus decided that although he had flown at Mount Soledad before, the lift at this site was not sufficient for a record on this day so he moved the entire soaring operation to Point Loma.

At 5:47:03 p.m. that evening, Bowlus was launched into a 30-mile-per-hour wind that sent the S-18 sailplane rocketing 500 feet into the air over Point Loma. This was later described as a "spectacular launch" by local newspaper reporters. Bowlus flew into the darkness as night fell over the area. It was reported that the wind blew steadily and sometimes gusted to 35 miles per hour, keeping Bowlus at an altitude of between 800 to 1,000 feet above the peninsula.

Red lanterns were placed along the Point Loma road and the narrow ledge between the foot of the cliffs and the ocean below, to guide Bowlus in case of a forced landing. A huge bonfire marked the landing area, and automobile headlights were used to serve as beacons along the course. More than 1,000 people drove to the point during the night and early morning to witness the flight, and watchers on the ground staged a number of stunts to entertain Bowlus as he soared back and forth above the cliffs.

Bowlus finally landed in the darkness (with the help of automobile headlights to guide him) at 2:43:30 a.m. on February 24th, after a flight of 9 hours, 5 minutes, and 27.4 seconds, according to official records. His landing was on the main road, less than 75 feet from his point of takeoff near the old Point Loma Lighthouse. This gave Bowlus a new official United States endurance record for sailplanes, and also was reported by local newspapers to have set a new U.S. altitude record for gliders. Yet, the 9-hour flight fell just short of the 10-hour soaring endurance requirement for the $2,000 Evans Prize.

After recovering from his early morning landing, Bowlus and Charles Lindbergh traveled to the top of Mount Soledad and readied a Bowlus sailplane (S-20) for its maiden soaring flight. This sailplane, *The Good Ship Anne*, carried the logo for the Anne Lindbergh Gliders Club. At 2:21 p.m. on February 24th, 1930, test pilot Charles Lindbergh was launched by shock cord. During the launch, the tailskid of the sailplane was knocked off, but Lindbergh "kept his plane on an even keel." After flying over Mount Soledad and La Jolla Shores, Lindbergh headed to the north, using the lift along the cliffs at Torrey Pines to maintain his altitude. Finally, he landed 20 minutes after takeoff on the beach just south of Del Mar at the end of the cliffs just to the north of Sorrento Valley. This flight made headlines in the local newspapers and was regarded as setting a "Western Regional Distance Record." It was also regarded as "the most spectacular glider flight ever made in this section." Most significantly, Lindbergh's flight represented the earliest recorded use of the lift along the cliffs at Torrey Pines by a pilot in a true sailplane. The flights by Bowlus and Lindbergh over these two days were reported in newspapers across the United States, as well as in *Time* magazine.

*Above: Charles Lindbergh taking off in the Bowlus Sailplane #20 (584V) from Mount Soledad. Five members of the shock cord crew pull the aircraft into the air. Tip ailerons used for lateral stability can be clearly observed in this photograph.*

*Right: Disassembly of the Bowlus Sailplane #20 following Charles Lindbergh's landing on the beach just to the south of Del Mar. Many curious onlookers who had observed the landing of an unfamiliar aircraft were surprised to meet the legendary Charles Lindbergh on the beach and learn of his distance flight from Mount Soledad.*

## *A Model Sailplane Meet*

By the end of February, 1930, the fever pitch for motorless aviation had spread ever more youthward and a large "miniature model glider meet" was announced for the La Jolla Playground on March 6th. Seventy-five boys made models for the contest. The Y.M.C.A. boys club was also preparing to compete in a contest for superior intellectual, athletic, and model sailplane accomplishment. The winner was offered a free training course in a real glider at the Bowlus Gliding School.

## *New Glider Rules Established*

By early March, the California State Chamber of Commerce introduced a set of rules governing the licensing of gliders. A large number of gliders in the state were flown unlicensed, especially homebuilt primary gliders. State officials wished to change this situation and increase the safety associated with the growing sport. In addition to the state requirements, three additional requirements were established for local glider construction and flight by San Diego City officials. These were:

1) Glider plans were to be approved by either Letain Kittredge (woodshop instructor at San Diego Senior High School) or I. N. Lawson, Jr. (Airtech School of Aviation, Lindbergh Field) free of charge.

2) The glider was to be tested and approved by air board officials at no cost to the owner.

3) Gliders were required to bear their official United States Department of Commerce registration number (a requirement already levied by the Federal government).

Pilots who disobeyed these requirements were subject to fines or arrest if they flew. Although developed with safety in mind, these new local ordinances had the unintended effect of curbing the rapid development of gliding in the region.

With strict state and local licensing requirements for gliders, the "Western Glider Meet" proposed for Mount Soledad April 12th and 13th was postponed indefinitely. Meet officials could not guarantee license tests for all gliders in question prior to the meet. On April 26th, new dates were selected for the Western Glider Meet, which were announced nationally by William Van Dusen as June 26th through July 8th. The dates were arranged to coincide with an historical pageant in San Diego.

## The South Bay Glider Club

On March 2nd, 1930, Bowlus sponsored a one-day testing of a new location for glider flying next to Third Avenue in Chula Vista, on a paved road at the ranch home of Mr. and Mrs. High B. Rose. Approximately 1,000 spectators from a wide region around the San Diego area attended the flight activities. Pilots were launched by shock cord. Bowlus, William Van Dusen, and E. Lowell Bullen flew between 2:00 p.m. and 4:30 p.m. Afterwards, Bowlus announced that "the site was ideal for gliding."

The newly formed South Bay Glider Club became "official" at a meeting at Sweetwater Union High School on March 25th, 1930. Major T. C. Macaulay became President, E. Lowell Bullen Vice President, Harry Munson and Al Seabright were named Boys' Directors. Major A. B. Snead, Alfred Brooks, Roland Tyce, William Van Dusen, Hawley Bowlus, Forrest Hieatt, and Douglas Kelly were all named as members of the Advisory Board.

## The Girls' Division of the Mount Soledad Glider Club

La Jolla glider enthusiasts, George W. Pardy and George Irvin, attempted to bring heightened public awareness of the glider activities at Mount Soledad. On March 7th, 1930, they showed a series of glider films to the La Jolla Kiwanis Club at the La Valencia Hotel.

La Jollans had developed such an interest in gliding that the local Mount Soledad Glider Club proposed the notion of a separate Girls Glider Division under their auspices. Four members of the Anne Lindbergh Gliders Club were influential in this regard and a meeting of many girls and women was held at the Community House in La Jolla on the evening of March 8th. Mrs. George Pardy was elected temporary president of the Mount Soledad Glider Club Girls' Division on March 13th, with Mrs. Harry Haw elected as vice-president, Mrs. Beatrice Waggoner, secretary, and Mrs. Stella Thamer, treasurer. About 15 women and girls attended this first official meeting. By March 25th, Mrs. Pardy and Mrs. Beverly Stapler started taking glider lessons at the Bowlus Glider School.

## Glider Flights Near Oceanside

Local Oceanside car dealer, Dewitt Martin, became interested in the sport of gliding in early 1930. After a preliminary discussion, Martin secured Bowlus' interest in establishing a glider school in the vicinity of the coastline between Oceanside and Del

Mar through the auspices of the Pacific Coast Gliders, Inc. At the fourth annual flower show in Encinitas held February 19th-23rd, 1930, Bowlus set up a glider at the Martin Motor Company booth and helped introduce the sport to the public. Considerable local interest in gliding was generated at the flower show and it was hoped that once the glider school became operational, it would become famous along this part of the coast.

On March 6, 1930, Martin announced that Bowlus would make several demonstration glider flights in the Oceanside area on Sunday, March 7th. The demonstration was to be held near the Monroe Street reservoir at the south end of the Monroe Street in Carlsbad at 2 p.m. Following the demonstration, a public lecture on gliding and soaring was scheduled for the Oceanside-Carlsbad Union High School auditorium in conjunction with Mr. C. E. Line's aviation class. The *Oceanside Blade-Tribune* reported that "those who have doubts about the safety and practicability of this branch of aeronautics, particularly parents whose children are interested in flying, are especially invited."

Unfortunately, the weather did not cooperate. On March 7, 1930, the typical coastal seabreezes that are suitable for ridge soaring were nonexistent. Bowlus made two attempts at gliding on relatively flat terrain. Soon after each shock cord launch, he was forced to land. A large crowd of people had gathered to witness the activities, but was forced to watch the glider travel a rather unimpressive short distance before coming back to Earth. Later, former U.S. Congressman and Oceanside resident Lionel Van Deerlin recalled:

> *Bowlus...came up and had several trials on those high cliffs just south of Carlsbad. We considered it a great honor to be in the crew that would have these rubberized cords, and you would form a "V" in front of the glider, which was anchored. Maybe a dozen of us on one side and a dozen on that side, it was sort of like a tug-of-war except you pulled until the cord got just as tight as possible, then they would release the glider and it would come zipping over your head and out over the cliff. In looking back, I think we were taking something of a chance being in front of that damn thing as it took off, but I never wanted to be in it as it went off the cliff either!*

Due to the poor weather conditions and lack of interest, the lecture at the high school was postponed until March 13th. Bowlus disassembled the glider and drove back to San Diego.

On March 13th, 1930, Martin announced that Oceanside was selected as the first location for a chain of glider schools to be established on the west coast. He and Bowlus expected to establish several glider schools through the western United States. Bowlus returned to Oceanside that evening to give a public lecture at the high school on gliding. About 100 people attended the lecture. Bowlus showed films of the Lindberghs in their first soaring attempts, and also informed the audience of glider training methods "of the type that would be used at Martin's proposed glider school in

*Hawley Bowlus (r) prior to a demonstration flight at Oceanside.*

Oceanside." However, for unknown reasons, the glider school at Oceanside never became a reality. It is quite likely that the financial hardships of the Great Depression played a role in keeping Oceanside from becoming a glider capital.

In an attempt to renew local interest in gliding, pilots A. Clare Rand and Dick Essery arranged for two glider demonstrations in Oceanside off the bluff from Pacific Street to the beach below. These demonstrations were held on June 29th and July 4th, 1930. Given enough enthusiasm, Rand and Essery rekindled the idea of starting a glider school in Oceanside. Both pilots were members in the popular Escondido Glider Club. The flights of June 29th did indeed raise quite a lot of local interest. Several Oceanside boys took turns flying the Escondido club glider. Without a sufficient seabreeze to keep the plane aloft, the glider flights were made at a baseball field on Wisconsin Street. Both Rand and Essery had wanted to soar along the coastal bluffs, but were forced to think of other ways of keeping the glider aloft. Not to disappoint the crowd, Dick Essery made a two-mile flight along the beach in the glider while being towed with a rope behind an automobile. Rand and Essery returned for more flights on July 4th, 1930, from a location on a bluff two blocks south of the Oceanside pier.

The famous Bowlus sailplane S-18 was sold by the Bowlus Sailplane Company, Ltd. to the Pacific Coast Gliders, Ltd. on April 4th, 1930. Dewitt Martin of San Diego was then acting as the General Manager of the Pacific Coast Gliders, Ltd. In August of 1930, the identification mark was changed (G-586V) to reflect its status as a glider. Only one year later, in August, 1931, the license was allowed to expire.

## *Bowlus Sailplane #19 (587V)*

Bowlus model "A" sailplane, serial S-19, was completed on December 30th, 1929. Application for official identification mark was filed by the Bowlus Sailplane Company, Ltd. on March 10th, 1930. Identification mark 587V was granted on March 17th, 1930. The aircraft was sold to the Cardiff and Peacock Aero Corporation, Ltd., of Bakersfield, California in April, 1930.

At some time between April, 1930, and December, 1932, Bowlus sailplane 587V was sold for Cardiff and Peacock by the Aero Brokers Service of Mines Field, Los Angeles. Papers dated February 21st, 1933, suggest that 587V was sold and exported to Honolulu, Hawaii where it crashed. Identification mark 587V was officially canceled on January 12th, 1933.

## *San Diego Senior High School Primary Gliders*

San Diego Senior High School woodshop instructor Letain Kittredge was a strong influence in the development of construction skills for high-school-aged glider pilots in the San Diego area. He was born on April 2nd, 1888, and recalled his mother telling him as a child that he "missed being a [April] fool by five hours."

At the start of World War I, Kittredge entered flight school at the Naval Air Station, Pensacola, Florida, and was soon assigned to the Pacific Fleet Air Force, Naval Air Station North Island, in San Diego. During the late 1910s and early 1920s, Lt. Kittredge saw duty with the Station Flight Training Department and Seaplane (Patrol) Squadron VJ-1. On one occasion, during gunnery practice near Point Loma, Kittredge was thought to have created a world's record for accuracy in aerial gunnery when he made 194 hits out of 194 shots on a sleeve being towed by a DH-4 motor plane.

Following honorable discharge from the service, Kittredge and his wife remained in San Diego, where he began a career in education, teaching at San Diego Senior High School. As woodshop instructor, he taught students in building boats and gliders and, in 1928, he added a class in aircraft rigging to the school curriculum. He remained woodshop instructor at San Diego Senior High School for 26 years, retiring in 1948.

On March 12th, 1930, students in San Diego Senior High School's aircraft rigging class exhibited 12 new primary gliders built by the class on the school grounds. Primary glider #12 was completed by the woodshop class on February 28th, 1930. Application for an identification mark was forwarded to the United States Department of Commerce by Kittredge. The identification mark 61W was issued on March 27th, and the glider was flown at several locations in San Diego for high school student flight instruction. However, by the end of 1932, the glider was dismantled and salvaged, perhaps in load tests by the aircraft rigging class. The identification mark 61W was canceled officially on January 11th, 1933.

By March 13th, 1930, San Diego Senior High School student David Robertson had completed construction of his primary glider, serial number P-T-2 (implying that this was his second primary trainer, but no records are known of his first glider). The primary had a gross weight of 160 pounds. The glider was issued identification mark 17W from the United States Department of Commerce on March 21st, 1930, and was flown in the San Diego area for at least one year. The identification mark 17W was canceled on August 1st, 1931.

San Diego Senior High School students were rapidly applying for glider identification marks with the United States Department of Commerce in preparation for future glider meets in the local area. On March 25th, 1930, Robert Dickson, Jr. wrote to the United States Department of Commerce suggesting that an identification mark was needed prior to the proposed glider meet on Mount Soledad. Identification mark 311W was granted April 4th, 1930. However, 311W was unassigned in January, 1933, following attempts by the Department of Commerce to send Dickson a questionnaire. When the questionnaire was returned unclaimed by the United States Postal Service, the identification mark expired.

## *Lindbergh Soars at Carmel, California*

On March 4th, 1930, Charles and Anne Lindbergh arrived in Carmel, California in an attempt to set new soaring endurance records with Hawley Bowlus. Jack Barstow arrived on the site with a Bowlus sailplane that had been shipped from San Diego to San Francisco aboard the steamer *Harvard*. Bud Perl helped at the test site after bringing the primary glider, *Tillie the Toiler* from San Diego to Monterey by car, with the help of Lester Earhart. Unfortunately, the leading edge of *Tillie the Toiler's* wing was compressed en route up the coast. Necessary repairs were made during the following week at Carmel.

By the afternoon of March 4th, Bowlus, Charles and Anne Lindbergh, and the rest of the glider group surveyed the area for a potential launching site. Charles Lindbergh was friends with personnel at Sidney Fish's ranch near Carmel. Focus was directed on finding a proper launching site on the Fish Ranch.

On March 5th, Charles Lindbergh was launched in a Bowlus sailplane from a hillside two miles south of Carmel Heights. He was able to soar two miles to the south of the point of takeoff, but was forced to land after a total duration of six minutes, due to unfavorable winds. A barograph was carried in the sailplane should any official records be broken.

As was the case with experimentation at Lebec, California, the winds never seemed to be in Charles Lindbergh's favor. On March 6th, there was so little wind that he decided to play polo instead of soar. Lindbergh's resulting fall from a horse (without injury), lead to a front page headline the following morning. By March 7th, word of Lindbergh's visit to Carmel had spread, and the throngs of curious onlookers made it difficult for the glider group to inspect alternate sites for takeoff. The winds were also not cooperative. Lindbergh told the press that he would try to fly again the following day, but would keep the location hidden from the public. The winds finally changed for the better on March 8th. Lindbergh was launched at 3:03 p.m. and soared in the westerly seabreeze for 1 hour and 10 minutes at altitudes reported to be over 1,000 feet.

> *Once when he came close to the takeoff place, Jack Barstow, his assistant, cupped his hands to his mouth and shouted: 'What's the matter? Can't you come down?' 'No.' Lindbergh replied. But he circled again and, leaning far over the side of his glider, amended: 'In about ten minutes.'*

As Lindbergh headed for the landing site at the estate of New York millionaire Sydney Fish, and was setting up for a landing, one of the tip ailerons broke loose and fluttered away from the right wing (quite similar to his earlier experience at Lebec). Lindbergh continued ahead to a rather abrupt landing without incident. About 200 to 300 people were gathered at the landing site, including Anne Lindbergh. After the landing, the Lindbergh's attended a tea party hosted by Sydney Fish.

On March 9th, Lindbergh was launched again before noon from a hill in Carmel Valley. The wind was light and Lindbergh was forced to land at the bottom of the hill after only a short flight. He was launched once again at about 2:30 p.m., but could only manage to remain in the air approximately ten minutes.

Between March 10th and March 13th, the winds continued to be light and variable. On March 13th, Lindbergh had two short flights for the more than 500 spectators. After the flights, Lindbergh assisted in the glider instruction of J. Cheever Cowdin, New York millionaire and director of the Transcontinental Air Transport Company. Flights in *Tillie the Toiler* occurred on the Del Monte polo grounds by auto tow in a method similar to that used by the Bowlus Sailplane Company in San Diego.

On March 14th, the winds were finally gusting to over 18 miles per hour, but they were from a southerly direction. A westerly breeze was required to ridge soar on the mountain slopes south to Big Sur. Lindbergh made a four-minute flight just before noon from a hill on the opposite site of the Carmel valley from the Sydney Fish ranch. It rained immediately before and after the attempt. After the storm on March 14th through 15th, the winds ebbed yet again and continued light and variable all the way through March 20th, when the Lindberghs ended their glider experiments and left Carmel for San Francisco.

Major C. C. Moseley, vice-president and general manager of the Curtiss-Wright Flying Service School at Los Angeles Airport also observed the soaring activities of the Lindbergh's at Del Monte. Upon returning to Los Angeles, he was so enthusiastic that Moseley immediately ordered a Bowlus glider for student training at the Curtiss-Wright school.

## *Harland Ross*

After enlisting with the United States Navy, Harland C. Ross was stationed at North Island, near Coronado. With an interest in aviation, Ross began glider instruction at the Bowlus Glider School while Bowlus and the Lindberghs were soaring at Lebec. Ross made 34 flights on *Tillie the Toiler* between February 3rd and February 20th at Lindbergh Field. On February 25th, 1930, Ross made his first successful hop in Bowlus sailplane S-16 from a 50-foot hill at the base of Mount Soledad (perhaps near the same locations of the 1929 Pacific Beach Glider Meets). His first soaring flight was just two minutes in duration. It was a short start to the career of someone who would eventually become one of America's most important sailplane designers.

Between February 26th and March 10th, 1930, Ross made ten more flights at Lindbergh Field in *Tillie the Toiler*. With sufficient knowledge, Harland Ross succeeded in making his first soaring flight on March 10th by flying the ridge at Plumosa Park near the north end of Point Loma. His flight of seven minutes in the Bowlus sailplane S-16 was long enough to qualify for a third-class glider license, but remained unofficial because no official observer was present at the time.

On May 10th, 1930, Harland Ross took off in the Bowlus sailplane S-16 by shock cord from an altitude of 100 feet on the hills east of Mission Bay near Morena. He was finally able to qualify for an official third class glider license with a flight of two minutes.

## *The Y. M. C. A. "Y" Triangle Club*

Claude T. Burns, Assistant Probation Officer for San Diego County also served as leader of the "Y"-Triangle club. On March 11th, 1930, an application for identification mark was filed by Burns to the United States Department of Commerce for a secondary trainer glider. This glider was granted identification mark 357W on April 11th,

1930, and was flown by club members at several locations in San Diego. For unknown reasons, the glider was salvaged, and by January, 1933, identification mark 357W was canceled.

On March 29th, 1930, the Y.M.C.A. sponsored an athletic, intellectual and character contest for local boys in the "Y"-Triangle club. When the contest began, Bowlus announced that he would give the winner of the contest free regular primary and secondary glider training at Lindbergh Field. At the end of the contest, Melvin Steiner and Richard Missman had tied for first place. Informed of the tie, Bowlus announced that both boys would receive free glider instruction. William Van Dusen, San Diego Chamber of Commerce official, was the chief judge for the contest.

On October 8th, 1931, 14-year-old Melvin Steiner of National City was awarded a private glider pilot's license by the United States Department of Commerce, following successful flights at Ryan Airport. Steiner became a member of the Y.M.C.A. "Y-Triangle" Glider Club, and his flight was made in a Bowlus sailplane. At the time, he was believed to be the youngest boy in the state to receive a private pilot's license. Steiner had finally realized his dream.

In 1930, members of the "Y" Triangle club built and licensed four of their own primary gliders (identification marks 10123, 10124, 10125, and 10126), but no records have been obtained for these aircraft.

## *Dedication of the Emerald Hills Golf Course*

With the grand opening of the Emerald Hills Golf Course in Bonita, a large glider meet was planned at the site for Sunday, March 16th. In attendance was Captain Frank Hawks, United States speed record holder for powered aircraft and pilot for a proposed cross-country glider tow from San Diego to New York using a Franklin secondary glider named *Eaglet.* This glider had been shipped from Michigan to San Diego in time for display at the Emerald Hills meet. Other pilots attending the event included Jack Barstow, Richard Benbough, William "Bill" Dickenson, Robert Dickson, Dick Essery, Robert Goebel, Wyatt Ingram, Albert E. Jones, Letain Kittredge, Joe Thurston, J. H. Rainwater, Bob Robbins, David Robertson, Lloyd Standley, William Van Dusen, and several members of the Anne Lindbergh Gliders Club, including Ruth Alexander, Hazel Kelly, Peaches Wallace, and Helen Van Dusen.

William Van Dusen made a local aviation "first" by flying the Western Flyers Glider Club primary glider #3 (identification mark 372V), equipped with pontoons, to a successful water landing on a small lake near the clubhouse. Richard Benbough and Vernon Brown helped run the shock cord for this launch among several others. This flight was billed as the world's first "amphibian glider" by the local media (perhaps unknown to the participants were earlier attempts with "hydro-primaries" in Germany and at other locations in America). Van Dusen had test flown the amphibian primary glider 372V in February, 1930. Five movietone companies were on hand to record the water landing of the amphibian at the Emerald Hills meet.

James A. Moore made two hops in his glider, and Peaches Wallace demonstrated women's gliding with a flight of 23.2 seconds. Similar flights were made by Hazel Kelley and Ruth Alexander. Members of the Pacific Beach Glider Club were in attendance, but did not fly as they were between gliders at the time. Proceeds from the dedication event went to promote a proposed Dirigible Base at Camp Kearney (at what is now the location of Marine Corps Air Station Miramar). An unfortunate crash by Bob Robbins on the maiden flight of a new secondary glider was the only mishap of the event.

The March 26th edition of the *San Diego Sun* printed a subheadline "Three Musketeers of Gliderdom are only 17...But what they know about aerodynamics would fill a big book." The "Musketeers" were Dick Essery, Bill Dickenson, and Joe Thurston, builders of the pontoon hydro-primary piloted by William Van Dusen. The primary glider #372V had as many as 275 flights to its credit up through the Emerald Hills meet when it was equipped with pontoons built at the Pacific Technical University in San Diego.

Anne Lindbergh Gliders Club historian Helen Van Dusen wrote many detailed, humorous recollections of the activities at the Emerald Hills meet:

> *Emerald Hills--and the long periods of posing for the movie cameras, and Hazel and Peaches and Ruth talking for the movietones on our behalf. Then more publicity stunts--Eddie Peabody, comedian from a local theater posing in the cockpit of the sailplane which has just been returned from San Francisco. Grease-paint covered chorus girls trip a fantastic toe. Crash--one of the kicking feet has torn clear thru the blue fabric of the fuselage. Now Peaches, winner of the draw for first demonstration flight in the sailplane, takes her place, and does not know how close this flight will bring her to disaster. For Jack Barstow, standing close, assisting, forgets the sweep of the flippers on the tail. The plane lurches forward, Jack is struck from behind and hurled high into the air and when Peaches lands she finds one flipper useless--held in place by only a screw or two.*

For those who attended the Emerald Hills glider meet, it represented a unification of many of the local glider enthusiasts and a chance to share some fun.

## *A Formation Glider Flight*

Thursday, March 27th, 1930, found Hawley Bowlus (in Bowlus sailplane S-17, identification mark 599M) and Jack Barstow (in Bowlus sailplane S-20, identification mark 584V) soaring above Mount Soledad and the surrounding region, in what was

*Above: Vernon Brown (2nd from left) and Richard Benbough (3rd from left) assist in the shock cord takeoff of William Van Dusen in the hydro-primary glider.*

*Above Right: Touchdown of the hydro-primary glider in a lake at the Emerald Hills Golf Course dedication ceremonies.*

*Right: Sarah Brisbane (l) and friend pose for photographers on the Western Flyers hydro-primary glider. Sarah was the daughter of Arthur Brisbane, a highly-regarded newspaper columnist.*

WESTERN
FLYERS
ESSERY

*Above: Hawley Bowlus and Jack Barstow make the first "formation" glider flight in San Diego following a launch from Mount Soledad.*

*Right: Construction of sailplane fuselages, wings, and ribs at the Bowlus Sailplane Company adjacent to Lindbergh Field. This building was also used for the construction of the Spirit of St. Louis and is currently part of the Solar Turbines factory at the southeast corner of Lindbergh Field.*

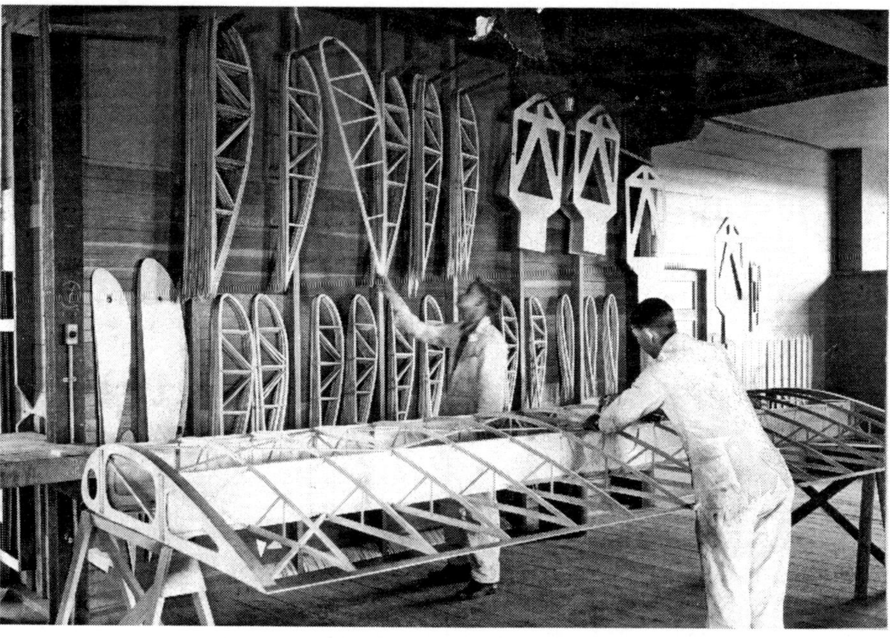

FÉDÉRATION AÉRONAUTIQUE
INTERNATIONALE

NATIONAL AERONAUTIC
ASSOCIATION OF U. S. A.
INC.

Certificate No. 2

The above named Association, recognized by the Fédération Aéronautique Internationale, as the governing authority for the United States of America, certifies that

William Hawley Bowlus

born 8th day of May, 1896 having fulfilled all the conditions required by the Fédération Aréonautique Internationale, for a Glider Pilot is hereby brevetted as such.

Dated May 26, 1930

CONTEST COMMITTEE

Orville Wright
Chairman

Executive Vice-Chairman

Signature of Pilot:

Wm. H. Bowlus

*Fédération Aéronautique Internationale (National Aeronautic Association of U.S.A.) certificate number 2 granted to William Hawley Bowlus and signed by Orville Wright. Certificate number 3 was granted to William Van Dusen.*

billed as "the world's first formation glider flight." The pair landed at La Jolla Canyon Road near the Biological Grade within ten feet of each other. Twenty-eight men reportedly pulled the shock cords for the launches from the top of Mount Soledad.

The paired flight was scheduled in honor of Arthur Brisbane, noted newspaper columnist who came to watch glider activities in the area. In 1949, Former Associated Glider Club of Southern California Vice President, Thomas F. Bomar recalled:

> *In the spring of 1930, Arthur Brisbane, the newspaper columnist, brought his family to San Diego for a vacation. Through T. C. Macaulay and W. A. Van Dusen of the Chamber of Commerce, Brisbane became interested in the glider activities. One afternoon, Hawley Bowlus and Jack Barstow took off from Mount Soledad in sailplanes and soared north along the low ridge of hills extending to Biological Grade. Brisbane and his parts stood on the road below and watched in amazement as the two soared back and forth, one behind the other. In all earnestness, Brisbane said, 'If I hadn't seen it, I wouldn't believe it.' That little exhibition got San Diego more national publicity than anything that has ever happened.*

On March 27th, 1930, Peaches Wallace had an unfortunate crash in the Bowlus Sailplane S-16 (identification mark 493) and the center section of the wing and fuselage were damaged. Fortunately, Peaches survived the crash without critical injury.

## *Maurice Collins*

Prior to 1930, a number of glider enthusiasts in the Los Angeles area started gliding and soaring from hills in the surrounding region, including those near the cliffs at Palos Verdes. One of the first pilots to use gliders in this region was Maurice Collins. After making a glider of his own design in 1930 (identification mark G-421), Maurice Collins and friend John Barclay made a trip to the Bowlus Sailplane Company factory in San Diego to learn more about the record-breaking Bowlus sailplanes. Later, Collins described what he found:

> *Hawley Bowlus' factory, a medium-sized, two-story building on the edge of the Bay, was a decided surprise with an impressive array of the long-spanned sailplanes in various stages of construction. Hawley was capitalizing on his successful prototype. A long line of bodies resembling streamlined barracuda occupied one side of the two-story loft and the other section was crammed with an assortment of wing panels, rudders, stabilizers, and ailerons. Looking out a nearby window, a passing flash of silver drew our attention to the field below. The proving ground for these graceful birds was conveniently located adjacent to the factory. We learned that a club had been*

*formed for ground training and soaring instruction and the membership composed of both sexes was rapidly expanding.*

*The price tag on a Bowlus complete with trailer and ready to ride the thermals was completely out of our budget but Hawley, instead of treating us like foreign spies, generously let us take notes and proffered some of his trade secrets.*

Following the trip to San Diego, Collins immediately began drafting plans for a copy of the Bowlus model "A" sailplane. Construction of the 64.5-foot wingspan sailplane took place over the latter half of 1930. The sailplane even used tip ailerons in a fashion similar to the original Bowlus sailplanes. A sister ship to Collins' Bowlus sailplane copy was built by Walter Pierce and his son. Both sailplanes were constructed in a workshop in Glendale, California.

In January, 1931, Collins' sailplane was hauled to the top of Mount Verdugo, to the north of Glendale. The orange colored sailplane was "plainly visible to a major portion of the residents of Glendale, their curiosity naturally aroused by the strange appearing aircraft perched atop Mount Verdugo." A crew of 18 men ran the shock cords as the Collins' sailplane was lifted into the air. During takeoff, the stabilizer struck one of the shock cord runners, damaging the tail section. Collins negotiated his way to the airport without attempting a soaring flight and landed successfully on the runway.

Shortly after this first successful flight, Collins was launched once again from the top of Mount Verdugo in Pierce's sailplane. This time, however, he carried nearly 1,000 pieces of glider mail to be delivered to the airport below. Collins soared back and forth along the hillside and made a landing at the airport, much to the pleasure of the crowd that had gathered to witness the event.

Collins' copied Bowlus sailplane was flown shortly thereafter from the hill overlooking the "Hollywoodland" sign just north of Hollywood. Less than full control on the tip-ailerons led to an unexpected landing shortly after takeoff near the famous sign.

## *The Escondido Glider Club*

On March 30th, 1930, 35 Escondido men signed up as members of the Escondido Glider Club. Members of the Western Flyers Glider Club (Dick Essery, Bill Dickenson, and Joe Thurston), William Van Dusen, and Hawley Bowlus made exhibition flights at Escondido's airport. An organizational meeting was held March 31st, 1930, for the election of officers. The glider used in the exhibition by the Western Flyers

Glider Club was the same primary used by Van Dusen as an amphibian (identification mark 372V). A large crowd witnessed the events at the local airport and was fascinated by motorless aviation.

## *A Transcontinental Glider Tow*

Frank Hawks' first experience with a glider occurred at the Detroit Aircraft Show in the spring of 1929, using a primary glider that had been imported from Germany. Hawks made three or four short flights after a shock cord launch in this glider. His next glider flight came later that same year at the National Air Races in Cleveland. The National Glider Association, forerunner of the Soaring Society of America, helped sponsor a number of glider events during the show. One of these was a "Famous Motored Pilots' Glider Derby." Entrants included Amelia Earhart, Casey Jones, Reed Candis, and others. Using an auto tow for launch, the competition centered on duration and spot landing using Franklin utility gliders. Hawks made several practice glider flights directly before the competition and with this preparation, he won a silver cup for the championship with a duration of 1 minute 20 seconds, and a spot landing located 13 paces from the landing mark. Amelia Earhart did not fare as well, as she was not as familiar with gliding flight. "Miss Earhart very narrowly escaped injury when she tried to execute a turn...and fell into a spin, which she did not pull out of until the glider was within a few feet of the ground."

Hawks' first towed flight came the day after the glider derby when J. D. "Duke" Jernigin, Jr. towed Hawks in an open cockpit Franklin Utility glider behind an OX-5 Waco biplane. Hawks commented that "it was a great trip...the whole upper part of my body was exposed to the rush of air that is inevitable in any kind of [glider] flying. As a result I nearly froze during the three-hours-and-a-half that it took us to cover the 150 miles from Pontiac to Cleveland" After reaching Cleveland, Hawks gladly cut loose over the Air Races and landed in front of the spectators.

With his interest in gliders increasing and a successful aerotow under his belt, Hawks put forward the idea of a transcontinental glider tow to the officials of the Texaco Oil Company, his sponsor on previous speed record flights. Hawks was convinced that gliders were an inexpensive introduction to aviation for the youth of America, and that Texaco Oil might benefit from the publicity of this new sport. Although many people in the aviation community initially thought the idea of a gas and oil company sponsoring a glider flight was ridiculous, Hawks was able to convince the officials of Texaco that those who learned to fly on gliders would soon turn to other forms of flight...perhaps even those that used Texaco gasoline.

Originally, Hawks proposed an 8-day flight from San Diego to New York, with 21 stops along the way. At these locations, Hawks wanted to demonstrate soaring for the crowds, and at the same time, allow the towplane to be refueled. Hawks demanded that the glider be fitted with brakes, a two-way plane-to-plane telephone system, and a stronger airframe to accommodate the increased demands of such a long aerotow. Due to his previous experience with Franklin Utility gliders, Hawks approached the Franklin Brothers (Roswell and Wallace Franklin) of Ann Arbor, Michigan, to design and build this glider. The Texaco *Eaglet* was constructed during the winter of 1929; Hawks commented later that the *Eaglet* was "the first completely enclosed cabin craft of its kind ever made." Perhaps Hawks' previous experience with cold open-air cockpits and streamlining influenced this decision. The *Eaglet* was also "one of the first (gliders) featuring a welded steel tube fuselage" and it had a wingspan of 46 feet. Standard Franklin PS-2 utility gliders carried a 36-foot wingspan.

The *Eaglet* was flight tested by Hawks at the factory in Michigan, and then shipped to Lindbergh Field in San Diego, where it was unpacked, displayed at the Emerald Hills Golf Course dedication, and prepared for the cross-country flight. Duke Jernigin, the same pilot who had towed Hawks previously, was selected as the tow pilot for the journey using the Texaco No. 7 Waco biplane. A special 500-foot manila towline was used, which included the unique plane-to-plane two-way telephone cable that Hawks had requested. This audio connection was releasable at either end in case of emergency. The cable could be reeled in by the copilot of the Waco after the *Eaglet* had released. On March 27th, 1930, the towline telephone cable was tested in San Diego with the help of Max Miller, a local San Diego newspaper reporter, riding as a passenger in the Waco and with Hawks in the *Eaglet*. Hawks prepared eagerly for his cross-country glider flight by practicing aerotowing from Lindbergh Field. The *Eaglet* was released at an altitude of 3,200 feet. These aerotows were in all likelihood the first of their kind in San Diego County.

On the March 28th, two days before the actual flight was to begin, Hawks and Jernigin practiced aerotowing on a flight from San Diego to Mines Field in Los Angeles. This short hop coincided with Hawks' 33rd birthday, and Hawks' parents (who lived in Hollywood at the time) gave him a home-cooked birthday celebration. The *Los Angeles Times* reported that "Angelenos...today are scheduled to witness the first glider to be cut loose from a towing airplane over Los Angeles," and that the short hop between San Diego and Los Angeles was "the first round trip by glider between the two cities."

On the 30th of March, Hawks loaded up the *Eaglet* with a sack of glider mail bound for the East Coast. At Lindbergh Field, a large crowd had gathered to witness the takeoff. The flight began at 7:45 a.m. with Duke Jernigin and Wallace Franklin in the Waco and Hawks in the *Eaglet*. The first leg was to contain three stops in Arizona: Yuma, Phoenix, and Tucson. Ominously, the air was very turbulent and became worse throughout the day. The "sky-train" landed after dark in Tucson, with "at least 10,000 people waiting to see (them) land." Hawks used the navigation lights of the Waco and the automobile headlights on the ground to aid in his approach and landing.

Day two was worse than day one. After takeoff, a strong gust buffeted the two planes snapping the towline in half. Luckily, it happened with sufficient altitude for Hawks to turn back and make a safe landing at the airfield in Tucson. The rest of the day was spent repairing the tow cable and telephone connections. Attempting to stay on schedule, they were forced to miss stops at Lordsburg and Pecos.

The following day, the pair headed east again toward El Paso, Texas. Upon reaching El Paso, "we found such a gale blowing that practically all flying had been suspended, and were forced to exert all our skill to get down without mishap." This leg of the trip covered 710 miles and ended in Sweetwater, Texas, after quick refueling stops in both El Paso and Midland, Texas. The weather finally showed signs of improvement, and on the fourth day of the trip, the *Eaglet* stopped in Wichita Falls, Texas, Oklahoma City and Tulsa, Oklahoma; the fifth day in Springfield, Missouri and East St. Louis, Illinois; the sixth in Terre Haute and Indianapolis, Indiana and Columbus, Ohio; and the seventh in Cleveland, Ohio and Buffalo, New York, where the bad weather unfortunately returned.

The eighth day of the trip was scheduled originally to include one stop for refueling at Elmira, New York, but a howling wind forced them to land at Syracuse and Albany instead. Hawks reported that he encountered tremendous upcurrents over Syracuse after releasing from the Waco. He climbed as much as 3,000 feet in lift, but realizing he needed to stay on schedule, Hawks felt compelled to land shortly thereafter. As he was always pressed for time, Hawks quickly headed out for Albany. Upon arrival at 3,000 feet over Albany, Hawks encountered a 55-mile-per-hour gale that nearly forced them to land. Hawks knew, however, that postponing the last leg any further would disappoint the officials who were waiting in Van Cortlandt Park at New York City for his final landing. Both pilots agreed to attempt a finish of the flight that day and prepared the "air-train" for takeoff. On the takeoff from Albany, Duke Jernigin encountered severe turbulence over a row of trees at the far end of the field. "The Waco heeled way over on one wing and shuddered there as if she could never recover before stalling and crashing on the field." But the Waco finally pulled up over the ground, Hawks stayed on tow, and the two were on the final leg of their adventure. Hawks later recalled, "Indeed, if we had been left to our own choice in the matter, we never would have stirred out of Buffalo that day in view of the near-gale that was blowing."

The last day turned out to have the worst weather of the entire trip. Hawks later commented in *The Literary Digest*:

> *Between Syracuse and Buffalo I experienced the toughest towflying of the entire flight. Twice I began to fear that I might be forced to quit the ship and join the Caterpillar Club, via my parachute. The wind was so strong and gusty that, nose the Eaglet down as I might, at sharper and sharper angles, I could not make it descend until the wind abated.*

After flying in the gale continuously down the Hudson river to New York City, the winds finally subsided long enough for Hawks to release, set up an approach, and glide into Van Cortlandt Park in a "triumphant finish of her unique ocean-to-ocean flight." After waiting in the rain, a crowd of approximately 15,000 people cheered as Hawks landed. Jernigan in the towplane landed at Newark Airport. While waiting for Jernigan to return to the park, Hawks and several officials from New York planted a

*Above: Captain Frank Hawks (cockpit) shows the glider-to-towplane intercom system to Hawley Bowlus (l) prior to takeoff from Lindbergh Field on his transcontinental aerotow.*

*Above Right: Duke Jernigin, standing beside the Texaco No. 7 Waco biplane, and Frank Hawks standing in front of the Texaco Eaglet during their transcontinental flight.*

*Right: A sample of glider mail carried from San Diego to New York City by Hawks and the Eaglet.*

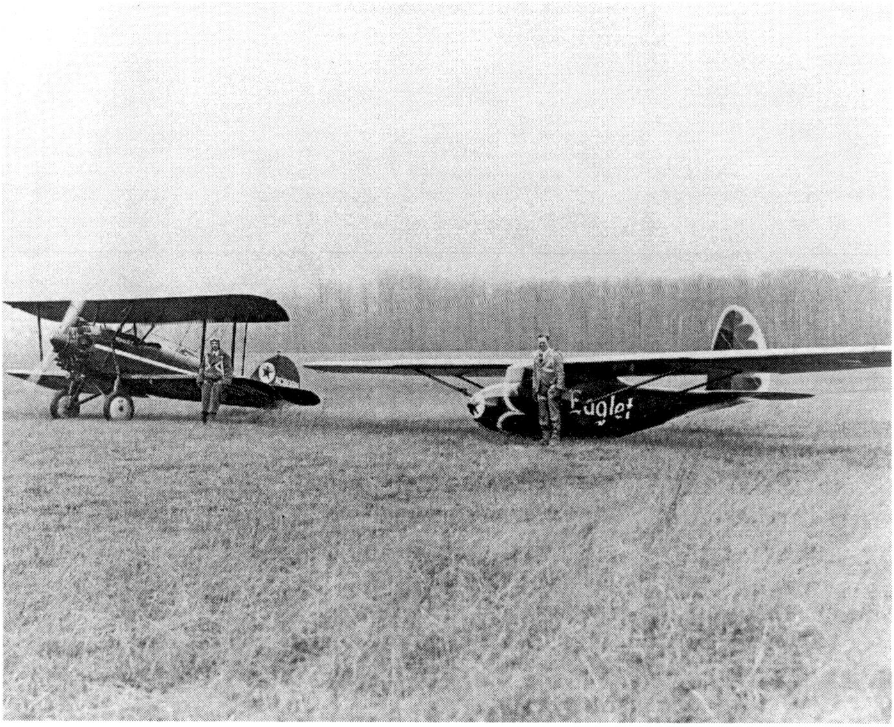
Eaglet

FIRST TRANS-CONTINENTAL
GLIDER FLIGHT
SPONSORED BY
THE TEXAS COMPANY
SAN DIEGO - NEW YORK
FRANK HAWKS, PILOT
NEW YORK, N.Y. 16
APR 6
6-PM
1930
ADDRESS YOUR MAIL TO STREET AND NUMBER
VIA AIR MAIL
Mr.George D.Hart,
General Delivery,
New York City,
New York.

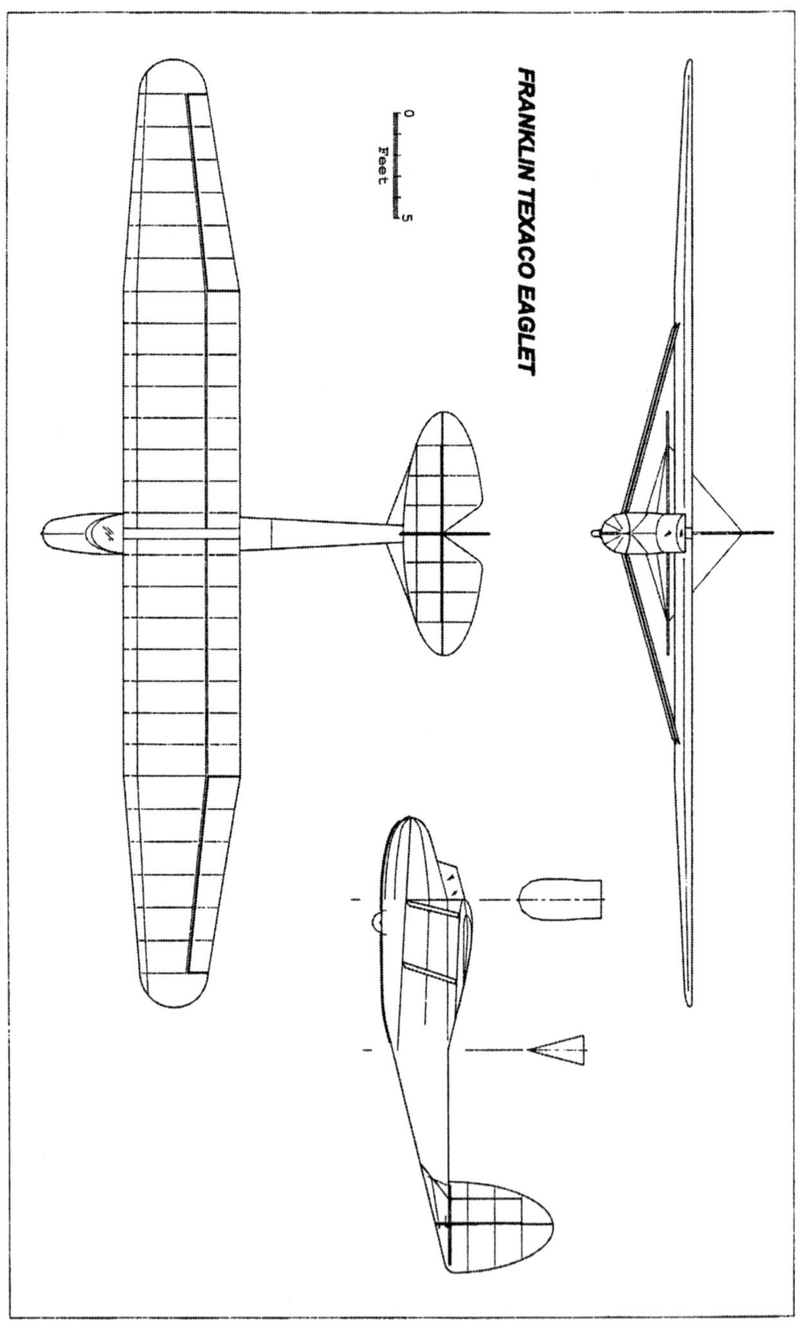
FRANKLIN TEXACO EAGLET
0
Feet
5

small potted palm tree that Hawks had carried in the *Eaglet* across the country as a gift from the City of San Diego to the City of New York. The entire trip took 44 hours and 10 minutes of flying time over 8 days; 35 hours were on tow, and 9 hours were spent in soaring demonstrations for the public at the airports along the way. Hawks estimated that on the average, 5,000 people turned out at these airports, interested in seeing this unique transcontinental excursion firsthand. The *New York Times* stated:

> *Not since the world flight of the Graf Zeppelin has the whole nation turned out to watch as it did for the aerial train. Over cities where his advance man had preceded him, the flier looked down on building and housetops blackened with people. In New York, many who were fortunate enough to be at Van Cortlandt Park last Sunday expressed the opinion that no flier since Lindbergh had received the reception accorded Hawks, Wallace Franklin, designer and builder of the glider, and Duke Jernigan, pilot of the Whirlwind powered Waco towing craft.*

The *Eaglet* was flown subsequently by Hawks at the 1930 National Air Races in Chicago, at the first National Glider Meet at Elmira, and at meets in Philadelphia and in Springfield, Massachusetts. Later in 1930, the *Eaglet* was dismantled and towed by truck from Curtiss Field in Valley Stream on Long Island to Bolling Field in Washington, D. C. In a presentation of the *Eaglet* to the Smithsonian Institution's National Air and Space Museum on December 8th, 1930, Hawks and Jernigin combined once again to tow the sailplane; Hawks cut loose and both Jernigin and Hawks landed simultaneously in front of the officials. Hawks was quoted as saying that gliding "obviously offers opportunity for a fine sport and one which may make the nation feel much more at home in the air than it could ever feel if it had to depend on planes alone." The *Eaglet* remains in the collection of the National Air and Space Museum in Washington, D.C. The *Eaglet* has a wing span of 46 feet, length of 21.6 feet, empty weight of approximately 230 pounds and gross weight of 410 pounds. The fuselage and tail are of steel tub construction with fabric covering, whereas the wing is made of wood and fabric.

## *Public Relations and Glider Lessons*

Colonel Pablo Sidar, chief of the Mexican Air Force, met with Hawley Bowlus in San Diego on April 2nd, 1930. Col. Sidar wished to train Mexican aviators using Bowlus gliders and sailplanes. After their meeting, Col. Sidar was optimistic about obtaining authority from the Mexican government to purchase several Bowlus gliders. On April 3rd, yet another lecture and demonstration of glider activities through motion pictures was held in the American Legion Hall building in Balboa Park. Letain Kittredge, Peaches Wallace, William Van Dusen, and Major Macauley were lecturers. Several members of La Jolla's various glider clubs also attended. Between April 9th and April 29th, Helen Van Dusen of the Anne Lindbergh Gliders Club was taking more primary glider instruction in *Tillie the Toiler* at Lindbergh Field, with Forrest Hieatt and Jack Barstow as instructors.

By April 12th and 13th, things took a turn for the worse for the San Diego's women glider groups. Peaches Wallace checked in to Mercy Hospital with appendicitis, underwent an operation on April 13th, and was listed in serious condition. The meeting of the Mount Soledad Girls' Glider Club was postponed to April 24th.

## *A Trip to the East Coast*

In early April, Bowlus traveled east across the United States with Bowlus model "A" sailplane, serial S-21 (identification mark 588V). Bowlus wished to increase awareness and sales for his line of gliders and sailplanes. Serial S-21 was covered in Chinese silk cloth and painted white with gold trim. This sailplane was exhibited along with many other motorless aircraft at the 1930 Detroit Aircraft Show, one of the largest aircraft shows in the country. While Bowlus was away, Pacific Coast Gliders, Inc. of Los Angeles purchased the rights to the Bowlus Glider School at Lindbergh Field in early April and Jack Barstow was named chief instructor. At the Queensboro Golf and Country Club at Bayside, New York, Bowlus entered a large glider carnival that was held under the auspices of the National Glider Association and Aeronautical Chamber of Commerce. The New York Glider Carnival was held May 1st and 2nd, 1930. Other famous aviators in attendance were Captain Frank Hawks and Amelia Earhart. Several aeronautical journals carried articles on Bowlus' gliding records and flights with the Lindberghs; Bowlus was becoming well-known on a national level. On May 1st, 1930, Bowlus accomplished the longest duration flight of the meet, flying for 44.1 seconds, and similarly won the duration event on May 2nd with a flight of 34.17 seconds.

While in New York, Bowlus encouraged aviation author Assen Jordanoff to take a test hop in a Bowlus sailplane at a 165-foot ridge near Montauk Point, Long Island. An extensive account of this flight appeared in the September issue of *Popular Science Monthly*, wherein it was suggested that *Popular Science Monthly* purchased the ship from Bowlus for Jordanoff to fly. Of his soaring experience, Jordanoff wrote:

> *Of all motorless flying, soaring teaches the pilot most. My opportunity to ride the wings of the wind on a Bowlus sailplane taught me things that have made me a better pilot of motored machines. Soaring is a flyer's postgraduate course.*

After the New York Glider Carnival, Bowlus sailplane S-21 was sold to the Cassell Flying Service of New York, displayed by the Westchester Glider School, and finally ended in the hands of the New York University Glider Club. An unfortunate crash without injury to the pilot wrote the final chapter for S-21.

## *Bowlus Sailplanes #22 (589V) and #23 (590V)*

Bowlus model "A" sailplane, serial S-22, was manufactured at the Bowlus factory on January 20th, 1930. Application for an identification mark was filed on March 10th, 1930, and identification mark 589V was granted on March 15th, 1930. The sailplane was sold on April 9th, 1930, to William J. Scripps of Detroit, Michigan for the sum of $975.00. In turn, Scripps sold the sailplane to the Chicago Gliding School at Chicago, Illinois for the sum of $1.00 on July 16th, 1930. Paul C. Skeels and B. M. Stimpson of Glenview, Illinois purchased the sailplane on June 6th, 1931, however, by September 1st, 1931, the license was allowed to expire. The eventual fate of this sailplane remains a mystery.

It is assumed that Bowlus model "A" sailplane serial S-23 was manufactured at the same time as serial S-22. Identification mark 590V was assigned to the sailplane in 1930, and it was sold to Mr. Smith and Mr. Myhres of Los Angeles, California. Unfortunately, all official records of this aircraft have been lost.

## *An Unofficial World Record*

On April 29th, Jack Barstow was lifted into the air by a steady sea breeze at Point Loma, on what was originally planned to be a typical afternoon soaring flight. He was launched by shock cord into a southerly sea breeze from the very southern tip of the point at 12:44 p.m. It was very rare to launch from this location, as the southern cliff face was quite narrow. The flight was planned as a leisurely flight...Barstow wore only golf knickers, a sweater, and a short leather coat, and carried no water or supplies. Much to everybody's surprise and delight, Barstow landed 15 hours and 13 minutes later at 3:57 a.m. to set a new unofficial world record for sailplane duration. During the flight, he spent the night exposed to rain squalls and winds of varying intensity. Upon landing, with the aid of the light from several automobile headlights and the local campfire, Barstow immediately asked for a cup of hot coffee.

He carried no barograph on his flight, and although National Aeronautic Association official William Van Dusen was present at the time of the landing, the flight could not be considered as "official" by the Fédération Aéronautique Internationale. During his flight, Barstow was reported to have attained an altitude of about 1,000 feet. The official world record for sailplane duration at the time was 14 hours, 10 minutes held by Ray Schultz of Germany and the unofficial world record was set by Lt.

*Above: Jack Barstow soaring in the Bowlus Sailplane #24 (315W) at Point Loma during his unofficial world soaring endurance record.*

*Left: Jack Barstow, who had learned to fly gliders and sailplanes at the Bowlus Gliding School, became so proficient that he was hired as an instructor in later months.*

Dinert of Germany at 14 hours, 45 minutes. A full account of Barstow's flight was published in *Popular Mechanics Magazine*.

*Ten hours went by, busy but slow hours; busy, because every nerve, every muscle, was working to take advantage of every gust, to lift the sailplane up the wind, to carry it across the air currents and still lose no altitude or lifting power. It was like being the mind and body of a bird, dependent only on the very wind itself for movement and elevation. Several times I sailed out over the ocean, which I could hear pounding on the rocks below.*

Two days later, Barstow attempted a repeat performance...this time carrying a barograph for an official record. However, after only three hours, he was forced to land due to a lack of wind. By May 24th, it was announced that Jack Barstow and the Pacific Coast Gliders, Inc. would share the coveted Edward S. Evans American Duration Prize. Because of the numerous affidavits signed by witnesses after the completion of the flight, the prize money, $2,000 for 10 hours and $100 for every extra hour, was given to Barstow, even though his flight was unofficial under the rules established previously by the Fédération Aéronautique Internationale.

Barstow was keenly aware that if he had been better prepared for an endurance flight prior to his 15-hour journey and if the winds had held up, he might have stayed up even longer. Barstow was convinced that a flight of over 15 hours could be made on the slopes of Point Loma.

On May 3rd, 1930, Barstow took off from the Point in the Bowlus S-18 sailplane in an attempt for a flight of over 24 hours. The launch occurred just prior to an approaching storm. Barstow's sailplane was tossed about by high winds and rain and the squalls became increasingly severe. After 8 hours and 1 minute, Barstow was forced to make a crash landing in a canyon along the side of the ridge. A portion of the wing was sheared off and Barstow was "lucky" to survive the crash with a fractured spinal vertebra and several cuts and bruises. He was rushed to Mercy Hospital. A large crowd, including Mrs. Barstow and Thomas Bomar, had gathered at Point Loma to watch the record attempt, only to eventually hunt in the darkness and rain for Barstow and the sailplane wreckage. Thomas Bomar recalled:

*It was past midnight...when suddenly out of the southeast came a terrific gale of wind and a cold rain. In a matter of minutes, a real chubasco (gale) was upon us. We anxiously strained our eyes trying to see the glider. We yelled ourselves hoarse, and we fought to keep the bonfire bright. Minutes that seemed like hours passed, but there was no sign of Jack.*

*We finally decided that Jack must have glided across the narrow harbor entrance and landed on North Island, which is large and flat and would therefore make a safe landing place...*

*Meanwhile, some of us with flashlights started crawling and sliding along the east side of the Point, looking down the ravines to see whether Jack might have crashed there. Daylight was just breaking when we found him. The first big blow of the storm had caught him off guard and had forced him down, hard, at the bottom of a ravine. He had been knocked unconscious and had suffered a back injury which made it impossible for him to move...*

*Dean Blake, the meteorologist of the Weather Bureau, who knew that Barstow was in the air, had tried desperately to warn him of the sudden storm, and was en route to the Point in his car when the blow struck.*

After learning of the crash in his morning paper in Detroit, Michigan, National Glider Association Manager Donald F. Walker sent a letter to William Van Dusen expressing deep concern over the condition of Barstow. On June 16th, 1930, Jack Barstow received a letter from Edward S. Evans. Enclosed was a check for $1250.00. The letter read:

*I take the greatest pleasure in handing you herewith my check in amount of $1250 as your share of the prize money for flying 15 hours and 13 minutes for a new world record.*

*My associates and I join in what we know is your regret that this flight was not official under the rules of the Fédération Aéronautique Internationale, and we are pleased to have received the co-operation of the contest committee of the National Aeronautical Association in restoring the primary money to me in order that I can, as an individual, pay it out to you as a token of my deep appreciation of your splendid work.*

*I have learned with the deepest regret of your accident in connection with your effort to repeat your flight officially but am pleased to know that more recent reports indicate that you are recovering rapidly.*

*I hope at some future time to make your personal acquaintance and congratulate you in person for what you have done to further the cause of American motorless aviation.*

*With deepest personal regards, I remain, very truly yours.*

*(signed) E.S. Evans*

## *Glider Activities in San Diego*

Yet another glider crash occurred when Dick Essery, president of the Western Flyers Glider Club, crashed his primary glider No. 2 (identification number unknown) on May 8th at the tip of Point Loma. At an altitude of 30 feet, a wind gust tossed Essery's glider *No Doubt* to the ground, breaking the nose of the glider in half. Essery was tossed from the glider while still attached to his seat. Richard Benbough helped pull the shock cord for launch and was an eyewitness to the incident. Newspaper accounts incorrectly suggested that Essery was tossed free from the glider at an altitude of 30 feet. He suffered only bruises from this mishap and returned to San Diego Senior High School shortly thereafter.

Over the period of May 9th through May 11th, 1930, Helen Van Dusen continued her primary glider instruction from Ruth Alexander at the Bowlus Glider School on Lindbergh Field using *Tillie the Toiler.* Mrs. H. K. W. Kumm was re-elected club president of the Anne Lindbergh Gliders Club during their "semi-annual election of officers" held May 20th. Others elected were: Mrs. Douglas Kelly, vice president, Miss Julia Twisleton, secretary, Miss Delores Griggs, corresponding secretary, Mrs. Margaret Burnett, treasurer, Mrs. William Van Dusen, historian, and Mrs. J. H. Rainwater, parliamentarian. Mrs. Anne Lindbergh continued as the club's honorary president. A benefit theater party was proposed and scheduled for the Savoy Theater on May 27th. The club was interested in raising money to purchase a trailer for the *Good Ship Anne* sailplane. Peaches Wallace underwent her third operation May 13th, following complications from her previous bout with appendicitis in April. She was reported to be recovering in serious condition following the operation.

Production of the Pacific Beach Glider Club sailplane was moving along swiftly. The boys were hopeful of using the sailplane to complete their first class glider licenses. On May 29th, 1930, under the supervision of Mr. Johnson and Mr. Heckleman the Pacific Beach Glider Club boys drove to Los Angeles and demonstrated glider flying to the students at La Brea High School using their primary glider (identification mark 303W). Some members of the Falcons Glider Club also attended, including Spencer Wilson. The flights were successful and it was hoped that students at La Brea would follow suit with glider experimentation.

On May 29th, 1930, San Diego Senior High School students Richard H. Benbough and Vernon M. Brown filed an application for identification mark for their primary glider. By June, 1930, identification mark 10258 was granted to the glider. However, by December, 1932, the glider had been permanently dismantled and the identification mark was canceled.

After returning from his trip to the East Coast, Bowlus announced to the local media that he had orders for 29 new Bowlus gliders (both primaries and sailplanes). The Bowlus glider factory was in the process of being moved from its previous waterfront location in the old tuna fish cannery to a new building one block to the south. The previously slow production of gliders was stepped up such that by late May, a rather optimistic Bowlus factory spokesman suggested that five primaries and five sailplanes were being completed every week. By June 20th, Clarence Young, assistant secretary of commerce, planned to come to San Diego for glider training at the Bowlus school.

In June of 1930, R. E. Fisher, chairman of the aeronautical committee of the State Chamber of Commerce, appointed C. F. Linesch of the aviation department of the Union Oil Company chairman of a committee to study the needs of the gliding industry in California. Other members of the committee included former San Diegan Waldo Waterman, manager of the Los Angeles Airport, William Van Dusen, secretary of the Associated Glider Clubs of Southern California, automotive instructor W. L. Winston of the Merced High School, Charles F. McReynolds of Los Angeles, Ross Peacock of Bakersfield, M. E. Coulter of Sacramento, and Emory B. Bronte of San Francisco. Their task was to establish California as the foremost gliding region of the United States.

## *Sterling Owen and Robert Goebel*

San Diego Senior High School students Sterling Owen and Robert Goebel were finishing construction on their single-place tapered-wing sailplane with trailing edge ailerons in May, 1930. The ship resembled the Bowlus sailplanes quite closely, complete with a very similar fuselage and tail assembly. Flights were made in the *Condor* (identification mark 10245) at Point Loma, and on at least one occasion (September 7th, 1930) a landing was made on the ledge below and to the west of the famous old Point Loma Lighthouse. At that time, a small polo ground was situated near the road that comes down the west face of the ridge to the small ledge and cliffs below. This polo ground was a favorite emergency landing strip for the glider pilots on the off-chance that the wind ebbed during flight. The *Condor* carried the words "R. K. O. Orpheum" on the top of the left wing. It is believed that the Orpheum theater helped finance construction by paying for some rather unusual advertising space.

Harland Ross made several flights in the *Condor* sailplane at Plumosa Park (July 28th, and September 17th) and at the Morena Hills site (August 18th). In his logbook, Ross suggested that the flight of July 28th was a test of a new ship, the "*Secondary Owens*," suggesting that this may have been the aircraft's first flight. This secondary was also known as the *Condor.* On September 21st and October 10th, 1930, Ross soared the *Condor* at Point Loma. His flight of October 10th lasted 2 hours and 26 minutes, covering a distance of 16 miles out and return. Ross suggested in his logbook, however, that an internal cable failure led to aileron flutter during the flight and as a result, Ross landed quickly. On October 18th, 1930, the *Condor* sailplane was "washed-out" in a crash at Point Loma and registration was canceled by the United States Department of Commerce on November 1st, 1930. The direct cause of the crash remains unknown.

## *Bowlus Sailplane #24 (315W)*

On March 26th, 1930, the Bowlus Sailplane Company, Ltd. filed paperwork for an identification mark on Bowlus sailplane serial number S-24. The model S-1000 sailplane was granted 315W on April 11th, 1930. 315W was sold to the Pacific Coast Gliders, Ltd. on April 17th, 1930, with the sailplane officially stationed at Lindbergh Field in San Diego. This same sailplane was used by Jack C. Barstow on his record-setting 15-hour endurance flight. The fuselage was heavily destroyed following Barstow's crash at Point Loma in May, 1930. Official paperwork suggests the intent was to rebuild the aircraft, but by 1933, identification mark 315W was officially canceled due to a lack of correspondence.

## *Bowlus Sailplane #25 (316W)*

After completing Bowlus sailplane S-25 in the late winter of 1930, an application for an identification mark was filed with the United States Department of Commerce on March 26th, 1930. The model S-1000 sailplane was granted identification mark 316W on April 11th, 1930. The aircraft was sold to Marshall S. Boggs of the Aeronautics Branch of the Department of Commerce in Washington, D.C. in May, 1930. Confusion resulted from the fact that the Department of Commerce assigned a second identification mark (1-Y) to this same aircraft in May. As a result, identification mark 316W was canceled and identification mark 1-Y remained with the ship until October, 1930, when it was changed to G1-Y to reflect its status as a glider. Official inspection reports at Oakland, California suggest that Marshall S. Boggs did not fly 1-Y prior to October, 1930. The aircraft was sold by Marshall S. Boggs to Carl D. Whalen of San Francisco, California on November 3rd, 1930. On January 15th, 1931, the aircraft was sold yet again to Raymond S. Stafford of San Francisco, California.

On March 8th, 1931, Ray S. Stafford soared for 47.5 minutes, covered approximately 16 miles, and rose to 200 feet above his point of takeoff near Salada Beach, San Francisco. He was a member of the Dragon Fly Club at the time. Stafford's flight did not break any official records, but set local records for endurance and distance for the region of Northern California.

> *It was the first Sunday of this season...that there has been wind. It was blowing about 12 to 15 miles an hour and conditions were good. I took off from the top of the ridge above the beach and found myself in a strong up current, which enabled me to rise to 200 feet. I soared along the ridge, back and forth in figure eights, 12 times and then, losing buoyancy, was obliged to land.*
>
> *I could not land near the takeoff on account of cultivated ground, so I had to dip down to the beach: I circled out over the water at an altitude of about ten*

*feet and then curved in to the beach. I was mighty glad to see everybody scuttle away when I shouted and to land without striking anybody.*

The local pilots in San Francisco used several Bowlus sailplanes built in San Diego and secondary gliders in the early 1930s. But by October of 1931, the identification mark 1-Y was officially canceled due to a lack of correspondence. Clearly, the sailplane (or at least the wing) survived to 1937. Ernest Langley, Jim Gough, and other members of the Northern California Soaring Society, flew a sailplane that used the rebuilt wing from G1-Y and a monocoque fuselage. This hybrid sailplane was flown at Point Reyes and other locations in the San Francisco Bay area with some flights over one hour in duration. Following this, the whereabouts of G1-Y remain a mystery.

## *Bowlus Sailplane #26 (317W)*

Bowlus model S-1000 sailplane, serial S-26, was completed at the Bowlus factory in the spring of 1930. An application for an identification mark was filed with the United States Department of Commerce on March 26th, 1930. Identification mark 317W was granted on April 11th, 1930. On May 13th, 1930, the aircraft was sold to the Varney Air Service, Inc. at the Oakland Municipal Airport, Oakland, California. Between September, 1930, and January, 1931, the nose of the fuselage and tip ailerons were repaired. Ownership was transferred to N. W. Bagley, W. H. Birch, and W. J. Bagley of Oakland, California in February, 1931, and continued until May, 1939 when the license officially expired. The aircraft, however, survived. It was later displayed at The Flying Lady restaurant near Morgan Hill, California and found its way to the Wings of History Museum, in San Martin, California where it is currently under restoration.

## *Bowlus Sailplane #27 (318W)*

Bowlus sailplane S-27 was completed at the Bowlus factory on March 26th, 1930. Identification mark 318W was granted by the United States Department of Commerce on April 11th, 1930. The aircraft was purchased by Hayes Aviation, Inc. in Syracuse, New York, but the identification mark was canceled on November 23, 1931, when the purchaser failed to submit the required documents for transfer of title. In 1933, the aircraft ended up in the hands of Floyd Gustin of Elmira, New York, who subsequently contacted the United States Department of Commerce in the interests of obtaining proper license and registration. Confusion regarding the incomplete transfer

*Howard Jope (center) and assistant (left) taking a publicity photo of Hawley Bowlus (right) and the Bowlus Sailplane #29 (320W). Jope lived in San Diego an accompanied Bowlus to various soaring locations in San Diego as official photographer. Jope was an eyewitness to many of the record flights made at Point Loma.*

of title between the Bowlus Sailplane Company and Hayes Aviation thwarted Gustin's attempted application. Following this, the whereabouts of 318W remain a mystery.

## *Bowlus Sailplane #28 (319W)*

On March 26th, 1930, an application for identification mark was filed by the Bowlus Sailplane Company, Ltd. for Bowlus sailplane S-28. Identification mark 319W was granted on April 12th, 1930. Mysteriously, S-28 ended up with Reuben H. Fleet, of Buffalo, New York later in 1930. While attending the 1930 United States Soaring National Contest at Elmira, New York, Hawley Bowlus borrowed S-28 and damaged it in one of the flights. In 1931, the damaged sailplane was purchased by the D. W. Flying Service, Inc., in Le Roy, New York. Wing struts were added as well as a new rudder. Russell Holderman, owner of the D. W. Flying Service, Inc. entered S-28 in the 1931 United States Nationals at Elmira, New York, and both Mr. and Mrs. Holderman earned their first-class glider licenses in S-28. Due to the confusion following the close of the Bowlus factory in San Diego and subsequent loss of paperwork, the identification mark was canceled on November 24th, 1931.

It is possible that Soaring Society of America pioneer Warren Eaton subsequently purchased the sailplane from Russell Holderman. Russell Lowe of New Berlin, New York bought the sailplane from Eaton, flew it on occasion, and sold it to Walter "Tommy" Tucker of Deposit, New York in 1941. Tucker entered the United States Army Air Corps and sold it to Raymond Hartz in Windsor, New York. Following this, the history of S-28 remains a mystery.

## *Bowlus Sailplane #29 (320W)*

By mid-June, Bowlus was interested in improved methods for glider training at Lindbergh Field. His answer was the Bowlus sailplane S-29, the "convertible Albatross." This single sailplane fuselage could be outfitted for ground training, primary and secondary gliding and soaring, and could even be converted into a motor-glider or amphibian glider. It was truly a plane with many faces. Bowlus was convinced of its utility in the training role and discontinued production of primary gliders, according to reports by Mr. R. E. Pollock, General Manager of the Bowlus Sailplane Company, Ltd.

The convertible glider was fitted with a 2-foot center section instead of the original 14-foot center section. By removing the outer wing panels entirely, and attaching a special landing gear, the plane was towed by car and the training pilot received ground instruction on the manipulation and feel of the tail assembly. For primary instruction, the outer panels were added, but the special two-foot center section gave a dihedral of 5°, making the plane inherently stable.

With the landing gear still attached, the glider was auto towed down the runway, and the pilot could release at a low altitude and glide straight ahead to a landing. For soaring, the 2-foot center section was replaced by the original 14-foot center section, giving a total wingspan of 60-feet and the landing gear was removed. For "hydro-gliding," a special canvas boot was fitted over the fuselage and pontoons were added. The "convertible" albatross sold for $1,095 from the factory and was reportedly cheaper than the combined purchase of a primary and a secondary glider.

By June 28th, the Bowlus factory was reported to be manufacturing two "convertibles" a month, and a similar training system was adopted by the Ferron Aviation School in Berkeley, California. The original "convertible," was the 11th sailplane to be produced at the factory, and its original identification mark of 320W was issued in March, 1930. Plywood pontoons were designed by Hawley and Glenn Bowlus and constructed at the Pacific Technical University, a ground school for the various flight schools based at Lindbergh Field. According to Bowlus historian Richard Benbough:

> *The twin floats were fastened to existing landing gear fittings in the sub-skid of the sailplane and strutted to attach points below the wing on both sides of the two main fuselage bulkheads. Trial and error, numerous changes in design and one capsized fuselage (no wings) due to an improper angle of tow, finally resulted in a gear with sufficient reserve buoyancy to accomplish the desired purpose.*

Test flights of the hydro-glider were conducted on several portions of San Diego Bay behind a motorboat.

For motor-gliding, the aircraft was equipped with a 9.5-horsepower outboard motor set on top of the wing. The motor was borrowed from Glenn Bowlus. A pilot could start the motor directly from the cockpit by means of a pull cord. Flight tests were made at Lindbergh Field, but the results were less than spectacular, due to the low horsepower and lack of a paved runway. Motorized flights were made successfully, but only with the initial assistance of auto tow. Bowlus hoped that this new combination sailplane would entice more people to sign up with the Bowlus Gliding School.

By July 7th, 1930, lessons in the Bowlus hydro-glider were offered as a prize to one of the winners of the Fox Theater Popularity Contest. Other prizes included a complete course at the local Kelsey-Jenney Commercial College, a new 1930 Chevrolet sport roadster, a 3,000-mile trip given by Western Air Express, and $5,000 equity in a $10,000 Point Loma home. Local newspapers reported that the combination glider received its United States Department of Commerce approval August 6th, 1930. In 1931, sailplane 320W was sold to Frank A. Van Bezel as part of the purchase of the Bowlus Sailplane Company, Ltd. The identification mark was canceled on June

17th, 1933, when the Van Bezel Aircraft Company, Ltd. failed to reply to a questionnaire on the status of the sailplane.

## *Bowlus Sailplane #30 (321W)*

Completed by March 26th, 1930, at the Bowlus Sailplane Company in San Diego, Bowlus sailplane S-30 received identification mark 321W on April 12th, 1930. The sailplane was a standard issue model S-1000 sailplane. Model S-1000 sailplanes were essentially a slightly modified version of the model "A." On June 1st, 1930, title for the aircraft was transferred to the Cassell Flying Service of New York City. In rapid order, the ship was sold to United States Army Captain Thomas Phillips of Hempstead, Long Island, New York on July 16th, 1930 complete with a shock cord for $900. Prior to shipment, repairs and modifications were made to the sailplane following a "faulty landing." Repairs were made by C. H. Biddlecombe of the Cape Cod Glider School in South Wellfleet, Massachusetts. The wing and cabane (a cabane was not part of a standard issue series S-1000 sailplane) were damaged and repaired.

Captain Phillips served in the Panama Canal Zone, and the sailplane was shipped to Fort Clayton (Miller Field), near Corozal, Panama where it could be properly inspected. While in Panama, Canal Zone regulations required proper Canal Zone identification marks and license. Hence, sailplane 321W was redesignated as CZ 502-G. Captain Phillips wrote immediately to the United States Department of Commerce notifying them that while flying in the Canal Zone, identification mark CZ 502-G would be displayed on the wing, and if the sailplane were to ever be flown in the United States again, the number 321W would be used instead. But upon hearing that a Canal Zone identification mark had been placed on the sailplane, the Department of Commerce canceled identification mark 321W immediately, with the understanding that this identification mark could be reinstated with proper paperwork.

Captain Phillips returned to America in early 1931, and brought Bowlus sailplane S-30 with him. The sailplane was "washed out" in a crash at Elmira, New York on August 18, 1931, during the United States Soaring Nationals while operating under the Canal Zone license CZ 502-G.

## *Bowlus Sailplane #31 (10144)*

On April 14th, 1930, Bowlus sailplane S-31 was completed at the Bowlus Sailplane Company at San Diego. The sailplane was a standard issue S-1000 series sailplane. By May 15th, 1930, application for an identification mark was filed with the United States Department of Commerce, and number 10144 was granted on May 22nd, 1930. The following month, the sailplane was sold to Henry G. Chapman of Bonita. During

Chapman's ownership, the sailplane was renumbered G-10144 to reflect its status as a glider. Inspection of airworthiness was held at the Chula Vista Airport on September 25th, 1930. Chapman owned the sailplane for a full year, placing it in storage until eventually selling the aircraft to the "Y" Triangle Club. Claude T. Burns signed the required paperwork on September 22nd, 1931.

After transfer to the "Y" Triangle Club, the sailplane was modified by replacing the standard ten foot center section with a two foot section. Extra dihedral and a light landing gear were also installed. The glider was flown by younger members of the "Y" Triangle Club through the majority of 1932, until October of that year, when the license was allowed to expire. The eventual fate of 10144 remains unknown.

## *H. Grafton Chapman Flies a Hydro-Glider*

On June 25th, 1930, H. Grafton Chapman test flew a glider equipped with pontoons at the south end of San Diego Bay near Tyce Airport in Chula Vista (850 G Street, next to the bay). After completing initial tests, Chapman suggested that the pontoons needed to be redesigned and subsequent tests were postponed. By July 1st, Chapman announced that the first "aquatic glider school in America" would open near the famous Coronado Tent City. Many United States aircraft companies, such as Cessna and the Detroit Aircraft Company, were making similar hydro-glider primaries at the time.

Headquarters for the Chapman Hydro-Glider School were established in the Arcade building of the Hotel del Coronado resort, and further tests of the glider equipment were conducted by James A. Moore and William Van Dusen of the San Diego board of air control.

## *Exhibition Glider Flights at Morena*

From July 4th to July 6th, 1930, a three-day glider exhibition was held at Morena "one mile east and two miles north of the bend in the highway opposite the Hardy slaughter house at Old Town," so that gliders in the area could be officially inspected and approved. Fifteen gliders were scheduled to attend, and flight activities were sponsored by the Associated Glider Clubs of Southern California. On July 2nd, gliders were brought to Lindbergh Field for structural tests and, on July 3rd, similar tests were made at Ryan Field. Airworthiness tests were held at the Morena exhibition. The exhibition was billed as the "largest number of gliders ever assembled in the west." Between 3 and 6 motorless aircraft were aloft simultaneously. Harland Ross made one flight on July 4th, and three flights on July 5th in the Bowlus sailplane S-16 using auto tow as a means for takeoff.

## *Dedication of the Peaches Wallace Gliderport*

Miss Peaches Wallace died of complications due to pneumonia and emphysema on June 22nd, 1930, as a result of her appendicitis. She had soloed in a motorized airplane at Ryan Field in September, 1929, with only 6 hours, 15 minutes of dual instruction and was a charter member of the Anne Lindbergh Gliders Club. Her funeral was held at Glenn Abbey Memorial Park in Bonita on June 24th. Her death was a shock to female glider pilots in the area. Unfortunately, several newspaper accounts incorrectly stated that she died in a glider accident.

With the passing of Peaches Wallace, interest in local women's gliding activities began to wane. An article describing the Anne Lindbergh Gliders Club written by Peaches just prior to her appendicitis was published in the July-August issue of *Aviation Mechanics* magazine. Similar attention was given to Peaches and the women of the Anne Lindbergh Gliders Club in *Popular Mechanics Magazine*. San Diegans held a sense of personal loss for Peaches; the Anne Lindbergh Gliders Club and other local women's aircraft clubs would never be the same without her. Earlier in her aviation career, Peaches was named "Queen of the Air" by local newspapers, as she was the subject of daily reports in the local *San Diego Sun* newspaper. Many San Diegans were aware of her skills as a pilot and followed her interest in aviation closely.

An area near the Emerald Hills Golf Course clubhouse was cleared of brush by local glider enthusiasts and developed as a gliderport. It was reported to be the "second [official gliderport] in the United States and [the] first in California." Local enthusiasts, especially those from the Anne Lindbergh Gliders Club, dedicated the site as the Peaches Wallace Gliderport in her honor.

A San Diego County-wide glider meet was held on Sunday July 27th, 1930 in conjunction with the official dedication program. San Diego Mayor Harry C. Clark addressed the crowd and Mrs. Rainwater of the Anne Lindbergh Gliders Club spent a great deal of effort to coordinate the event. Dr. Charles Good, Chairman of the County Board of Supervisors, and Dr. H. W. K. Kumm, President of the Associated Glider Clubs of Southern California, also addressed the crowd.

At 10:00 a.m., elimination contests were staged and the best glider pilots were selected for contests and awards that afternoon. A model-glider contest was also held and a silver loving cup was awarded to the first-place contestant. Mrs. Rainwater stated that "the site is one of the best in the country for gliding and training purposes." The field, presented to the glider enthusiasts by Mr. C. C. Crouch, an owner of the country club, included a wide glider landing area below the launching point.

During the ceremonies, Ruth Alexander circled over the field in a powered plane, spiraled down from 3,000 feet, and dropped flowers on the gliderport in memory of Peaches Wallace. Two formations of planes from local aviation companies at Lindbergh Field (Airtech School of Aviation and Ryan) circled the field in her honor and flew off into the distance.

The following aircraft were registered in the contest: David Robertson's primary glider G17W, Harry H. Haw's primary glider 367W, Bud Perl's Bowlus sailplane

*A large assembly of local gliders and sailplanes at the dedication of the Peaches Wallace Gliderport.*

G493/599M, the Escondido Glider Club primary glider G681W, Dick Essery's primary glider G372V, and the Anne Lindbergh Gliders Club Bowlus sailplane 584V. Harry Haw's primary glider was disqualified after failing to meet United States Department of Commerce requirements for license. Pilots who entered the meet included Dick Essery, Harry H. Haw, David Mendenhall, M. J. McIntire, Henry Morgan, Sterling Owen, Bud Perl, Landis Perry, A. Clare Rand, David Robertson, and Harland C. Ross. The entrance fee was 50 cents.

In the distance category, David Robertson placed first in the novice category with a distance of 1,681 feet. Using Robertson's primary, Sterling Owen took first prize in the advanced category for distance with a flight of only 1,628 feet, shorter than Robertson's mark by 53 feet. In duration, David Mendenhall managed to fly 24.4 seconds to take first prize in the novice class, while Dick Essery nearly doubled that mark with a flight of 42.4 seconds. Landis Perry took first place in the novice class in spot landing, stopping only nine feet from the mark with G681W. A. Clare Rand took first place in the same ship with a distance of 36 feet from the marker. David Robertson was awarded the Overall Novice Class trophy, and Dick Essery was awarded the

*Ruth Alexander (left) and William Van Dusen (right) reviewing a barograph following one of Ruth's record altitude flights in powered aircraft.*

Overall Advanced Class trophy for the meets based on the averaged score for takeoff, flying, landing, and duration of flight. Harland Ross made three flights in the contest using the Robertson Primary each of one minute in duration.

After the contest, the distinction between "novice" and "advanced" categories was complicated by the fact that, in many cases, the "novices" appeared to outcompete their "advanced" counterparts when using the same gliders. No award was made in the distance event for sailplanes as the only entry was Ruth Alexander in the *Good Ship Anne*. Silver loving cups were presented by various banks and community associations to the winners of the contests. News reports suggested that 5,000 curious onlookers attended the dedication and glider flying at San Diego's newest gliderport. It was a fitting tribute to the memory of Peaches Wallace.

## *Western Flyers Club Gliders #4 (681W) and #5 (682W)*

Acting on behalf of the Western Flyers Club on April 19th, 1930, Dick Essery applied for an identification mark for the club's 4th primary glider. The glider was manufactured by Dick Essery, Joe Thurston, and Bill Dickenson. Identification mark 681W was granted on May 2nd, 1930. By early June, 1930, primary glider 681W was sold to the Escondido Glider Club. John White, president, and Howard Donaldson, secretary/treasurer jointly purchased the glider for the sum of $1.00. A. Clare Rand acted as the primary agent in this transaction. Airworthiness inspection was made at Howell Airport in Escondido, California. The glider was flown in the Escondido area until September, 1932, when the license was allowed to expire.

As a sister ship to 681W, the 5th primary glider of the Western Flyers was completed in early April, 1930. Application for an identification mark was filed on April 19th, 1930, and identification 682W was granted on May 2nd, 1930. Confusion resulted from the fact that the original application for identification was filed under the name of the Western Flyers, and on subsequent paperwork, the glider was listed as being owned by the Western Flyers Glider Club. By August, 1930, Dick Essery wrote a letter to the Department of Commerce stressing the fact that the Western Flyers and Western Flyers Glider Club were one and the same and operated under the auspices of the Western Flyers Glider Company. To this the government responded that a form documenting the transfer of title over the aircraft was required. Such a form was completed in October, 1930. However, by April, 1933, identification mark 682W was allowed to expire for unknown reasons.

## *Essery, Dickenson, Freedman Glider #2 (683W)*

On April 19th, 1930, Dick Essery and Bill Dickenson applied for an identification mark on yet a third glider. This glider was originally completed on July 4th, 1929, by Essery, Dickenson, and Freedman (first name unknown to author) and flown unlicensed. Official records note that the aileron system was changed and fuselage repaired by Essery and Dickenson prior to relicensing. It is quite possible that this same glider was flown by Essery at the 1929 Pacific Beach Glider Meet. Identification mark 683W was assigned on May 7th, 1930, however, the only other records on this aircraft suggest that the identification mark was canceled on June 17th, 1933, following a lack of correspondence.

## *Gliding Activities in Fall, 1930*

La Jolla's junior glider guiders had their moment in the spotlight with the "baby glider meet" held at the La Jolla Playground on August 15th at 2:30 p.m. Balsa-wood free-flight gliders were used by the "playground glider class" to teach the fundamentals of aeronautics and for a genuinely fun outdoor activity.

Mrs. Gertrude Kumm, club president and Hazel Kelley, vice president, met to discuss plans for the latter half of 1930 and club finances. By August 8th, plans were being made by the Anne Lindbergh Gliders Club to raise money for the payment of several post-due bills. To pay for expenses, a dance was scheduled for August 20th at the Emerald Hills Golf Course. Sincere gratitude was expressed in a letter written by Mrs. Gertrude Kumm to the various members of the club for the work of Mrs. Rainwater in arranging the dedication ceremonies of the Peaches Wallace Gliderport.

In August, 1930, the National Glider Association reported that of the 64 glider clubs officially registered in the United States, the Bowlus Glider Club contained more third-class glider licenses (33), second-class glider licenses (16), and first-class licenses (8) than any other club in America. Also high on the list was the Anne Lindbergh Gliders Club with 4 third-class licenses, 3 second-class licenses, and 1 first-class license (Anne Lindbergh). The Bowlus Glider Club was leading the way in glider club activities. One of the Bowlus Glider Club's youngest members, Bud Perl, published an account of his training activities at the Bowlus Glider School in the August, 1930, edition of *Popular Mechanics*.

During 1930, virtually any open hillside in San Diego was a potential gliding site. On at least one occasion, a primary glider was flown from the west side of Black Mountain, just north of Kearney Mesa. As many as five high school students were involved in the activities. The glider was launched by shock cord or auto tow and brought back up to the launching site on top of the hill by car. San Diego Senior High School student Richard Benbough attended these activities on one occasion during the summer of 1930.

Gottlieb Goller, a 21-year-old recent immigrant to the San Diego area from Germany, crashed in a glider (most likely the primary glider 17W) at Morena on August 3rd, 1930. Goller came to America with the knowledge of over 50 glider flights in Germany. His wounds required a trip to the emergency room at the County hospital. Upon shock cord launch, Goller appeared to not have sufficient airspeed for flight and crashed from an altitude of approximately 40 feet. Goller had been in the air less than a minute when the accident occurred.

On September 16th, 1930, Homer D. High of San Diego filed for an identification mark on a newly constructed primary glider. Identification mark 902Y was granted on October 7th, 1930, by the Department of Commerce. However, by June, 1933, the identification mark was canceled due to a lack of correspondence.

At least 12 more gliders or sailplanes were licensed officially in the San Diego area in 1930, but records for these aircraft have not yet been obtained. These include the Justice Marine Glider #1 (159W) made by J. Justice, the McElheny sailplane #1 (189W) made by Clinton B. McElheny, the McMahon-Wiedel primary glider (198W) made by Herbert McMahon and Carl Wiedel, the Rainwater ST Glider (543V) made by J. H. Rainwater, the Robbins sailplane #1 (591V) made by Bob Robbins, the Gottschalk glider (40W) made by M. E. Gottschalk, the Ace Glider #1 (91W) made by the Ace Glider Club, the Miller glider #1 (92W) made by B. Miller, the Goebel primary glider #12 (928Y) made by Robert Goebel, the Gage and Faxon glider (10095), a Northrup primary glider (10134) made by Vincent Loop, and the Penguin sailplane (929Y) made by the Penguin Glider Club. Members of the Penguin Glider Club included Albert Gabbs, Vincent Loop, and David Robertson. Albert Gabbs later recalled:

> *I do remember one test-hop with a glider built by a glider club. Another fellow was chosen as the test pilot. We hooked up the glider to the auto tow rope. The glider didn't have wheels or springs, only a wooden skid. As the car started speeding up and the skid was sliding on the dirt field, there was a rut it its path. The skid took a terrible bounce, and each of the wings broke above the fuselage and simultaneously dropped like a wounded eagle. I don't remember whether that project ever went on to glorious soaring or whether the glider was taken to the scrap heap!*

## *Dr. H. Karl William Kumm*

On August 22nd, noted scientist, explorer, horticulturist, and first president of the Associated Glider Clubs of Southern California, Dr. H. Karl William Kumm, died of heart disease. This disease was reportedly induced by "a fever contracted in the African jungles in the region of the Congo" several years earlier. Dr. H. K. W. Kumm was 56 years old. Born in Hanover, Germany in 1874, he studied at schools in London,

Freiburg, Cambridge, and Paris. During his explorations of Africa in the late 1800s, he was reported to be the "first white man to traverse the north central African divide between Congo Shari and the Nile." He arranged seven such journeys as the director of the board for medical education and research in Africa. His focus of research was sleeping sickness, which was believed to be contracted by Kumm on his seventh expedition.

*Dr. H. Karl William Kumm*

After moving to New Jersey, his doctors suggested that a warmer climate might be more suitable for his health. He and his wife moved to San Diego in 1925, settling in Pacific Beach. He was crucial to the development of enthusiasm for glider activities in the San Diego area, especially in Pacific Beach and La Jolla. As the first president of the Associated Glider Clubs of Southern California, he brought together glider clubs from all over San Diego and Los Angeles, making the Associated Glider Clubs of Southern California one of the largest glider clubs of its time. At present, the Associated Glider Clubs of Southern California is the oldest surviving active glider club in the United States and continues to fly sailplanes at a variety of locations in Southern California.

## *Ruth Alexander*

In the very early morning of September 18th, local glider aviatrix Ruth Alexander readied her altitude record-setting Barling NB-1 powered aircraft (identification mark NR880M) for a one-stop flight from San Diego's Lindbergh Field to New York. Her one stop was to be in Wichita, Kansas. Heavily loaded with 117 gallons of fuel, she took off from the airport at 3:28 a.m. into a thick marine layer of low clouds and fog which had developed overnight in the area. Ten minutes after takeoff, she crashed nose-first at Plumosa Park near Bodega Street in Loma Portal. Although no fire occurred on impact, Ruth died instantly still strapped to her seat. She was the third local aviatrix to die within a year following Marvel Crosson (1929) and Peaches Wallace (1930). In her memoirs of the Anne Lindbergh Gliders Club, Helen Van Dusen recollected:

*The crowd of friends who have risen at 2 a.m. is surprisingly large; and none of us will forget the happy self-confidence in Ruth's voice as she spoke of seeing her mother and father, and of her joy that circumstances were permitting her to takeoff at this time...She is off the ground easily. We watch the lights of the plane pass over the Marine Base, then the lights dim as she enters the fog, tho' for a moment more we can still hear the muffled tones of the motor. 'If I can't get thru, I'll be back in fifteen minutes,' she had said. We wait a full half hour--and return home unknowing that even as we waited Ruth had crashed to her death on the north end of Point Loma.*

Ruth Alexander

News of Ruth Alexander's death was too much for the local glider pilots to bear, especially those connected with the Anne Lindbergh Gliders Club. After the quick succession of Peaches Wallace, Dr. Kumm, and Ruth Alexander, gliding just was not the same as it had been only a few months earlier. Their leadership and inspiration were crucial to the local development of the sport. Waning enthusiasm for women's glider activities would soon find its way throughout the San Diego glider clubs. It would take several years before enthusiasm for gliding activities in San Diego would again reach the fever pitch of early 1930.

## *Bowlus Sailplane Company Closes*

By November, 1930, operations at the Bowlus Sailplane Company in San Diego had closed due to the extreme financial pressures of the Great Depression. Mr. Frank A. Van Bezel and Ray Jones had a partnership in the Van Bezel Aircraft Company based in El Centro, California. The company sold four-cylinder engines for light aircraft, and investors were interested in increasing engine sales. Van Bezel was looking for a set of pre-built airplanes that could be retrofitted with his engines. With this idea in mind, in early 1931, Van Bezel purchased the Bowlus Sailplane Company as well as the sailplanes and gliders therein, so that they could be converted to powered planes using Van Bezel engines. A two-place, side-by-side motorglider was later constructed, but production on the aircraft type never started. Three or four of the old Bowlus sailplanes were sold, as were three or four of the old Bowlus primary gliders. Then, with the Great Depression in full swing, sales dropped and the Van Bezel Company folded. During the time that Van Bezel owned the products of the former Bowlus Sailplane Company, Bud Perl stayed on as chief test pilot and instructor, giving sailplane demonstrations over Point Loma on a regular basis.

## *Bowlus Leaves San Diego*

Shortly after leaving San Diego for the East Coast, Hawley Bowlus and Wolfram Hirth teamed up to form the Bowlus-Hirth Institute of Soaring Schools, Inc. based in New York. The Bowlus-Hirth school lasted only a short time, and closed when Hirth returned to Germany in the spring of 1931.

At the 1931 United States Soaring Nationals at Elmira, New York, Hawley Bowlus made a flight of 10.95 miles in a Haller Hawk, sailplane soaring for a total of four hours and 25 minutes in the contest. Following this, Bowlus teamed up with Russell Holderman of Le Roy, New York, and opened another glider school, but Bowlus returned to California in December, 1931, to serve as an aviation instructor for the Curtiss Wright Aviation School. While at the Curtiss Wright School in Glendale, California, Bowlus designed a number of sailplanes including the prototype for the famous Albatross I.

In 1933, Bowlus and Richard duPont teamed up to form the Bowlus-duPont Sailplane Company, based in San Fernando, California. Bowlus and duPont continued with the construction of Warren Eaton's *Falcon*, the Albatross II, and the Bowlus Utility Glider. In 1933, Bowlus designed his own camping trailer, the Bowlus Road Chief, which was sold via Bowlus Trailers, Inc. Construction of gliders continued with the Bowlus Utility Glider X-1, which was entered in the 8th United States Soaring Nationals, as well as the Bowlus Baby Albatross and Super Albatross sailplanes. Bowlus even continued designing gliders for the United States military during World War II, and also designed the *Bumble Bee*, an auxilliary-powered sailplane in 1945. Bowlus left a truly remarkable legacy of designing gliders and sailplanes, and is considered by many to be one of the most important persons in U.S. soaring history.

## *Aerial Shows at Lindbergh Field and Ryan Field*

On October 12th, 1930, an air show was held at Lindbergh Field to demonstrate powered acrobatic flying to the public. Airtech Chief Pilot and Glider Instructor Earle Mitchell made several glider flights at the air show. Earle Mitchell was the first pilot in San Diego to receive a United States Department of Commerce commercial glider pilot license. At the Lindbergh Field air show, Mitchell used a Bowlus sailplane similar to the one in which Barstow set his 15-hour duration mark. He took a short hop by auto tow at 1:30 p.m. to open the festivities, and also flew at 4:30 p.m., prior to the aerobatic demonstration.

Early in November, an annual air show commemorated the eighth anniversary of Ryan Field. Many new airplanes were on display and flown for the enjoyment of the crowd. At the air show, Dick Essery was reported to have staged a glider exhibition for the crowd.

## *Harland Ross and the "Silver King" (908Y)*

Harland Ross' first flight instruction was completed at the North Island Naval Air Station in San Diego on United States Navy Stearmans. He received aviation mechanics training with the Navy, and was soon captured by the glider activities surrounding Bowlus and the glider school. While earning his glider ratings, Ross built his first sailplane, the Ross R-1000 *Silver King,* while still enlisted in the Navy at North Island. The *Silver King* was closely patterned after the large 60-foot wingspan Bowlus S-1000 series of sailplanes, but used trailing edge ailerons instead of the typical tip ailerons. Albert Gabbs helped Ross construct the *Silver King* over a period of 2 to 3 months. Ross was hired by the Bowlus Sailplane Company soon after he completed his stay with the United States Navy.

First flights of the *Silver King* occurred on November 2nd, 1930, at Lindbergh Field by auto tow. On November 3rd, the ship was test flown along the beach at the north end of the Torrey Pines cliffs on five separate flights with about six minutes average duration. Soon thereafter, identification mark 908Y was granted by the United States Department of Commerce. Ross made an attempt at high altitude soaring along the mountains east of San Diego, with a 35-minute glider flight on November 9th, 1930. Following a shock cord launch, Ross was able to soar the *Silver King* above the Volcan Mountains near Julian at approximately 6,000 feet above sea level. It was the first high-altitude mountain soaring flight in the United States.

On November 10th, Jack Barstow flew to Julian in a powered plane to pick up his friend Harland Ross. Barstow landed in a large empty meadow near the Julian High School. Upon taking off for the return trip to San Diego, with Ross as a passenger, Barstow was surprised by the proximity of several telephone wires at the end of the field. The plane became entangled in the lines and crashed. Barstow received cuts to his left eye, while Ross fractured both his knee cap and ankle and sustained numerous cuts. They were driven to Mercy Hospital in San Diego for treatment, the same hospital that Barstow had been recovering in until about two months prior to this crash from his earlier sailplane mishap at Point Loma.

*Harland Ross soaring in the Ross "Silver King" above the waves at Torrey Pines in November, 1930. This is the earliest known photo of soaring at Torrey Pines.*

## *Primary Gliders at Torrey Pines*

At the age of 18, Henry Severin and his high school friends were flying primary gliders by shock cord launch at the foot of the Torrey Pines Grade between La Jolla and Del Mar at the north end of the Torrey Pines cliffs. The beach was easily accessible by car and the hard packed sand made driving on the beach possible. The gliders were launched by auto tow parallel to the beach. On some lucky occasions, pilots were able to soar on the updrafts created by the 100-200 foot cliffs south toward Flat Rock. Several students from San Diego Senior High School were involved with these activities, some of whom learned about glider construction from Letain Kittredge. In late 1930, San Diego Senior High School students Dave Robertson and Henry Severin constructed a 50-foot tapered sailplane wing in the hopes that they would finish a true sailplane by the 1931 spring soaring season at Torrey Pines. Construction was slow. By the end of spring, in order to speed up construction, they completed a framework primary glider "fuselage" for the sailplane wing in under two weeks. They were soon flight testing it at Camp Kearney, near Mira Mesa, and along the beach at Torrey Pines. This two-place glider was used by Robertson and Severin to train other teenage boys in the art of gliding, and was even used to soar on the cliffs on days with a sufficiently strong westerly sea breeze. Launches in the primary were made by auto tow along the beach at the north end of the cliffs at Torrey Pines, north of Flat Rock. At high tide, Flat Rock sometimes posed quite a challenge to the young aviators. John Robinson recalled:

> *...At low tide, you could get a car around that rock. And then there were several miles down to where a whole bunch of rocks had fallen off the cliff...we had somebody who had landed on the beach, south of this pile of rocks. When they went down to get this plane, instead of disassembling the plane and walking it through the rocks, to where the car was...they got the car around the first rock no problem, but they started to drive around the pile of rocks. And even though it was low tide, why, they got out in two feet of water and got stuck. They unhooked the trailer, which was logical, and then tried to drive the car around the rocks to get to where the plane was. But they couldn't do it with the waves, you know how the waves run under something that's standing there like feet or tires. The tires got washed, the sand got washed out under the tires, the thing was sinking down to where it couldn't be driven. So, the tide was coming in, and so they said 'well, we'll come back tomorrow at low tide, and finish the job.' And meanwhile, they put the plane on the trailer. When they came back to the car the next day, the frame of the car was way up in the middle of the rocks, and there were parts of the car scattered two miles down the beach. The waves had taken the car apart and really, really creamed it. So, we made a rule that you never drive around Flat Rock for any reason. If you have to land down that far south, why you take the glider apart and walk it over across the rocks to get it out.*

John Robinson learned to fly in the Robertson-Severin two-place primary glider. Robinson was a student at San Diego Senior High School, but was not involved with Letain Kittredge's woodshop class. Another San Diego Senior High student, Richard Benbough, also made a test hop in the two-place primary at Torrey Pines. At the time, Dave Robertson was the most experienced glider pilot in the group. This primary glider has been recognized as having particular importance, in that it was one of the first two-place gliders used for training on the West Coast. Flights in primary gliders were common at Torrey Pines during the latter part of 1930.

While launching on the beach north of the cliffs at Torrey Pines on December 17th, 1930, Henry Severin crashed in a primary glider after striking the car of Thomas Blair, another young glider enthusiast. Severin was reported to be knocked unconscious by the blow and recovered at his parents' home on El Cajon Avenue. The bungee cord used for launching snapped before the plane achieved sufficient airspeed for flight. The glider tip stalled, fell to one side, and crashed onto the top of Blair's car before finally coming to rest on the ground. During December, 1930, Vincent Loop and Henry Severin flew both a sailplane and a primary glider at Torrey Pines, the latter glider destroyed in this crash.

At least six of the students from San Diego Senior High School flying gliders along the beach at Torrey Pines were interested in other hobbies. On occasion, while waiting for suitable soaring conditions to develop, they would take rides on cut-down surfboards while being towed from a car driving along the beach. While on tow parallel to the beach, they could play and jump the waves. They also made short boards for each foot and were towed into the surf at about a 70° to 80° angle from the tow car. This was prior to the widespread use of water skis.

# *CHAPTER 4*

# *1931-1940*
# *From Point Loma to Torrey Pines*

## *Glider Activities in 1931-1933*

Starting February 22nd, 1931, the Jack Barstow Glider Club of San Diego advertised a series of regular glider "meets" on the last Sunday of every month along the slopes of Point Loma. Soaring was still fine, even though enthusiasm was not as high as the year before. Early in 1931, Harland Ross also made some soaring flights in the *Silver King* from Point Loma.

To honor Dr. Kumm and Ruth Alexander, a glider exhibition was held at the Peaches Wallace Gliderport on Sunday, March 1st, 1931. Flights were made by Alfred Higgins and Wyatt Ingram, Henry Morgan, and Spencer Wilson. The following day, the Falcons Glider Club boys from La Jolla Junior-Senior High School took their primary to Camp Kearney and made several auto tows. The only accident occurred when a boy from Escondido fractured his wrist after ground looping his glider.

Manager of the National Glider Association, Donald F. Walker, suggested in a letter to William Van Dusen in March, 1931 that the well-known German glider pioneer Dr. Wolfgang Klemperer planned to visit San Diego. In 1921, Dr. Klemperer made a 13-minute flight in Germany that beat Orville Wright's previous duration record and earned Klemperer the first "C" award in the world. Dr. Klemperer was searching, at least in part, for potential sites capable of hosting a National Glider Contest proposed for the West Coast in 1932. His visit came in early-mid April, 1931, when he was shown various soaring locations by William Van Dusen and Jack Barstow. Dr. Klemperer arrived on the night of March 14th, 1931, and was entertained by members of the Associated Glider Clubs of Southern California. Two glider demonstrations were scheduled in his honor: one at Point Loma and the other at Emerald Hills.

In June, 1931, the yearbook for the La Jolla Junior-Senior High School contained a photo of the Falcons Glider Club in front of their Northrup primary glider. It also contained a poem regarding their glider ambitions.

*His one dear ambition*
*was to fly an aeroplane*
*His parents wouldn't let him*
*And it sure gave him a pain*

*But soon would come a day*
*of sunshine or of rain*
*When he would sally forth alone*
*In his own aeroplane.*

In the interests of increased publicity for his sailplane company, Van Bezel contacted the United States Navy and arranged for a special aviation "first," the landing of a sailplane on an aircraft carrier. The United States Navy agreed to anchor a carrier in San Diego Bay between Point Loma and North Island, whereupon a sailplane could be flown east from high over Point Loma to a landing on the deck. It sounded like good publicity for all concerned.

At the very last minute, the United States Navy backed out of the proposition. Van Bezel, Bud Perl, and several members of the local press were on hand at Point Loma on July 26th, 1931, but it looked as though the event would become a public relations catastrophe for the Van Bezel Company. To make matters worse, the wind did not cooperate. Bud Perl took off in a sailplane from the top of Point Loma and landed at the polo field at the base of the ridge near the ocean due to insufficient wind.

The sailplane was hauled back to the top of the Point, and by 3:30 p.m., the wind came up from the west. Following another launch, Perl climbed in the light westerly wind as high as was possible under those conditions. Shortly thereafter, the wind ebbed off once again. From the ground below, Perl heard Van Bezel shouting "try to land on North Island!" Not to disappoint the cameramen, Perl headed east, and descended on the leeward side of the ridge. He soon realized, however, that he did not have the required altitude for the three-mile distance. He made several turns and headed for a beach at Ballast Point on the east side of Point Loma.

> *My original plan was to settle down close to the water and then stretch the glide so I could set her down across the strip of sand, but I noticed some bathers in the surf and I was afraid of hitting one of them. There wasn't any place else to go but into the water--and all the water looked the same, so I landed. Wasn't any use sailing around.*

Perl swam to a motorboat and both the pilot and plane were brought to shore. There was no damage to the glider or the pilot.

In 1931, Carl Joseph Weidel and Herbert McMahon of San Diego built a sailplane (identification mark 976Y), but no records have been obtained for this aircraft.

In 1932, Postmaster Ernest Dort, Chairman of the Aviation Committee of the San Diego Chamber of Commerce, announced plans for a model airplane contest to be held in July. San Diego glider pilots H. G. Chapman, I. N. Lawson, Jr., and Letain Kittredge were all named as the advisory committee.

Students of the San Diego Senior High School aircraft rigging class were putting the finishing touches on their new sailplane (identification mark 13745). By March, 1932, the airframe was completed and ready for a fabric coating. With a talent at woodworking and yet a lack of talent in sewing, the boys posted a notice in the school newspaper:

> *WANTED: 20 seamstresses to sew fabric on our glider framework. Must be willing to serve without pay.*

Out of the high school students, two girls volunteered for the task. One was Miss La Verne Benz who was just 16 at the time. This was the 22nd motorless aircraft produced by Kittredge's aircraft rigging class. It was their first true sailplane. Successful test flights of the sailplane were made at Morena Hill on May 20th, 1933. Additional flights were made at Plumosa Park (Loma Portal) and Point Loma. Kittredge always served as test pilot in the gliders before allowing any students to fly. As with the previous gliders, Kittredge would serve as temporary glider instructor, with prior parental consent, and as a result, the students nicknamed him "Skipper." Kittredge made the first hop, and student Charles Freel also flew on the first day. During one flight, Kittredge remained aloft 1 hour and 45 minutes. Students Frank Cooper and Blair Burkhardt also flew the sailplane at Morena for as many as five flights each. On the hills above Morena, sailplanes were launched from a location south of Clairemont Blvd. towards the west, and landings were made at the base of the hill, prior to crossing the highway (Morena Blvd.). Sailplane pilots aimed toward Kennedy's Road House on the highway to maintain a proper heading.

According to Blair Burkhardt, Kittredge excelled at building things out of wood. An all-wood trailer was built for the high school sailplane. Over one weekend, Kittredge and some students drove with the sailplane to the top of Volcan Mountain near Julian. Kittredge was launched to the east into the wind in a series of 2 or 3 flights. On the last flight, Kittredge got below the launching point and was forced to fly out towards the desert to the east for a landing. The student group drove with the trailer down the Banner Grade to retrieve Kittredge and the sailplane. Upon arriving at the landing scene, they noticed that the sailplane was badly damaged due to a landing in a group of ocotillo cacti. Kittredge sustained minor scrapes, but it is believed that the sailplane was never flown again. Back at San Diego Senior High School, the sailplane was load tested with sand bags on the wings and fuselage, until the entire framework

*Members of the San Diego High School aircraft rigging class launching Letain T. Kittredge in the school sailplane from Point Loma. This sailplane was closely patterned after the early Bowlus sailplanes but utilized conventional ailerons that were extended to the very tip of the wing, similar in style to Bowlus tip-ailerons.*

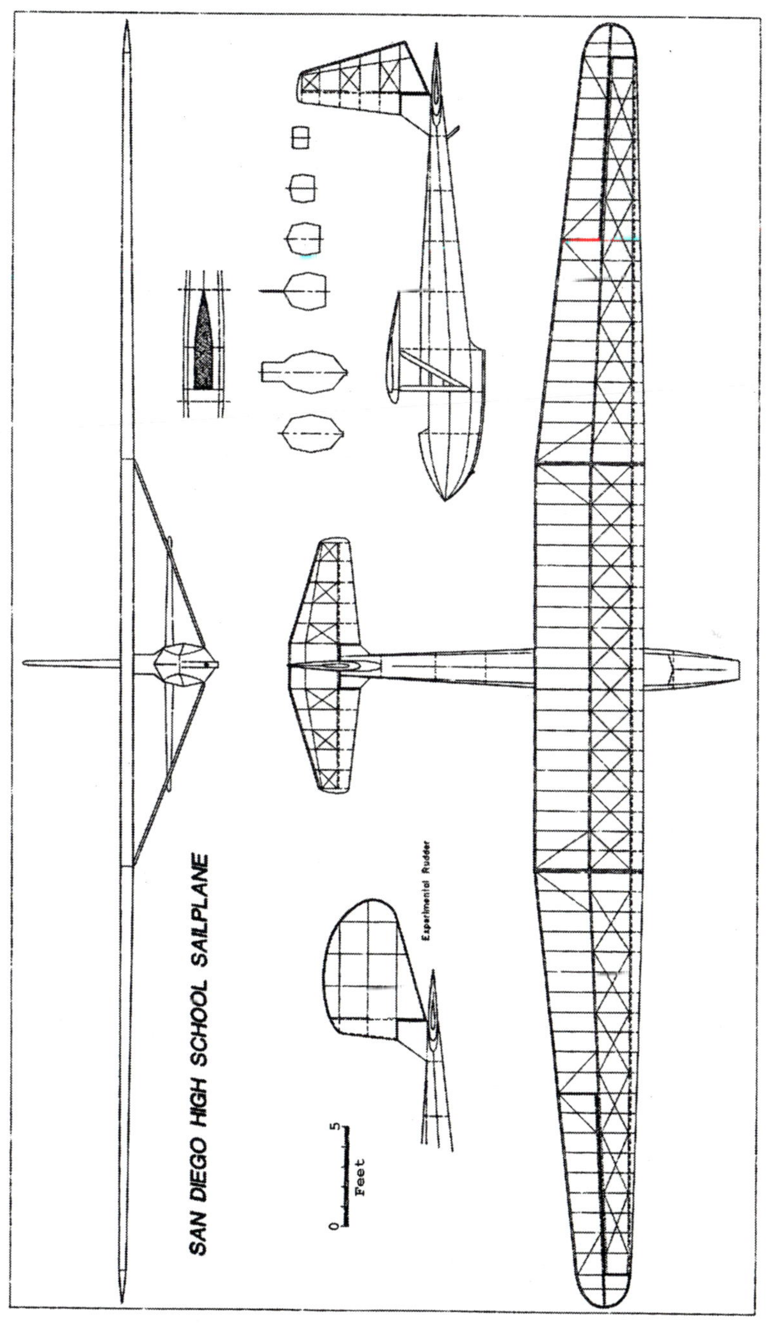
SAN DIEGO HIGH SCHOOL SAILPLANE
Experimental Rudder
0
5
Feet

was stressed past the point of fracture. This confirmed the mathematical calculations on the stress limitations of the airframe made by the students during construction. Succeeding shop classes salvaged the metal fittings and control system parts for use in other designs.

The San Diego Senior High School sailplane had a wingspan of 63 feet, 5 inches, empty weight of 350 pounds, gross weight of 550 pounds, and had a wing surface area of 281 square feet. A Göttingen 387 modified airfoil was used. This was reported to be the first and only sailplane in the west designed and built by high school students. Students Robert Marshall (Chief Engineer of construction), Charles Freel (who helped cover the rudder), Frank Cooper (who built the elevator), Chester "Chet" Sweetland, and Scott Johnson were all involved with the sailplane construction at San Diego Senior High School.

## *A Connection to San Diego*

Even though the Bowlus Sailplane Company had closed in 1930, Bowlus' sailplane designs continued to be flown at a variety of locations across the nation. Some of these sailplanes were copies of the Bowlus designs, while others were original products of the sailplane factory. It was a legacy that would continue for many years.

On July 20th, 1931, Second Lt. William A. Cocke, Jr. flew his *Nighthawk* sailplane on the north short of Oahu for a new Hawaiian sailplane endurance record of 3 hours and 55 minutes. The *Nighthawk* was nearly identical in appearance to the Bowlus model "A" sailplanes and there is confusion over whether or not the sailplane was designed and built by Cocke or might have been a rebuilt version of the Bowlus S-16 sailplane. Lt. Cocke claimed to have designed and built the *Nighthawk* with the assistance of Air Corps pilot Lt. John C. Crain.

On the 25th to 26th of July, 1931, Lt. John C. Crain flew the *Nighthawk* through rain and darkness for 16 hours and 38 minutes for a new unofficial world duration record. The cliffs surrounding Crain's sailplane were lit throughout the night by United States Army searchlights. This flight broke the previous duration mark set by Jack Barstow over Point Loma. His takeoff was at 2:30 p.m., and part of his flight was made above clouds.

Glider events continued on November 21st, 1931. Lt. W. A. Cocke entered the *Nighthawk* sailplane, Lt. W. J. Scott entered another sailplane, the members of the Honolulu Glider Club entered a sailplane, and Air Corps officers at Luke Field entered a two-place glider. Lt. William J. Scott set what would have been a world record for distance in a glider. After taking off at 12:39 p.m., his 6 hour and 36 minute flight covered an estimated distance of between 150 and 160 miles, at times reaching an altitude of approximately 2,400 feet. However, officials of the Fédération Aéronautique Internationale denied the distance records as the flight was not of a one-way distance or "out and return" type; they were measured on a two-and-a-half mile closed course. This accomplishment was particularly interesting in that the sailplane he used was a Bowlus-type sailplane, purchased from the Van Bezel Aircraft Company in San Diego. It was essentially the same design as the sailplane used by Jack Barstow and Hawley Bowlus for many of their record flights in 1930. On November 27th, the two-place sailplane crashed in a test flight, slightly injuring Lt. J. M. Thompson, the pilot.

Overnight, from December 17th to 18th, 1931, Lt. W. A. Cocke, United States Army Air Corps Reserve, landed the *Nighthawk* after soaring along the cliffs on the north shore of Oahu for 21 hours and 36 minutes. It was a new world record for sailplane endurance. Cocke's landing came at 12:34 p.m., after having been aloft since 3:00 p.m. the previous day. The flight was also believed to set a closed course distance record and new United States altitude mark of 3,400 feet. After landing, Cocke suggested that he could have continued soaring even though he was very tired, but preferred to make a landing in the daylight when the winds close to the landing site were low.

Lt. Cocke accomplished his flight unaware of the fact that his friend and soaring companion, Lt. W. J. Scott, was killed in a failed takeoff attempt a half hour after Lt. Cocke's launch. Expecting Lt. Scott to join him in the air, Lt. Cocke dropped a note from the *Nighthawk* inquiring about the condition of Lt. Scott. He was informed that Scott was "O. K." by persons on the ground who drew the letters "O" and "K" out of fire during the night. Lt. Scott had been pronounced dead several hours previously. Eyewitnesses to the crash suggested that the tow cable fouled the rudder during takeoff. Lt. Scott's Van Bezel sailplane descended in circles and came to Earth 300 yards from the point of takeoff. Lt. Scott passed away an hour later at Kaneohe Hospital. The historic *Nighthawk* sailplane survives to this day and is currently on display at the Santa Monica Museum of Flying in Santa Monica, California.

## *Gliding Activities in 1934-1935*

In 1934, John Robinson flew his own ***Robin #1*** sailplane, which was a fabric-covered, open-cockpit sailplane built by Robinson and Barr in partnership. The cantilever wing spanned 52 feet. In 1935, John Robinson designed and built a new sailplane. The *Robin #2* had an open cockpit, 52-foot cantilever wing with a slight gull shape from the root to the tip. The sailplane was made entirely of wood except for the metal fittings.

On March 31st, 1935, Jack Barstow died as a result of a midair collision during an air race at Corpus Christi, Texas. Although his name had not been associated with soaring in several years, his early achievements in soaring flight at San Diego and instruction at the Bowlus Glider School were not forgotten. He was the first pilot in the world to soar for over 15 hours duration in a single flight. The Jack Barstow Airport in Midland, Michigan was named in his honor.

*Above: Mary Wind (l) receiving glider instruction from Roland Fetters (r) in the early two-place primary glider on the beach near Torrey Pines.*

*Left: Carl Goller's sailplane aloft over Torrey Pines.*

*Above: John Robinson's Robin #2 on the beach below the cliffs at Torrey Pines circa 1936.*

*Right: John Robinson soaring in the Robin #3 at an early Arvin contest.*

The high school boys who used the beach below the Torrey Pines cliffs for gliding ran into some problems with the law during the early 1930s. A few unsympatheic ocean fishermen invoked a law prohibiting driving on all San Diego City beaches. It had never been applied to this stretch of beach before, but within a short amount of time, police officers were enforcing the restriction. The title of the Associated Glider Clubs of Southern California was transferred to the small group of young glider pilots. With this title, they could use the security of an incorporated club to bargain with the City of San Diego for flight activities.

At nearly this same time, Woodbridge "Woody" Brown headed west from his home on the East Coast to settle in La Jolla in 1935. Born in 1912, in New York City, Woody fell in love with flight and left school at the age of 16. He spent his spare time at the Curtis Airfield on Long Island learning about airplanes. Due to a desire to work with nature rather than against it, his interest in powered flight soon gave way to an interest in motorless soaring. Both he and his wife, Elizabeth Sellon, left New York in 1935, after Woody's cousin in La Jolla found a place for them to live.

With his prior interest in gliding and soaring flight, it did not take long for Brown to track down the young boys who were flying their primary gliders on the beach below the Torrey Pines cliffs. According to Woody Brown:

*The only trouble was, the best flying was in the winter, but the big storms would make such a high tide we did not dare to bring out cars on the beach to tow off, so we missed the best flying. So we decided to look for a place on top of the Torrey Pines cliffs, but it was all leased to farmers, but finally I found a place near the La Jolla end that was big enough to shock cord off [the site of the present day University of California Ecological Preserve south of La Jolla Farms]. But this was very dangerous, if anything happened or the shock cord broke, or the car stopped we could run off the edge with no flying speed.*

*One day after a big rain, the ground was wet and slippery. As my wife was towing me off with the car, the wheels slipped in the mud and did not give me full power in the takeoff. When I failed to get off the ground, coming near the edge, I put the wing tip in the ground, gave full rudder and ground looped to a stop with my tail sticking out over the edge of the cliff. So finally we found a better place at the best place on the cliffs and there seemed to be no farming there [the current site of the Torrey Pines Gliderport].*

*Now I decided to go to the City Council and ask them if we could have a lease on that small bit of land, but when they noticed it was leased to Senator Fletcher, they threw me out! I then decided to go right to Senator Fletcher. I told him our problem, and I told him the boys had no place to fly and that was the only possible location there was. And he said he would let go the lease on that small bit of land for us. When I brought his letter to the City Council, they gave me the lease without any question!*

*So we then dragged the field with a railroad iron to make runways. It was big enough to takeoff with a dead man in the ground [a type of pulley system for auto tow described later in this book]...the rope then going to the pulley on the back end of a car then to the glider. This gave the glider twice the speed of the car and it worked fine.*

*After awhile, someone told us it was against the law to fly unlicensed gliders in a Civil Air Way. So I wrote to Mr. Butell who was head of the civil aeronautics in Washington D. C. and told him our problem. The boys designed and built their own gliders, it was better than for them to be standing on street corners telling dirty stories, boy, I laid it on him thick! And besides, the gliders never got above 2,000 feet altitude. And by golly, he sent back a letter giving us permission to fly unlicensed gliders in a Civil Air Way, the only one in America!!!*

*After we had been flying for a while, the inspectors from the San Diego Airport came out to the field and gave us a real hard time. Telling us we were breaking the law and could not fly anymore. I let him go on and on until he was finished, then I brought out the letter and gave it to him, his face dropped and his mouth fell open. They never said another word, just got in their cars and left.*

Woody Brown also became famous in San Diego for his early attempts at surfing on his homemade surfboards. He was one of the first to try the waves at Windansea Beach in La Jolla, and is regarded as a pioneer in both soaring and surfing. With a knowledge of aerodynamics, he helped shape some of the first modern surfboards. Steve Kesckes joined the scene at Torrey Pines in the mid-1930s. Instructed by Woody Brown, Kesckes made several flights at the base of the Torrey Pines Grade near Del Mar in July or August of 1936, and added to the increased enthusiasm towards soaring.

To the northeast of San Diego, Camp Kearney was a one-mile long field, south of the barracks left by the United States Army from World War I. Dave Robertson and Henry Severin had been towing and landing gliders at Camp Kearney between 1931, and 1934, making training flights with the two-place primary glider and taking up passengers. During this time, Robertson and Severin designed and built the *Swift* sailplane (identification mark 14209). They flew it for one to three years, and eventually sold the aircraft to Woody Brown. Robertson concentrated on his job for the Vultee Aircraft Company while Severin's other "hobby," amateur radio, helped him find a job on a tuna fishing boat. According to John Robinson, Henry Severin was never seen gliding again. Camp Kearney was used for auto towing and gliding in the early years (1931-1934) and as a site for thermaling in later years (after 1934).

Bud Perl and Bill Beuby set up the San Diego Soaring Society and encouraged new members to join them in a *San Diego Union* article in November, 1935. They were both discouraged by the fact that interest in local gliding activities had waned and that most gliding records were now held by pilots from France, England, and Russia. Bud Perl and Bill Beuby were flying their modified Bowlus S-1000 sailplane (identification mark 14968) along the slopes at Torrey Pines. The United States Department of Commerce granted the identification mark to Perl and Beuby on September 17th, 1935. By October 1st, 1936, identification mark 14968 had expired.

## *1935-1936 California Pacific International Exposition*

San Diego was selected as the site for the California Pacific International Exposition held in 1935 and 1936. As a feature event of the opening of the 1936 Exposition, pilot Don Stevens of Glendale, California attempted to set a world record for continuous loops in a glider. On March 15th, 1936, Stevens took off at 11:00 a.m. via aerotow behind a plane piloted by Earl Ortman. Towed high to an altitude of 16,000 feet, the glider cut loose and Stevens began a series of loops. The loops were officially tallied by William Van Dusen, who watched from the ground with powerful binoculars. A smoke flare was used, and the loops were visible to the thousands of spectators who also watched the unusual aerobatic demonstration from the Exposition directly below. Stevens later recalled:

> *At about 16,000 feet the air was becoming so thin that I found it hard to breathe...I dropped my smoke bomb and then swung into the loops. After counting 25 loops I lost track. I pulled out at 3,000 feet in order to circle back to Lindbergh Field to land.*

A new world record of 54 consecutive loops was claimed. After his landing at Lindbergh Field, Stevens was aerotowed to Mines Field in Los Angeles. Later, in August, 1936, a "kid's glider contest" was held at the Ford Bowl as part of Kid's Day at the 1936 Exposition.

## Carl Goller

On September 17th, 1936, Carl Goller christened his new sailplane at Balboa Park and announced that he would attempt to break the world glider endurance record of 48 hours with this new ship at Torrey Pines. This sailplane was one of two sister ships that Goller constructed in 1935 and 1936 (identification marks 14943 and 14944). It was reported to have a 60-foot wingspan and weight of 300 pounds. These two sailplanes were designed and built by Goller, George Palmer, and Vernon Yates in San Diego. Although his longest soaring flight was 4 hours, the 28-year-old Goller was convinced that the cliffs at Torrey Pines were well suited for record breaking flights:

> *I built this glider not only to try to establish a new record, but to interest San Diego people in the sport. Gliders, when built by experts, are perfectly safe. Gliding is a wonderful sport.*

## Glider Badges

In 1931, the Silver "C" badge was created by the Fédération Aéronautique Internationale as a means to reward achievement in soaring. The requirements for this award consisted of a distance flight of 50 kilometers (31.07 miles), an altitude gain of 1000 meters, (3,280.80 feet) and a soaring flight of 5 hours in duration. The Golden "C" badge was established in 1935. Requirements included a distance flight of 300 kilometers (186.42 miles), a gain in altitude of 3,000 meters (9,842 feet) in addition to the 5-hour endurance requirement of the Silver "C" badge. In 1949, the Fédération Aéronautique Internationale added diamonds to the Golden "C" badge. The diamonds signified the requirements of a 5,000 meter (16,404 foot) gain in altitude, a distance flight to a goal 300 kilometers away, and an open distance flight of 500 kilometers (310.7 miles).

## The Robin #3 Sailplane

John Robinson designed and constructed the *Robin #3* sailplane in 1936. As a skilled welder, the *Robin #3* employed steel tubing (type 4130) in the fuselage. According to Robinson:

> *I could soar with an extra 100 to 150 pounds, and glide at 90 and 100 mph...and that was 1937...Same as with water ballast today... No one else was doing that 'til about 1960...it helped me win a lot of contests.*

The back of the pilot seat was detachable. With this design, there was enough room in the fuselage to carry a crouched passenger on the center of gravity. On many occasions, Robinson carried emergency equipment behind the seat when flying solo, especially in the event of an off field landing in the desert.

The *Robin #3* was a full cantilever, high-wing sailplane with new slightly gulled wings made of wood with a 52-foot wingspan. The fuselage was made of welded chrome-moly steel tubing covered with fabric and contained a fixed wheel. The entirely enclosed cockpit had a hinged canopy and the nose of the ship was covered with eight clear pyralin panels, giving an excellent view out the front of the ship. Instruments were arranged in a staggered position. Robinson noted:

> *This was the first sailplane on the West Coast to use a tight canopy for drag reduction, and to keep the pilot warm. I hated the cold on those long flights, and I anticipated high altitude flights, due to my study of meteorology in college!*

A new wing was under construction before July, 1938, using a NACA 24 series airfoil. This 48 foot wing decreased the wing area slightly to 177 square feet, gave a lower aspect ratio of 13:1, and decreased the empty weight to 335 pounds. Wing loading was roughly the same at 2.74 pounds per square foot or 3.59, with ballast for cross-country or with a passenger.

## *The Ross-Stephens R.S.-1 "Zanonia"*

While surveying the Southern California region with Charles Lindbergh in 1930, Hawley Bowlus had discovered a potential soaring site east of Bakersfield, in the foothills of Bear Mountain near Arvin. Bowlus and Lindbergh opted to stage their glider experimentation at Lebec, and the Arvin soaring site was forgotten until the spring of 1937. Several members of the Southern California Soaring Association in Los Angeles drove 125 miles north to fly at the site to make observations about the soaring conditions. This first gathering at Arvin opened up one of the most popular soaring sites in California. Pilots in attendance included Harland Ross and Harvey Stephens with the Ross-Stephens R.S.-1; Volmer Jensen, Jay Buxton with the *Transporter*; and Gil Walters with his *Pegasus*. Hawley Bowlus and his son, William, Jr., also attended the meet. Flying the R.S.-1, Harland Ross was able to make the best performance of the meet with a 20-mile circular course, gaining over 1,500 feet on a 1.5-hour flight.

The Ross-Stephens R.S.-1 sailplane was to become particularly famous in American soaring history. The aircraft was designed by Harland Ross, who years earlier had learned to soar in the San Diego area. It was patterned after the best German sailplanes of the time with one purpose in mind...cross-country soaring. The sailplane had a root chord of 4 feet, an aspect ratio of 17:1, and an unusually small wing area for the time of just 124.4 square feet. The R.S.-1 wing loading was considerably heavier than the similar German Minimoa sailplane, but in combination with the smaller wing area, the span loading was lighter at 10.2 pounds per square foot. The maximum glide angle was 24:1 at 48 miles per hour, and later modifications gave the sailplane a glide ratio of 30:1. Construction of the R.S.-1 was co-financed by Harvey Stephens. He and Ross flew the ship at the 1937 National Soaring contest at Elmira, New York. Ross placed fifth overall in terms of total points and also was awarded second place in the Eaton Design Competition.

Stephens, a well-known movie actor, was the first vice-president of the Southern California Soaring Association. He made his first soaring flight in 1933, with Ted Jenks above the cliffs in a two-place sailplane at Palos Verdes near Los Angeles. Soon

*Harland Ross and an early version of the famous Ross-Stephens R.S.-1 "Zanonia" sailplane. Ross became well-known for his ability in sailplane design.*

thereafter, Stephens resumed his interest in soaring with Don Stevens and Speed Westphal in 1936, in their Franklin Utility. With the Franklin, he made several flights with durations over one hour at Palos Verdes. Later, he made a flight in the Briegleb BG-1 at Palos Verdes for 1 hour and 30 minutes, to an altitude of 3,300 feet. In late 1936, he and Ross began construction on the R.S.-1. By 1938, Stephens had redesigned the tail surfaces and flown the ship at various locations in Southern California, including Torrey Pines and Hemet.

The R.S.-1 sailplane would eventually change owners later in the 1930s from Stephens to Woody Brown, and then to John Robinson. The sailplane was renamed *Zanonia* after a tree, *Zanonia macrocarpus*, with an unusually successful free-flying seed pod. Robinson and *Zanonia* became legendary, winning three national championships and setting numerous national and world soaring records.

*Jerry Litell in the cockpit of his highly modified Bowlus sailplane at Torrey Pines.*

## *Jerry Litell*

As Machine Shop Inspector at Consolidated Aircraft Corporation, Jerry Litell was no stranger to rebuilding aircraft. By June, 1937, Litell had obtained parts of an original Bowlus sailplane and had reconfigured them to "suit his ideas of what a good glider should be." The plane weighed 290 pounds and had a 44-foot wingspan, essentially using only the outer panels of an early Bowlus sailplane. With the center section removed, a cabane was added with additional brace wires for increased strength. Flights with the sailplane were made at Torrey Pines and Camp Kearney. There are records of Litell obtaining an identification mark for a glider in San Diego in 1934 (identification mark 14216), but it is unknown if this and his rebuilt Bowlus sailplane were the same.

## *The Freel Flying Wing (18131)*

Charles Lewis Freel was born in 1916, in Tonopah, Nevada, and soon thereafter, his family moved to San Diego. He was admitted to San Diego Senior High School in September, 1931. By serving as a draftsman and construction engineer in Kittredge's aircraft rigging class, Freel learned about many aspects of aerodynamics and glider flight. Before his graduation, Freel designed a 36-inch experimental free-flight model of a flying wing glider. It was a revolutionary design for the time. The model flew well and, in 1933, construction of a full-scale flying wing glider began in the San Diego Senior High School woodshop class under the supervision of Freel and Kittredge.

Control of the flying surfaces became an immediate problem. Freel designed a remarkable control system where the ailerons could also function simultaneously as elevators (elevons). This system was finalized and drawn by Freel on January 28th, 1935. A number of students helped with the construction of the flying wing, including Ralph Sawade, Bill Buyer, and Reynaldo V. Vinole. The glider was completed in 1935, and flight tests were conducted by Kittredge and Freel at a hill near Morena. The glider was licensed in 1937, and was granted identification mark 18131. The glider suffered from poor directional control, possibly due to a lack of sufficient dihedral or sweep in the wing. It became quite difficult to recover the ship from a turn. It has been suggested that one or two flights were made with the flying wing from Volcan Mountain near Julian, but further soaring flights were not attempted.

The wing was a full cantilever wooden structure made in two 26-foot sections bolted together at the center chord. Main spars running the full length of the wing were "I" beams, with plywood webs and spruce cap strips. A reflexed NACA M-6 airfoil was used; the wing and all control surfaces were covered with fabric. Directional control was provided by seven-foot movable surfaces at the outboard trailing edge of the wing. Operating on a drag principle and working independently of each

*San Diego High School student Charles Lewis Freel holding a free-flight model of the proposed Freel Flying Wing.*

*Construction of the Freel Flying Wing in the woodshop of San Diego High School. The aircraft was made as left and right halves that could be joined at the root.*

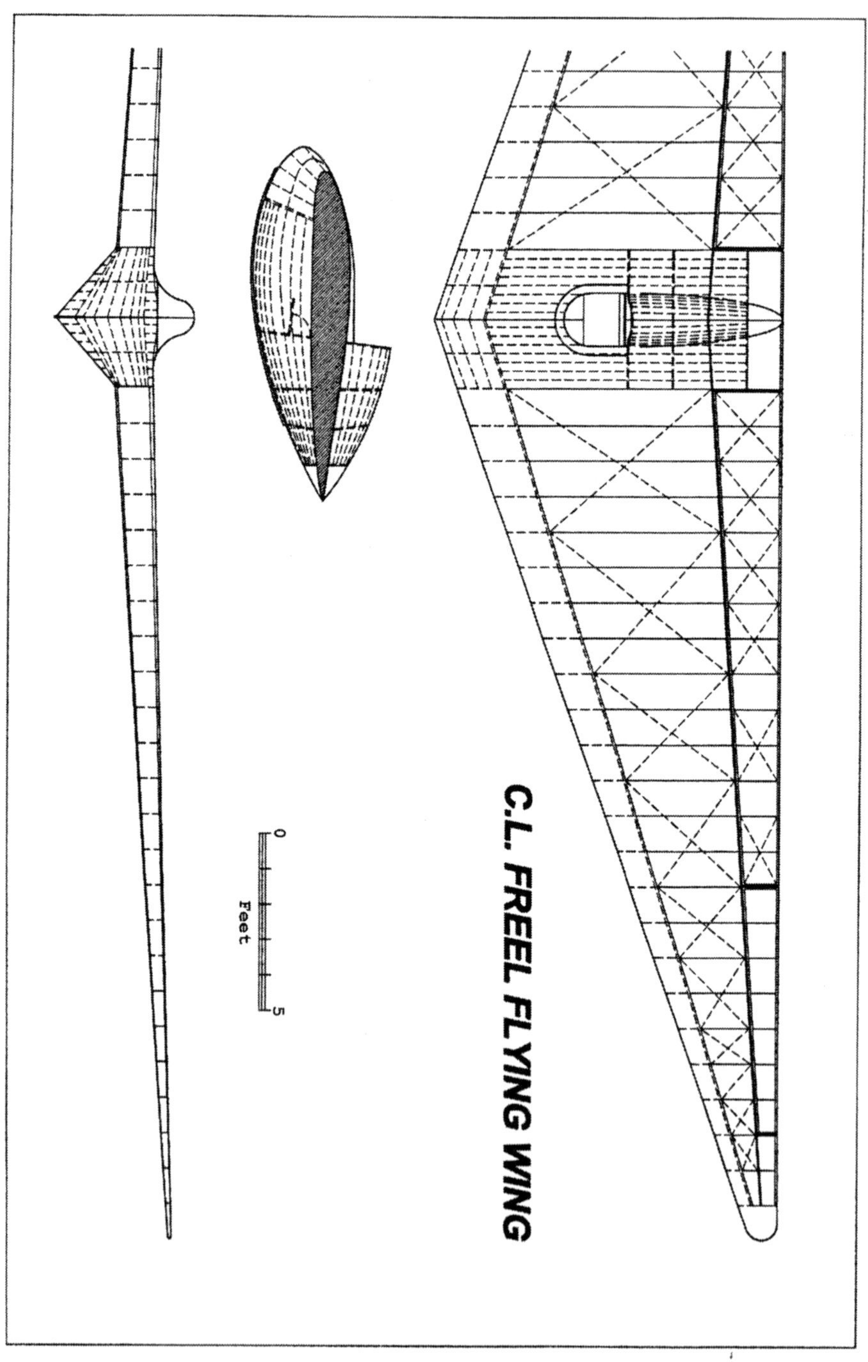
C.L. FREEL FLYING WING
0
Feet
5

other, the trailing edge surfaces were actuated by cable and foot control and took the place of a rudder. When empty, the 270 square feet of wing area weighed 280 pounds. The *Freel Flying Wing* sailplane was highly advanced for its time and was the most challenging design ever constructed at the San Diego Senior High School woodshop/aircraft rigging class.

A description of the flying wing glider followed in *Consolidator*, the monthly magazine for the Consolidated Aircraft Corporation in San Diego. Curiously, even at this early time, the flying wing was recognized as having possible military importance akin to the yet-to-be-developed Northrop flying wings or B-2 stealth bomber. In 1937, author C. L. Hibert, suggested that:

> *Along with the commercial aspect, the military Flying Wing will present itself in the form of a deadly ultra-high speed bomber capable of placing enemy fortifications at an extreme disadvantage, due to having approximately 90% clear firing range for defense and provision for an enormous load of bombs situated in the wing proper. In view of the vast advantages and possibilities, a perfection of the Flying Wing is warranted in the evolution of aeronautics in the near future.*

In Los Angeles, Jack Northrop was working on similar flying wing designs and models as early as 1929, but did not produce his first successful pure flying wing aircraft until July, 1940. After his high school graduation, Freel was hired immediately by Consolidated Aircraft Corporation and held the title of "junior engineer."

## *Soaring at the Salton Sea*

On August 21st, 1937, Woody Brown and John Robinson set out to explore soaring conditions at the Salton Sea, east of San Diego. The Salton Sea is a large lake in the desert approximately 10 miles wide by 30 miles long. Brown and Robinson wondered if a temperature gradient existed next to this lake such that thermal conditions would be superior. Upon arriving at the site in the afternoon, the pair set up the *Swift* sailplane in a quick 12 minutes for some test hops. Brown later wrote that this quick assembly was "a fact we appreciated as the temperature was 110°F in the shade with no shade." Launches were by auto tow with both pilots taking turns in the single-seat sailplane. Brown and Robinson noticed that although the air was very still, it was quite buoyant. The following day, they made successful thermal flights from 10:30 a.m. to 1:30 p.m., when Brown hooked a large and slow rising thermal, ascending to 2,000 feet in a 30-minute flight. With two similar soaring expeditions during the Fall of 1937, Brown and Robinson concluded that the thermal activity around the Salton Sea was in mass form rather than as distinct small thermals. The average rate of climb was slow, at approximately 1.5 feet per second.

*Above: Woody Brown soaring in the Swift sailplane at Arvin, California.*

*Bottom: John Robinson (l) and Woody Brown (r) standing in front of the Swift sailplane at the Torrey Pines Gliderport.*

# *The Associated Glider Clubs of Southern California*

By Fall, 1937, the Associated Glider Clubs of Southern California was gaining membership once again. Members from the Torrey Pines Soaring Club, Western Flyers Glider Club, and the San Diego Soaring Club combined efforts and merged with the Associated Glider Clubs of Southern California. Many new glider pilots were also employees of Consolidated, Ryan, and Solar aircraft corporations in San Diego. At this time, the local club had five gliders in flying condition, and this number was expected to increase to nine by Christmas of 1937.

By March, 1938, the list of members and gliders in the Associated Glider Clubs of Southern California had grown substantially. Included were Roland Fetters, Ernest Stout, and Steve Kecskes' two-place secondary glider *Sloanlo*; Carl Goller's two sister ship sailplanes (identification marks 14943 and 14944), Woody Brown's *Swift*; a Bowlus sailplane owned by Frank Graham and Jim Galagher; a side-by-side two-seater owned by Bill Baker, Bob Winters, and Ed Roberts; another Bowlus derivative flown by Jerry Litell; the *Freel Flying Wing* operated by Charles Freel, Letain Kittredge, and Dave Robertson; and a primary operated by Dick Essery. Under construction at the time was the *Nomad* by Robert Stanley, a *Grunau Baby* by Bill Stackhouse and Roland Fetters, the *Robin #4* by John Robinson, and the *Thunder Bird*, a Bowlus Baby Albatross being finished by Woody Brown. Dick Essery served as president of the Associated Glider Clubs of Southern California. In 1934, Roland Fetters and Gale Bartlett had built a glider (identification mark 13796) and later this glider was sold to Jack Dev Emery around 1937. Fetters and Warren Morrison teamed up in 1937, and licensed a glider (identification mark 17378), but official records of this glider have yet to be obtained.

The *Sloanlo* (pronounced "slow-an-low") glider was originally built by Jay Buxton in Los Angeles, and was flown on the cliffs above Palos Verdes for several years. Buxton was building his *Transporter* two-place sailplane while he was flying the *Sloanlo.* The *Sloanlo* was a very large two-place secondary glider with a rectangular wing of 300 square feet of 6 feet by 50 feet. Secondaries generally had rectangular wings and fabric covered "people wide" fuselages to streamline the pilot a little bit, in an "open cockpit," wind-in-the-face configuration. When Jay Buxton finished the *Transporter*, he sold *Sloanlo* to Roland Fetters, Ernie Stout, and Steve Kesckes. With a ten-inch diameter Goodyear tire mounted in the center of the *Sloanlo* skid, this two-place secondary was used for training by several members of the Associated Glider Clubs of Southern California. This glider was also nicknamed *Old Slow and Low.*

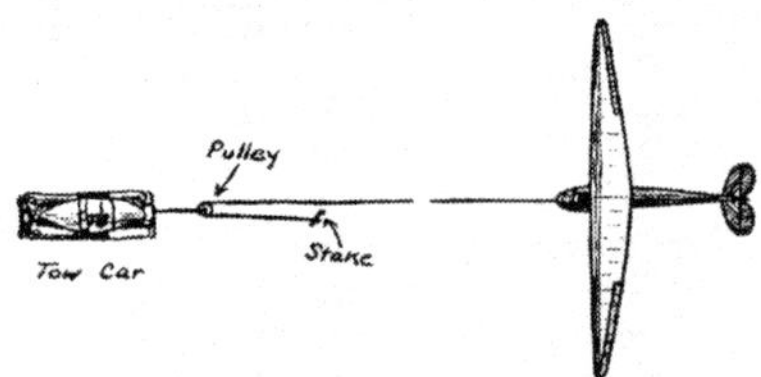


*Top: Steve Kecskes in the cockpit of the "Sloanlo" sailplane at Torrey Pines circa 1936.*

*Left: A diagram of the auto tow pulley takeoff system first used at Torrey Pines.*

*Top Right: Looking south towards La Jolla from the cockpit of the Swift sailplane piloted by Woody Brown. John Robinson's Robin #3 can be seen soaring below circa 1937.*

*Bottom Right: Looking east at the Torrey Pines Gliderport from the Swift sailplane. The main east-west runway is clearly visible as well as a southeast-northwest runway. A third runway running due north-south can also be seen. The two main runways are nearly identical in position to those used today at the Torrey Pines Gliderport.*

## *The Auto Tow Pulley Takeoff System*

With the necessity to have rapid speed sufficient for takeoff in a short distance, John Robinson invented the auto tow pulley takeoff system. This important launching system was first used at the Torrey Pines Gliderport. One pulley of about four inches in diameter with oversized flanges was attached to the car by a rope on the trailer hitch. One end of a 3/8-inch rope was attached to a stake in the ground (a "dead-man"); the other end was brought through the pulley and to the glider (with a steel ring at the glider end put in the glider release mechanism). The car was driven in low gear into the wind at half the climbing speed of the glider, and the car speed was reduced when the glider neared the apex of the launch. This method was particularly useful for launching fields of limited area and also saved wear and tear on the tow car due to the slower towing speeds.

Years later, Robinson introduced this launching technique to soaring enthusiasts on the East Coast. Afterwards, the Schweizer Aircraft Corporation produced 12" wooden pulleys for the same purpose. Precautionary measures in the event of a glider release failure were added by glider enthusiasts on the East Coast, but these problems never occurred during use in Southern California. On short fields, altitudes of 20 feet to 300 feet were normal. On long fields, or dry lakes, altitudes of 2,000 feet were common, using wire instead of rope, which wore out too quickly. The original "pulley" was donated by Robinson to the National Soaring Museum in Elmira, New York. According to Robinson:

> *With my welding equipment, I made the 1st pulley on a 4" ball bearing, with flanges, before I told Woody. On the first flight I flew Robin #3 and Woody drove the car. The pulley was to take the place of rubber shock cord launches which were prone to breakage when used with a car for power. After use, the rubber cord was left in the hot sunshine for another use and this made them brittle over time.*

## *A Regional Competition*

Harvey Stephens spoke to the members of the Associated Glider Clubs of Southern California in the Summer of 1937, on the possibility of a regional Southern California soaring meet. Proposed locations included Arvin, Point Loma, Torrey Pines, and a number of other locations in Southern California. Stephens felt that due to the absence of forests in the local area, chances for distance soaring were better in Southern California than at Elmira, New York (home of the annual national soaring contest).

Largely through the efforts of Harvey Stephens and Hawley Bowlus, by Labor Day weekend, September 6-8th, 25 local sailplane pilots met at Arvin for a fun-fly sailplane meet. Gliders included the Buxton *Transporter*, the Ross-Stephens R.S.-1, Dan Sanborn's Grunau 8, and Gil Walters' *Pegasus*. Woody Brown of San Diego brought his *Swift* to the competition and also helped arrange a double-pulley auto tow takeoff system. Brown had several thermal flights in excess of a half hour each, and the many attendees agreed that this meet was a sign of good things to come.

## A Lease for Torrey Pines

Ordinance number 1224 of the City of San Diego was adopted on August 24th, 1937. This ordinance allowed the Associated Glider Clubs of Southern California to lease the Torrey Pines Gliderport property from the City of San Diego. On November 23rd, 1937, that same ordinance was repealed and replaced by ordinance number 1285 to extend the length of the lease to five years commencing on the January 1st, 1938, and ending on December 31st, 1942. The yearly fee was $50.00 for a large portion of Pueblo Lot 1324. San Diego Mayor Percy J. Benbough signed the ordinance into effect. The property had been originally appraised at $40,000 by the City Auditor and Controller. A lease was drafted and signed December 31st, 1937, by Woody Brown on behalf of the Associated Glider Clubs of Southern California.

Just as the lease was signed with the city, a new ruling of the Bureau of Air Commerce prohibited unlicensed aircraft from flying on a federal airway. The Torrey Pines cliffs were only four miles away from the center of the Los Angeles-San Diego Airway, which was considered 50 miles wide. It suddenly became unlawful for the sailplane pilots to fly their planes at Torrey Pines.

Acting on behalf of the group, Woody Brown contacted the head of the Bureau of Air Commerce by phone and explained that the youngsters soaring at the site were not harming anyone nor polluting: they were simply exploring new and innovative aircraft designs without motors. Soon thereafter, a letter signed by the Bureau Administrator arrived allowing the members of the glider club to fly along the cliffs. It was the first time that unlicensed gliders were allowed to fly in a Civil Airway. Local authorities were flabbergasted. Following this, development of the Torrey Pines Gliderport progressed at a rapid pace. Three runways suitable for the operation of motorless aircraft were cleared on the site. The northwest/southeast runway was the only one long enough for powered takeoff. In the event that the wind subsided, the beach below the gliderport was used as an emergency landing strip. John Robinson wrote:

> *During the spring and summer the prevailing sea breeze from the west, although not very strong, is sufficient to make soaring possible most of the time. This is due to the fact that wind flowing over a vertical cliff is smooth and solid in front of the bluff--like an inverted waterfall. Thus one can soar here in less wind than he could over a rounded ridge of equal altitude.*

*For the past five years, we have accomplished soaring at this site by auto towing off the beach, or shock cord from any field that we were not denied permission to use. We were continuously bothered by high tides, unfriendly farmers, and shock cord failure. The year 1937 saw great improvements over these conditions. First, we developed to a high degree of efficiency the single pulley tow takeoff method. Second, we obtained a five-year renewable lease from the city of San Diego. Now we are continually improving the runways that we have cleared, and hope soon to have shelters erected for the ships.*

The longest duration flight by any pilot at Torrey Pines prior to mid-1938, was reported to be made by Woody Brown, who soared his *Swift* for nine hours in the constant ridge lift. Dick Essery operated a secondary glider at Torrey Pines for the Western Flyers Glider Club.

## *The Robinson Variometer*

In 1938, John Robinson developed a pellet-type variometer and began testing them during soaring flights at Torrey Pines. These variometers were unusually sensitive, and by using them along the ridge at Torrey Pines, Robinson could more easily find lift under puffy cumulus clouds that drifted east off the Pacific Ocean. He carried his own variometers with him, not only on flights at Torrey Pines, but also in the desert and at glider meets across the nation. The Robinson variometer was a significant advancement over what was commonly being used at the time, and were purchased by sailplane pilots around the world. His variometer business closed after the advent of the more efficient electric variometer following World War II.

## *The Bowlus Baby Albatross*

From his shop in San Fernando, Hawley Bowlus was working on his latest sailplane design, the Bowlus Baby Albatross in March, 1938. Classified as an intermediate or utility sailplane, the Baby Albatross was designed to be a reasonably priced combination of suitable features for pilot training and adequate performance for thermal and ridge soaring. The streamlined pod fuselage and tail boom were to become a classic in sailplane design. It had a wingspan of 44 feet, length of 18 feet, chord of 4 feet, and area of 153 square feet. The empty weight was 216 pounds, and the completed aircraft, ready for flight, could be purchased for $750.00. In kit form, the Baby Albatross was sold for $385.00.

Bowlus Sailplanes, Inc. was formed in February, 1940, in Los Angeles. Among its stockholders were Donald Douglas, Robert E. Gross, Richard W. Miller, and John

K. Northrop, presidents of Douglas, Lockheed, Vultee, and Northrop aircraft manufacturers, respectively. Douglas was quoted as saying:

> *Aviation as a career has an undeniable appeal for the young generation. To a certain degree we feel an obligation to provide the opportunity for satisfying these youthful ambitions. We believe the sailplane, safeguarded in design and manufacture through the experience of modern airplane production, is ideally adapted to this purpose....*

Additional machinery and equipment was added to the preexisting Bowlus San Fernando factory for the anticipated production of 15 sailplanes monthly. By 1941, Hawley Bowlus, Woody Brown, Harold Huber, Frank Kelsey, John Livingston, Don Mitchell, Gayle Ottley, Don Stevens, and Ed True were employees of the factory, producing Bowlus Baby Albatross kits as fast as they could be sold. Because of its popularity, the Bowlus Baby Albatross rapidly became synonymous with soaring activities across the United States, especially those in Southern California. The unique design was much more affordable than the imported German sailplanes, and yet had similar performance. Over the years, the Bowlus Baby Albatross became Bowlus' most well-recognized sailplane.

## *Glider Meets at Arvin*

The weekends of April 16th-17th and April 23rd-24th, 1938, were highlighted by the second soaring meet at the Arvin soaring site. No trophies, prizes, or ribbons were awarded. Pilots, instead, focused on enjoying the spring scenery and wildflowers from the air over the San Joaquin Valley. Admission of 25 cents per car generated revenue for the Southern California Soaring Association, as nearly 1,000 spectator cars (an estimated 3,000 spectators) came to watch the dozen or so sailplanes swoop along the ridge.

Even though conditions were less than favorable, Woody Brown, flying in the *Swift*, and John Robinson, in the *Robin #3*, made some nice thermal flights of 20 minutes each on the first day. Hawley Bowlus brought out his new Baby Albatross and Stan Hall flew the ship in a one-hour thermal. Other Southern Californian pilots who attended the meet included Volmer Jensen, Hal Huber, and Howard Morrison.

During the week between the 17th and the 23rd, no sailplane flights occurred, with the exception of two flights that nearly ended in disaster. Brown in his *Swift* and Huber in the *Yellow Peril* had been soaring the ridge for about 1 hour and 15 minutes. Huber was following Brown directly behind his tail. Unaware of Huber's proximity, Brown made a 180° turn using his instruments and came about directly in the path of the *Yellow Peril*. In their ensuing head-on collision, the center section and fuselage of the *Swift* sliced through the left wing of the *Yellow Peril* ten feet from the tip. With a loss of control, Huber crashed in the *Yellow Peril* along side the ridge, while Brown crash-landed the *Swift* on a rocky hillside at the base of the ridge. Miraculously, both pilots escaped serious injury, but both sailplanes were badly damaged.

On the 23rd, George Palmer of San Diego made a nice two hour thermal flight in his sailplane (identification mark 14944). John Robinson flew the *Robin #3* for a 1 hour and 10 minute cross-country flight 15 miles to the east of the glider field. He returned to land within two miles of his point of takeoff.

Suddenly, on the last Sunday of the meet, a squall line broke directly over the ridge, bringing high winds and heavy rain to the flying site. George Palmer's sailplane was lifted up into the air by the high winds and dashed to pieces. Everyone else dismantled their ships and tents as fast as possible and made a rapid exit from the flying site.

Over Labor Day weekend, September 3rd-5th, 1938, pilots once again gathered at the Arvin site for some soaring. Among the many pilots were Jay Buxton, Doug Hugill, John Robinson, Woody Brown, Dick Essery, John "Jack" Ludowitz, Andy Flicker, Volmer Jensen, Harvey Stephens, Howard Morrison, Hawley Bowlus, and Bob and Walt Heideman. Even with only a small amount of publicity, a large number of spectators turned out to watch the sailplanes soar. On the 3rd, Robinson made a launch from auto-pulley tow and thermalled to 5,000 feet in the *Robin #4*, and on the 5th, Robinson flew over Bear Mountain at a height of 5,200 feet. Many other soaring flights were made to a wide range of locations across Southern California.

## *Desert Thermals*

John Robinson had an exceptional soaring day on May 8th, 1938. Early in the morning, Robinson, Dick Essery, and Woody Brown drove to Clark Dry Lake, east of Borrego Springs in the northeastern desert of San Diego County. Robinson brought along his *Robin #3* for thermal flying in the warm desert air. At 10:45 a.m., Brown made the first flight of the day and landed 35 minutes later after a series of thermals. Those that remained on the ground sweltered in the desert heat. According to Robinson:

> *Before taking off, it was necessary to keep the cockpit enclosure open until the very last second, in order to reduce the painful similarity between the pilot in the cockpit and a roast turkey in an oven.*

Soon it was Robinson's turn to try the cloudless skies and climb toward the cooler air above. After a release from auto tow at 400 feet above the dry lake bed, Robinson immediately caught a strong thermal of 10 to 15 feet per second and climbed to over 7,000 feet without much trouble. An interesting technique of catching thermals was used; the tow car made a series of wide circles with the sailplane in tow at the end of the rope until a thermal was encountered and the sailplane released.

*John Robinson in the Robin #3 climbing on auto tow at Clark Dry Lake in 1938, and later on final approach for landing.*

After cruising around in sinking air, losing of an average of 8 feet per second, Robinson was down to 3,000 feet before he caught another thermal that carried him to 8,000 feet, at a best rate of climb of 17 feet per second. With this altitude, he headed north over the 8,000 foot Santa Rosa Mountains toward the Coachella Valley. At 3:00 p.m., he arrived with 5,000 feet altitude over Palm Springs. With the intent to land at the Palm Springs airport, at 1,500 feet Robinson entered another thermal and by 4:30 p.m., Robinson was soaring at 5,000 feet along the face of Mount San Jacinto.

For ten minutes, he circled in a strong thermal with the indicator reading over ten feet per second. He was carried up beside the snow-capped peak of Mount San Jacinto and shivered in his shirt sleeves as he flew over the peak at 10,800 feet. With a sink rate of 25 feet per second on the other side of the mountain, Robinson made a rather quick descent to a landing at the East Portal Camp of the Metropolitan Water District, approximately six miles from Banning, California, around 5:00 p.m. His total flight time of nearly 5 hours, 30 minutes, and airline distance of 50 miles, was a distance longer than any Californian glider pilot had achieved prior to that date.

Robinson set a new United States unofficial glider altitude record 4,000 feet above the established official mark. This unofficial United States altitude record was mentioned in an article entitled "Men-Birds Soar on Boiling Air" in the July issue of *National Geographic*. With this flight, Robinson satisfied the requirements for his Silver "C" badge. Since he did not carry a barograph on board the *Robin #3*, however, the altitude mark remained unofficial. Woody Brown drove to meet Robinson and the pair discussed the magnitude of Robinson's flight on the drive back to San Diego.

In an attempt to make a repeat performance for an official record, Robinson took off on May 23rd from Clark Dry Lake in the *Robin #3*. This time, he carried a sealed barograph in his sailplane and the flight was witnessed by a National Aeronautic Association official. He topped the Santa Rosa Mountains at an indicated altitude of 7,600 feet, breaking the official record held by Richard duPont of 6,233 feet. With a new official altitude record under his belt, a picture of the *Robin #3* soaring through the sky was featured on the front cover of the July issue of *Soaring* magazine.

Woody Brown and Roland Fetters had accompanied Robinson to Clark Dry Lake on May 23rd. Fetters had convinced Brown to demonstrate thermaling techniques with the *Sloanlo*. Brown agreed to help but was not convinced that the *Sloanlo* could withstand the strong thermal lift. While on auto tow at Clark Dry Lake, a wing of the *Sloanlo* collapsed, sending the aircraft plummeting to Earth. Woody Brown recalled:

> *We got up there on the tow line and hit this thermal and I said 'OK, now! See, it's lifting up your right wing, so you turn to the right! Now, turn to the right! Come on, turn to the right!' And Roland said 'I'm sorry, Woody. I cannot. The wing's come off.'*
>
> *That's all I can remember. We came down with no wings at all and we lived through it. It broke his legs in two or three places. His arms were all broke*

*up and I had a brain concussion; broke my windpipe. There was some tubing I went up against and hit my head and I was out for eight hours.*

*The only thing that saved us was that this glider was a terrible thing. It had a huge wing and it had wires going up top-called 'cabane,' wires up on top to hold her on the ground and then flying wires, underneath, when it lifted, see, instead of struts. So, it had all that stuff. So, when the wings came off, this tremendous area of these wings were going around like helicopter blades, see? They kept flying around on the end of these wires and that kind of broke our fall, as we didn't come down quite so hard, with no wings at all. That's the only reason we lived through it.*

Roland Fetters wrote:

*I had just taken off of the ground, and was still attached to the tow car, flying at about one hundred feet altitude. The tow car swung around the dry lake to the left and headed into the wind. I had picked up fifty feet on a few bumps, while I was still on the tow line. Flying a little further, I hit a good thermal, so I cut loose from the car and started to make a left turn. I glanced at the instruments and read: air speed 30 m.p.h., altitude 162 feet, and the variometer showed that we were rising between 4.5 and 5 meters per second. I had made one and a quarter turns when something seemed to hit the ship and make it tremble from one end to the other. I had just enough time to look at the air speed and noticed the needle making a new trail around the dial, passing seventy m.p.h. with ease, when I heard an unfamiliar crunching and cracking sound. I looked back over my shoulder and saw the left panel fold back against the fuselage. The ship started down in a right dive and then the right panel tore loose and back. Both panels broke about two feet away from the fittings. I tried to pull the ship out of the dive but that was useless, so then I just waited for the ground to come up and get me. It did. This casualty has taught the members of our club a good lesson concerning air currents at the dry lake and will not interfere with my further glider activities.*

The day after the crash, a group went to retrieve the wreckage of the *Sloanlo* and found that the sailplane was no longer at the crash site. Strong desert winds had blown the ship clear across to the northeast side of the dry lake bed.

## *Robert Stanley*

By January, 1938, Robert M. Stanley of the VT Squadron 2B, Fleet-A Detachment of the United States Navy, was in the process of building a new sailplane in San Diego. His hope was to complete the aircraft in time for the United States Soaring Nationals in Elmira, New York. The design of the sailplane began while Stanley was a cadet in Pensacola, Florida. Once he arrived in San Diego, he began construction in the basement of a bungalow, which he shared with four other cadets. Stanley wrote:

> *During the time that we were based ashore, I spent my spare hours in sawing out wing ribs, making form blocks, welding up fittings, and making all the component parts of a soaring plane having 57 feet of wingspan (more than a B-58), an aspect ratio of 18, a fabric-covered wooden wing with an all-metal monocoque fuselage and a total flying weight, including pilot of 510 pounds. With a wing loading of 3.1 pounds per square foot and a structural strength of 12 g, I hoped to create a sailplane of superior performance wherein to attack some of the national soaring records.*
>
> *My basement was so tiny that I had to build the fuselage in four sections, the aileron in two sections, and to assemble the long wing spars on the lawn. I didn't get much help from the other cadets, because none of them had the skills necessary to maintain the standards of workmanship that I demanded. They were most tolerant, however, of my bandsaw whining away at late hours of the night and my pounding out sheet metal ribs on Sunday mornings before the hours that late sleepers normally like to arise.*
>
> *My only encounter, while in uniform, with the great Admiral King occurred when I petitioned for leave of absence to take my sailplane to the national soaring contest at Elmira, New York. In the face of a fleet order over his signature that no officer could be granted leave prior to the completion of gunnery training, I had the audacity to ask for thirty days of leave, using the simple excuse that the organizers of the soaring competition had not seen fit to schedule their national meet to fit the Navy's gunnery training convenience.*
>
> *Eventually, my commanding officier...assured me that my leave would be granted and confessed to me that the only reason that he had been able to get permission for me to attend the soaring meet was because I was a lousy gunner (which was quite true). And so began my entry into competitive soaring, a sport which, for a brief few years, brought me considerable fame and a great deal of enjoyment.*

The *Stanley sailplane* (identification mark NX20645) represented Robert Stanley's long desire to design and build a high-performance sailplane embodying features from current transport and military aircraft. An aspect ratio of 18:1 and a semielliptical planform made it one of the more high-performance sailplanes of its day. Although the wings were made of spruce and mahogany plywood, the fuselage was all-metal and of monocoque construction.

The 9th annual National Soaring Contest was held at Elmira, New York, from June 26th to July 10th, 1938. The weather cooperated, and cross-country and high altitude soaring flights were common. On June 29th, Robert Stanley (the only attendee from San Diego) flew from Elmira to Reading, Pennsylvania, a distance of 144 miles. It was his first serious attempt at cross-country soaring, made in his newly completed *Stanley sailplane*. His soaring flight lasted 6 hours and 8 minutes, reaching an altitude of 6,380 feet.

On July 2nd, Stanley repeated his cross-country soaring with a flight of 122 miles to the Delaware Water Gap, in a flight lasting 6 hours and 18 minutes. After landing, and while calling Contest Headquarters to document his flight, a souvenir hunter stole a "flipper" (elevator) from the sailplane. Stanley was distraught and ready to leave for the return trip to San Diego, when he was persuaded to remain at the contest and continue flying in the *Ibis* sailplane (identification mark NX17623). The *Ibis* was designed by Harland Ross and owned by the Soaring Society of America. Contest rules prohibited flights in the Soaring Society of America's sailplane from counting towards their total points for the contest.

On July 4th, Stanley took off in the *Ibis* and proceeded to fly from Elmira to Washington, D.C., covering 219 miles in 7 hours and 26 minutes, with a maximum altitude of 5610 feet. This flight was longer than the current American distance record, but not by the 5% margin required for an official record. Despite not being able to use this flight for points in the contest, Stanley's accomplishment was well-received by the pilots back at Elmira. His flights during the meet were enough to qualify for a Silver "C" and gave him 9th place overall in the contest. He was also awarded the silver trophy for second in highest altitude during the meet, and the Air Trails Trophy for best performance of a "C" pilot for his altitude of 6,380 feet.

## *Thermals for Harland Ross*

On the morning of August 21st, 1938, members of the Wichita Falls Soaring Club started setting up their sailplanes. Included in the group was Harland Ross, who had recently relocated from California to Texas. Taking off by auto tow, a weak thermal was finally hooked by Ross. He worked the thermal past 4,000 feet, whereupon he located some growing cumulus clouds to the west and headed towards them, climbing to 5,500 feet in strong thermal lift. Soon, he realized the potential for a record-setting flight. The sailplane was carried to 7,400 feet above the ground (7,000 feet above the point of release) when the air became very turbulent. Ross later wrote:

> *While making a left turn, I was thrown completely over into a vertical right turn by the violent gusts. Without a parachute or blind flying instruments, I decided against trying to enter the cloud base a few hundred feet above, and left the updraft on my glide back to the takeoff point, a distance of 12 miles. How I wished for a Ross R-2 sailplane, equipped with a barograph!*

He landed at the point of takeoff after having flown for one hour. His round trip of 24 miles was the best distance and return flight made in that portion of the country.

## *San Diego Soaring Activities*

During the Fall of 1938, Carl Goller was busy repairing George Palmer's sailplane (identification mark 14944) that was flipped by high winds at the spring Arvin meet. At the same time, Palmer was reported to be working on another sailplane. Woody Brown was repairing the *Swift* in the hopes that it would be ready for slope soaring at Torrey Pines during the winter months. Jerry Littel was in the process of modifying his cut-down Bowlus sailplane. John Robinson had finished construction on the *Robin #4* sailplane, with a strut-braced Grunau Baby wing of 48 feet and welded steel tube fuselage. The airfoil of the strut was set at the same angle of incidence as the wing, acting as a lifting surface. This streamline tubing had a fineness ratio of 7:1, whereas the common streamline tubing of that time was closer to 3:1. A photo of the *Robin #4* sailplane appeared in the November issue of *Soaring* magazine. The wing for the *Robin #4* was acquired by John Robinson from Bill Stackhouse who had decided to discontinue work on the construction of a Grunau Baby sailplane with his partner. Robinson saw this as an opportunity to quickly finish his *Robin #4* sailplane.

Associated Glider Clubs of Southern California members prepared Torrey Pines for the official dedication ceremonies to be held on December 31st, 1938, and January 1st and 2nd, 1939. Dick Essery, president of the Associated Glider Clubs of Southern California, contacted the local press. Pictures of gliders and gliding activities were placed prominently in local newspapers. City officials were invited to the event and several sponsors were contacted.

Members of the Associated Glider Clubs of Southern California constructed a clubhouse on the field, and the site was well-suited to camping. The 25-acre site was believed to be the only airport in California devoted exclusively to soaring. Twenty members were active in the Associated Glider Clubs of Southern California, and monthly meetings proceeded with great enthusiasm. All pilots held great expectation

*A selection of glider mail from the first dedication of the Torrey Pines Gliderport.*

for the historic dedication to officially designate their club field as the Torrey Pines Gliderport at the start of 1939.

## *Dedication of the Torrey Pines Gliderport*

The first annual glider meet of the Associated Glider Clubs of Southern California started on December 31st, 1938, and continued through January 2nd, 1939. A local contractor gave the Associated Glider Clubs of Southern California use of his construction equipment and 2,000-foot-long dirt runways were graded. More than a thousand spectators and various members of the press arrived to witness the activities at the bustling Torrey Pines Gliderport.

The first day was quite uneventful, due to a lack of wind and visiting glider pilots. John Robinson opened the meet, however, by releasing the tow rope from the *Robin #4* at 300 feet and proceeded to make a large loop for the crowd. Hawley Bowlus, Frank Wolcott, and Bob Heideman followed Robinson into the air in quick succession. Ray Parker and Howard Morrison also made launches, but it was clear that the lack of suitable conditions curtailed any soaring flights.

Without activities in the air, focus shifted to the dedication ceremonies on the ground. Spectators were informed and entertained by Dick Essery and William Van Dusen. Van Dusen gave a history of gliding in San Diego, including Montgomery's glider flights in 1883, the flights by Nathan Rannels in 1910 (who attended the dedi-

4

*Left: Two photos of the Robin #4 sailplane flown by John Robinson. A clear nose gave excellent forward visibility.*

*Above: John Robinson in front of the Robin #4 in the foothills of San Diego County circa 1938.*

cation ceremonies as La Jolla's Postmaster), Hawley Bowlus, and Charles Lindbergh in 1930, and concluded by relating the history of the Associated Glider Clubs of Southern California. Councilman Crandall of La Jolla dedicated the Torrey Pines Gliderport to the youth of California. Some newspaper articles suggest that San Diego Mayor Percy J. Benbough made a similar dedication.

After the official ceremony, John Robinson took off in his *Robin #4* sailplane loaded with 295 pieces of cacheted (and an additional 50 pieces of uncacheted) glider mail. Postmaster Rannells awaited his landing, received the glider mail, and forwarded it through the United States Postal Department. One of the envelopes was addressed and sent directly to President Roosevelt, and another to the National Youth Administrator.

After a few more quick launches and landings in the still air, Robinson climaxed the day with an aerobatic flight. He was towed to 600 feet via auto-pulley, released, made three quick turns of a spin, dove to increase speed, and performed a loop. Diving to buzz the launch spot at 3 feet altitude, he pulled up to 150 feet, did a 180° turn, landed and rolled to a stop 1 foot from the starting spot.

> *During these maneuvers over the field, the crowd was cheering and auto horns honking. With the 'Ah's' and 'Oh's' and 'Pul-lease pull her out' of the loud speaker, it made quite a show.*

Pilots spent the night camped by their gliders near the clubhouse at Torrey Pines. By 10:00 a.m. the next morning, the wind came up, but it was running parallel and slightly offshore to the cliff, providing no lift at all. Several launches and landings were made until Ray Parker was forced to land on the beach below. The Heideman brothers kept the spectators interested on the public address system as they watched Parker's glider being buffeted by the winds. Robinson launched in the *Robin #4* when a large cloud came drifting along. He was able to circle under the cloud for several minutes, but was caught out over the cliff and was forced to join Ray Parker on the beach below. Rain eventually forced the end of the meet.

Despite the poor soaring conditions, the meet was a success for the Associated Glider Clubs of Southern California as a great deal of publicity was generated. The club netted a small profit from a modest parking fee levied for each car. Several new members also joined the club as a result of the meet. Woody Brown expected to soar in his new Bowlus Baby Albatross *Thunder Bird* at the meet, but he was not able to finish it in time. Brown had sold his repaired *Swift* to Jerry Litell and Steve Kesckes of the Associated Glider Clubs of Southern California.

For his outstanding efforts to please the crowd, Robinson was awarded the Bishop Trophy for the meet championship. The trophy was donated to the meet organizers by a brother of a famous Canadian War Ace by that name. Robinson was given the trophy at the monthly Associated Glider Clubs of Southern California club meeting.

*Dick Essery (l) and Hawley Bowlus (r) with the Bowlus Baby Albatross "Thunder Bird."*

## *Thermals from Torrey Pines*

On February 8th, 1939, John Robinson took off by auto-pulley tow at Torrey Pines into a wind of about 40 miles per hour, with a set of cumulus clouds at a base of 4,000 feet. By ridge soaring high enough, Robinson was able to "cloud hop" in the thermal lift under the clouds and traveled east with them, leaving the Torrey Pines Gliderport far behind. Soon afterwards, as he neared the local mountains, it started to snow and his wings started to ice up. He dove and made a landing in an empty field between Alpine and Descanso in the midst of a snow storm 33 miles away from Torrey Pines. Woody Brown and Dick Essery also made similar flights away from Torrey using thermal lift, these representing the first thermal cross-country flights made from Torrey Pines.

## *A Club Grunau 8*

In the hopes that the Associated Glider Clubs of Southern California could obtain United States Government aid to train new pilots, the club became interested in purchasing a suitable two-place training sailplane. The German Grunau 8 sailplane was billed as the "most widely used two-place trainer in the world" and the Associated Glider Clubs of Southern California was interested in finding such an aircraft in the United States. As it turned out, Don Sanborn of Redlands, California owned just such a ship. This sailplane (identification mark 16029) was manufactured in May, 1936, had been featured previously on the cover of *Soaring* magazine in April, 1938, and flown at various locations near San Francisco and Los Angeles. With a span of 47.5 feet, length of 21.9 feet, and gross weight of 605 pounds, it was a perfect design for a two-place club trainer. The Göttingen 619 airfoil was a key ingredient. The Grunau 8 was purchased by the club on March 27, 1939. Jerry Litell wrote:

> *The dream of a two-place sailplane in which every club member could fly, is now a reality. Since March 8th the Grunau 8 has been used every week at Torrey Pines. The ship is very stable and of rugged construction, being designed as an intermediate trainer. Yet it has flown to 1,100 feet with two up on a 15-mile-per-hour slope wind. With the aid of a cloud we once rose to 1,500 feet where the cliffs were only 200 feet high. The Grunau 8 is stored at the field and takes only 15 minutes to set up, so flying need not be limited to week-ends for those who work. Hence: wives and mothers of glider friends: when the wind is good, don't worry about your 'wandering boy tonite'-he'll just be out at Torrey Pines, soaring.*

James R. "Jim" Spurgeon, who moved to San Diego in 1940, to work at Consolidated Vultee Aircraft Co. (which later became General Dynamics/Convair), wrote:

*In 1939, our Glider Club, with a big cash loan from Ernie Stout, bought a Grunau 8 two-place wood and fabric German training glider that did a very credible job of introducing many, many people to soaring here at Torrey Pines. The instructors were Alan Essery, Woody Brown, Frank Graham, and the Parker Brothers, Ray and Harry.*

*I remember one time Harry had a green student up who 'slipped' a turn and that was too much for the old Grunau to take-so it was down to the beach and Harry, being not the kind to latch onto any unnecessary work, grabbed the controls and headed at the best glide angle up the beach toward the foot of Torrey Pines Grade to make the retrieve easier. Now you couldn't see a tall fisherman standing on the rock pile up toward the North end of the beach until it was too late to go OVER him, so-o-o-, they flew out to sea to go around the man and naturally, ran out of altitude about half way back--they made a beautiful Seaplane Landing, the Grunau coming to rest, then sinking right up to the wings. Harry and the student came clambering out and all three, the ship and two men, came floating in on the next wave.*

*We rushed down and dismantled the glider, put it on a trailer, and rushed it into town where we washed it down with fresh water. Well, we didn't get ALL the salt out and after it dried out and collected in the bottom of the 'V' of the fuselage, it would act as an excellent skid indicator-it would 'swish' across the plywood bottom every time you skidded your turns. We had very few instruments in those days and the skid indicator was welcomed.*

## *The Thunder Bird*

On April 1st, 1939, Woody Brown's wife, Betty Warner Brown, purchased a Bowlus Baby Albatross kit (serial number 106) for Woody from the Bowlus Sailplane Company. On May 18th, ownership of the Baby Albatross was transferred to her husband. Woody Brown completed his new Bowlus Baby Albatross, *Thunder Bird* (identification mark N18998), and test flew it with John Robinson at Camp Kearney. According to Robinson:

*Woody had finished construction and we set it up on Camp Kearney field. After set up, and a second look around, I laid out the tow rope and Woody climbed in for the first flight. I gave him good tow speed and he climbed well, went around the field, and made a good landing.*

*We moved the ship for another tow, and Woody said, 'Johnny you take this tow.' We had shared flying the Swift sailplane on previous occasions. I*

*Above: The Associated Glider Clubs of Southern California club Grunau 8 sailplane soaring overhead.*

*Right: A three-view diagram of the Schneider Grunau 8 sailplane.*

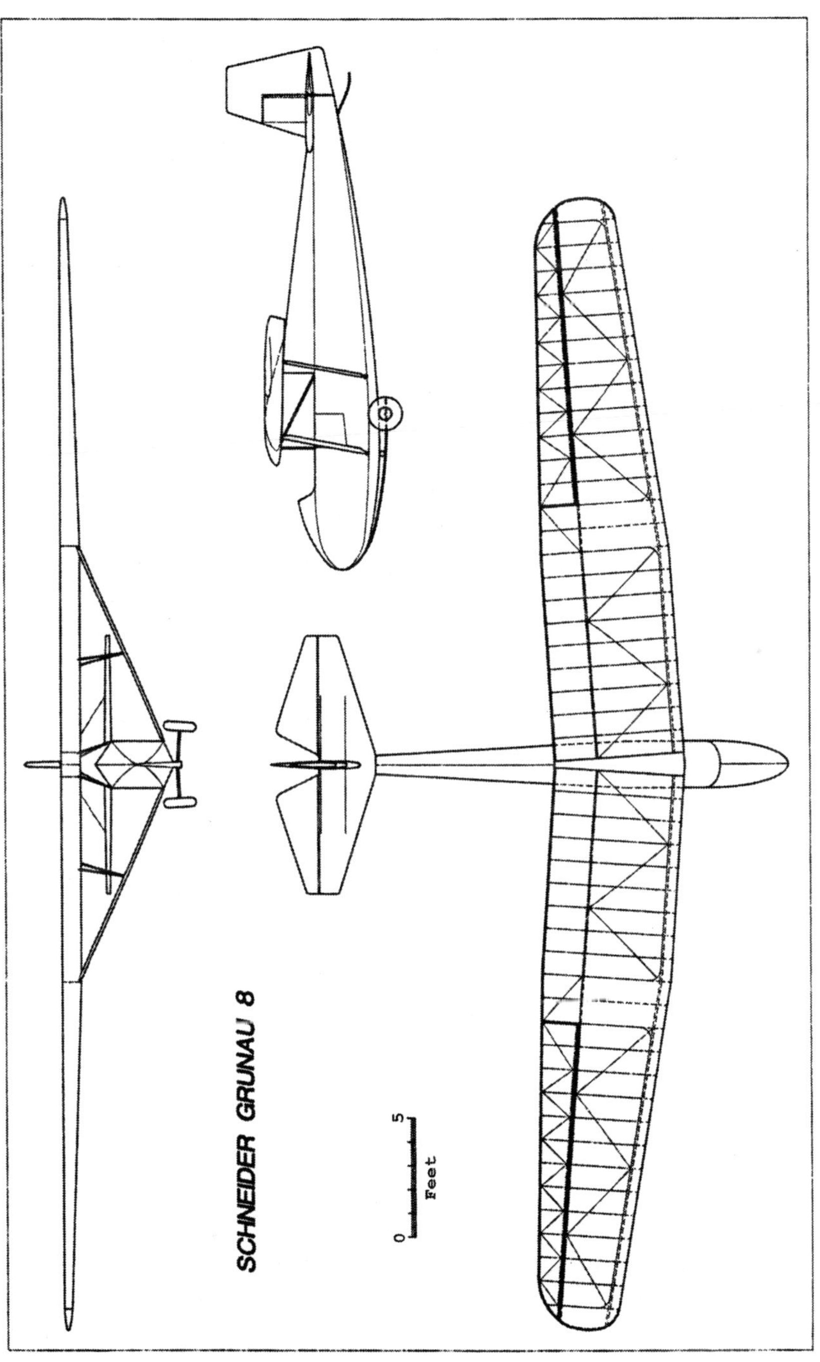
SCHNEIDER GRUNAU 8
0
5
Feet

*Woody Brown and the Bowlus Baby Albatross "Thunder Bird" at the 1939 Western Soaring Championships.*

*climbed in the Baby's cockpit, adjusted the seat belt for skinny Woody's 127 pound frame was smaller than my 147 pounds. I checked the controls and became used to the wheel operated ailerons, since all my sailplanes had been stick controlled. As the tow started I had to pull the control column back to get the skid off the ground. At flying speed I added more up elevator and slowly left the ground. At three feet altitude, the control post hit a stop, and the control wheel was against my belly!*

*By five feet altitude, my brain was screaming at my muscles 'release-Release-RELEASE!!!' I did! It did. And I landed immediately! This was dangerous! The plane was very nose heavy. That 20 pound difference in our weights was enough to turn the weight and balance beyond its limits! If I had climbed until the tow car stopped, I would have had to make a very speedy landing, without elevator control. Just whatever speed this nose-heavy condition would dictate, and that is not the way to go!*

After initial tests at Camp Kearney, Brown and Dick Essery flew the *Thunder Bird* at Torrey Pines on the beach at the base of the Torrey Pines Grade. Within 15 minutes, they had the ship set up and ready to fly. Using only 200 feet of tow rope and with Brown in the *Thunder Bird*, he cut loose, made a 180° turn, glided back over the launching point, made another 180° turn and made a perfect landing. Woody and Essery made several test hops and, before July, Brown allowed Essery to get over five hours slope soaring and five hours thermaling in the *Thunder Bird*. Essery later wrote:

*Although the pod is small, I found there was plenty of room for a chute, a large instrument panel, maps, water, and a couple of chocolate bars. I know you fellows who are making or getting one of these pods will be pleased with it, especially after you get used to its model airplane characteristics.*

## *The Dedication of the Arvin-Sierra Soaring Site and the Third Annual Western Soaring Championships*

The Southern California Soaring Association organized what was quickly becoming the western version of the United States National Soaring Contest. The third annual Western Soaring Championship/Southern California Meet was held at the Arvin-Sierra Soaring Site near Arvin in the San Joaquin Valley in 1939. The meet continued over two weekends, including April 8th and 9th, and April 15th and 16th. Over 200 flights were accomplished without incident. Associated Glider Clubs of Southern California pilots were keen on competition after their training at the Torrey Pines Gliderport and at other locations in San Diego County. Woody Brown, John Robinson, and Dick Essery all brought sailplanes from San Diego to Arvin. On the first Saturday of the meet, Paul Pierce of CBS radio was carried aloft as a passenger in the *Transporter* sailplane, with Lucretia Buxton as the pilot. The 15-minute flight was broadcast to 81 radio stations in the United States and 26 in Europe.

The Arvin-Sierra site was officially dedicated by a large group of honorees and politicians on April 8th. Hawley Bowlus, who discovered the site many years earlier, and Dr. Wolfgang Klemperer spoke at the ceremonies. As a completion to the ceremonies, Brown took off in his *Thunder Bird* Bowlus Baby Albatross sailplane loaded with 256 pieces of glider mail and landed in Arvin, to the west of the launching site. With this flight, he was honored as the first pilot to land in that city by the Arvin Boosters' Club. Bowlus carried the mail on the following day, and proceeded to land in a vacant lot a block away from the post office in Bakersfield. In his *Robin #4* sailplane, John Robinson soared for 6 hours and 40 minutes on the first day in two flights. His second flight of the day was a declared distance flight to Tehachapi a distance of 16 miles wherein he climbed to 4,000 feet. During the second week, both Robinson and Brown flew in separate sailplanes from Arvin to Taft, a distance of 43 miles. Dick Essery and Paul Hepburn joined in the two-seat *Transporter* sailplane in a flight to Taft. During the week, Robinson made a 27-mile cross-country flight to Grapevine; there seemed to be no stopping the San Diego trio. Brown was awarded first place and the William Hawley Bowlus Perpetual Championship Trophy. He was also awarded the Kern County Junior Chamber of Commerce Perpetual Championship Trophy, as well as the Arvin Booster Club trophy for best duration of 3 hours, 48 minutes. Robinson finished second, and won the Bakersfield Trophy for best altitude of 4,000 feet and the American Legion Trophy for greatest distance. Essery took third place, and received the Western Flying trophy for best distance and return flight of 18 miles.

## *Blair Dry Lake*

On Sunday, May 7th, John Robinson, Dick Essery, Woody Brown, and Sparky Koenig towed the *Robin #4* and the *Thunder Bird* to Blair Dry Lake, just east of Banner in San Diego County. They arrived at the lake at 10:00 a.m. and set up the sailplanes and an auto tow cable. After takeoff, Robinson was able to spiral in a weak thermal at 200 feet above the lake, until finally breaking loose to gain altitude at 10 feet per second. Brown attempted to find a thermal in the *Thunder Bird,* but was forced to return to the lake bed.

Robinson jumped from one thermal to another at 3,000 feet and continued increasing his altitude. Looking back at the lake, he saw the *Thunder Bird* circling below. Unknown to Robinson, Dick Essery was now at the controls of the *Thunder Bird*. Robinson climbed in lift as great as 20 feet per second to 9,700 feet above the takeoff point, over 12,000 feet above sea level. At around 9,000 feet Robinson heard a loud noise in the cockpit as one of the pyralin panels on the nose contracted, split, and broke loose. Cold air of 24° F soon filled the cockpit. He headed west toward the mining town of Julian, passed overhead, and continued on, reaching the Linda Vista Airport near San Diego with an altitude of 11,000 feet above sea level. The altitudes were later cross-checked to the barograph he carried on board.

Meanwhile, Essery continued to climb in the *Thunder Bird* to an altitude of 9,500 feet above the desert floor. He continued on a westerly course nearly parallel to Robinson, taking him over the highway to Ramona, and to a landing at Escondido. His flight time was 3 hours and he covered 40 miles distance. Near the end of his flight, Essery made use of a slight surface wind to slope soar his way for the last leg of the journey. Local newspapers reported the activities, but confused several details about the flights.

## *San Diegans at National Contests in 1939*

While travelling across the country to attend the United States National Soaring Championships in Elmira, New York, Dick Essery, John Robinson, and Woody Brown competed in the Southwestern Soaring Contest in Wichita Falls, Texas. Brown arrived one week prior to the meet to get in a few days of soaring in the *Thunder Bird* before the meet started. On Wednesday, May 31st, he made a flight of 5 hours duration, reaching an altitude of 9,000 feet in the Texas-sized thermals.

Brown took off as the first official contestant in the *Thunder Bird*. He carried 300 pieces of cacheted glider mail and announced a destination of Wichita, Kansas. Launching at 10:00 a.m., he headed due north and succeeded in reaching the Cessna Airport in Wichita, Kansas after a duration of 7 hours, 30 minutes in the cramped quarters of his Baby Albatross. His landing at the Cessna Airport came by mistake. He was expected to land at the Municipal Field seven miles across the city, but was so tired and had such little altitude that he headed straight for the first airport in sight. Although he carried a ham sandwich on board, he was so busy during the flight that he never had time to eat. His goal of 280 miles set a new American distance record. Within 20 miles of his goal and at and altitude of 3,000 feet, Brown recalled:

> *There, about 20 miles ahead in the haze was the biggest thrill of all. A huge city with its great while buildings reaching to the heavens, with the setting sun casting deep shades of red and purple--my goal--Wichita. But could we make it? With feverish hands, I caressed the Thunder Bird--Indian good luck sign. One more thermal, just one more, there has to be one somewhere! Finally, there was one; weak, yes, but it served the purpose. With the city beneath me at 2,000 feet, there was a moment of hesitation. It was 5:30 and there was a possibility of flying till 7:00, and on top of that a 2,000 foot start; possibly 40 miles more. But the goal would be lost, and perhaps only five miles more could be made. While trying to decide one way or the other, I was going with a tail wind, with a ground speed of about 70 miles per hour*

*A triumphant Woody Brown in the cockpit of the Bowlus Baby Albatross "Thunder Bird" made the cover of Soaring magazine following his record flight.*

*and the city was slipping away. So, I suddenly turned back to a ball field I had picked out in the middle of the city. But to my dismay, there was no forward speed at all, and the sinking speed was very high. Whereupon, the speed of the ship was increased to 80, just enabling me to squeak in over a row of trees to the ball park, which turned out to be the old Cessna Airport at Wichita, Kansas.*

As a result of his accomplishment, more than 200 people waited to receive him as he crossed the state line back into Texas. He was an instant local hero. He entered Wichita Falls heading a two-block long procession, with police sirens paving the way. The Mayor of Wichita Falls, W. E. Fitzgerald, and several other local politicians, rode in the car with Brown as he paraded through the streets. Essery later wrote:

*Huge crowds of residents of the area had gathered to aid Wichita Falls in the reception. Brown jumped out of the car and seemed to try to get behind the crowd as shouts arose from those standing on the river banks...The crowd rushed around the hero. The committee hustled Brown into the official car. They formed a parade through Burkburnett and almost every resident of that town turned out to hail the record-maker.*

For his exceptional record flight, Woody and his accomplishment received national recognition in Ripley's syndicated "Believe-It-Or-Not" cartoon feature.

On the last flying day of the meet, Robinson flew 200 miles to Buffalo, Oklahoma, by flying in several thunderstorms. This established the distance leg for his Golden "C" award. Takeoff was by winch launch to 300 feet altitude. Robinson recalled:

*Before landing at Buffalo, Oklahoma, flying my Robin #4, at 15,000 feet I left the last thunderstorm, heading north, my slide rule and map told me I could make the first of 2 small towns ahead without any more thermals. Approaching the first town, Selman, in a steady glide, I calculated that the second town was within reach if I turned to 280°, off course to the left. That would be less mileage than straight ahead, with no towns, but it would still be farther than stopping here, and in a contest every mile counts! It was about 8 miles in between towns.*

*Arriving at Buffalo, Oklahoma, there was a shortage of large landing spaces. The best one was a baseball diamond and this was a Saturday afternoon, with a game in progress! When I was on my landing downwind leg, the players all scattered. I turned final in line with 2nd base and home plate. After clearing the fence with 3 feet, I put the wheel on the ground in early center field, applied the brake immediately, and the nose skid at 2nd base, and stopped at home plate to the cheering of the spectators! (I could have stopped sooner)!*

Robinson later noted that the owner of a plane can often do things that should never be attempted in a borrowed, rented, or club plane.

*We quickly rolled the plane off to a safe tie down, and the game continued. After getting my landing card signed, etc..., I was told there was no motel or place to stay in Buffalo, but Selman had a hotel, and a kind soul offered to drive me back there to make my phone call to Contest Headquarters, and get a hotel room, for my wait for my crew. He had been sent in a northwest direction due to the information at the pilots meeting and the experimental radio we were trying out didn't work. When I got aloft, the conditions drew me to fly straight north.*

*After I ate dinner and settled in my hotel room, a horrendous loud noise outside drew me out to investigate. Hail the size of hen's eggs and golf balls was falling everywhere! And this lasted for the longest time. They were coming down from the last thunderstorm I had been flying in. It had been blown by the wind straight north!*

*Now I was thinking about my Robin #4 sailplane tied down 8 miles away. In my mind I could picture all the fabric stripped off, the steel tubing dented all over, and the bare spar, sticking out from the fuselage! When my crew finally arrived, the completely dented look of a couple of cars parked in front of the hotel told the whole story better than words.*

*After a good night's sleep, we headed for Buffalo, to view the wreckage and pack it in the covered trailer. When we arrived at the place where I had left my sailplane, it was sitting there, tied down as if nothing had happened! Wow, what a relief! Seven minutes later, we were towing the trailer, with the sailplane secured in it, on the road headed for Wichita Falls, Texas, and the Contest Headquarters.*

*I have often thought of the two pieces of good luck that saved my sailplane. One: my last second decision not to land at Selman, but to fly on. Two: That the 'hail portion' of the thunderstorm did not hit both towns! Just pure good luck!*

The trio of Essery, Robinson and Brown finished first, second, and third, respectively in the overall standings, and won cash prizes as well as trophies. Robinson's flight of 109 miles to Oklahoma City, which took 3 hours and 15 minutes, was also another exceptional flight at the meet. Woody and the *Thunder Bird* were featured on the cover of the July, 1939 issue of *Soaring* magazine. The cash awards helped to defray the costs of their transcontinental excursion to Elmira, New York, for the U.S. National Soaring Contest.

At the July, 1939 Wichita Falls meet, Harvey Stephens, in the R.S.-1 sailplane, cut from the tow line with Tulsa, Oklahoma, as his goal. Upon landing in a corn field near his goal, he proceeded to hit one of the only posts hidden in the field. The post completely demolished the leading edge of one wing and nose of the sailplane. It was thrown over on its back, and Harvey Stephens was not able to exit the sailplane until help arrived on the scene.

Stephens had planned to take the R.S.-1 sailplane to the National Soaring Contest and was now distraught by the fact that he would not be able to go. Realizing his opportunity, on June 12th, 1939, Brown traded his Bowlus Baby Albatross *Thunder Bird* for the wreckage of the R.S.-1 sailplane, even though he had just made a record-setting flight in the *Thunder Bird*. Stephens agreed to the deal and proceeded to take the *Thunder Bird* to the Nationals while Brown brought the wreckage of the R.S.-1 sailplane back to his home in La Jolla, convinced he could bring the higher performance sailplane back from the ashes.

Dick Essery and passenger Jack Begley of Wichita Falls took off at 1 p.m. on June 31st in the *Transporter*. Their landing at 5:20 p.m., on a vacant tract southwest of Oklahoma City, established a new United States record for distance with a passenger. Although they had covered an estimated 126 miles during the flight, the straight line distance was 109 miles. This was Essery's second distance record in under a week. Earlier in the week, Essery and a passenger flew from Wichita Falls to a point north of Lawton, Oklahoma, a distance of 64 miles. All totalled, the group from San Diego netted $650 in cash awards, numerous trophies, and aeronautical instruments.

After the Southwestern Soaring Contest, Robinson and Essery continued on to Elmira, New York, for the United States National Soaring Contest. On July 4th, 1939, Robinson was towed aloft in his *Robin* sailplane to 1,500 feet by aerotow. Soon, he entered a thermal and was carried to 4,000 feet and into the base of a cloud. Continuing on by instruments alone, his airspeed indicator clogged up with moisture and he popped out of the top of the cloud at approximately 10,000 feet. Upon seeing a higher cloud in the vicinity, he was soon spiralling upwards. His canopy frosted over; it rained and then started to hail. Robinson noted:

> *This was bad! If the hail stones grew very large, they could easily damage a sailplane. They made a terrific noise on the wings and hood and I decided the best way to keep my sailplane from getting holes in it was to get out of this cloud. This I did as quickly as possible, encountering a 25 feet per second downdraft in so doing. About this time I read my altimeter at 12,500 feet. Later the calibration of my barograph showed my highest point as 11,550 feet above point of release, which was 13,000 feet above the field.*

After flying south for some distance, Robinson spotted a hole in the cloud base below him, and spiralled down in a spin for 5,000 feet. He straightened his ship out just below cloud base. As it turned out, he was not far from Harris Hill at Elmira, and, with his extra altitude, he put on an aerobatic exhibition for the crowd. John Robinson placed fifth overall at the contest. He placed third in the National Sailplane Derby (for the fastest flight to Harrisburg, Pennsylvania), with a flight of 5 hours, 46 minutes on July 2nd, 1939. Robinson was the second American to complete the requirements for the Golden "C" award.

Robert Stanley's desire to complete his design of a superior sailplane came in 1939, with the renovation of his *Stanley Sailplane*. Rechristened the *Nomad*, the sailplane now sported a V-tail, the first aircraft in the United States to do so.

> *The Nomad was feverishly rushed to completion in June of 1938 just in time to leave San Diego and enter the National Soaring Contest at Elmira, New York. Even before it was finished, however, ambitious plans were fermenting in my mind for future aerodynamic and design problems which I would try out on this the only airplane at my disposal which I could do with as I saw fit. Even before it was finished the idea for the Vee tail had been formulated and was 'Number One' on the list of things to do next.*
>
> *Some vandal with a twisted sense of humor deprived me, following a flight from Elmira to Delaware Water Gap, of the single elevator which was easily detached from the tail of the ship and without which I obviously could not continue the contest. Confronted with the necessity of building a new tail anyway this seemed the proper time to try out the idea of the Vee tail.*
>
> *Such an empennage, having the same basic theoretical control characteristics as the original Nomad empennage was designed, built and flight tested immediately prior to the 1939 National Soaring Contest.*

At the 1939 United States Soaring Nationals, Stanley established a new American altitude record for sailplanes of 17,264 feet above the point of release on July 4th. He was awarded the A. Felix duPont Altitude Award.

> *Among the more spectacular incidents were two thunderstorm flights by Bob Stanley. Bob is one of the small number of high ranking soaring pilots in the United States with an instrument rating, and consequently, is one of the few who have attempted to fly into the raging interiors of these mountainous clouds. On both flights he was forced to leave the cloud because his instruments iced up. His first attempt left his ship with a broken seat and set of loosened control cables. Later during the meet, he again rode a storm to 17,264 feet above the point of release or over 20,000 feet above sea level, to*

*better his previous altitude mark and make what will be the new American record.*

Stanley placed second overall, took first place in the National Sailplane Derby, and was awarded a variety of other trophies for his goal flights during the meet. Stanley received his Golden "C," the third American to do so.

Dick Essery helped fly Jay Buxton's *Transporter* and give rides to passengers prior to the contest. Unfortunately, on the afternoon of June 23rd, a downdraft caught the sailplane on winch launch, forcing it into the ground just as the winch crew cut power. Essery's chance at setting more two-place American sailplane records was dashed.

## *Soaring in San Diego*

Back in San Diego, the Associated Glider Clubs of Southern California Grunau 8 training sailplane was moved from Torrey Pines to Prescott's Airport (near Camp Kearney) ten miles to the east. At Prescott's Airport, thermal flying was achieved by several students. Altitudes of 1,500 to 2,000 feet were easy to obtain on the common midday thermal activity. Writing to the editors of *Soaring* magazine, Associated Glider Clubs of Southern California member Platt McCartney suggested that it would be a good idea to have a National Winter Meet in Southern California. This was a popular idea with local gliding enthusiasts. Ray Parker became the primary instructor in the Grunau 8. Later that year, John Robinson took his mother up in the Grunau 8 for her first flight in an airplane.

On the evening of August 7th, 1939, approximately 60 soaring enthusiasts from across southern California gathered at the Hollywood Athletic Club for dinner and a discussion of the activities of Woody Brown, John Robinson, Dick Essery, Harvey Stephens, and others at the Wichita Falls and Elmira meets. It was a way for members of the Southern California Soaring Association and Associated Glider Clubs of Southern California to share adventures.

On Sunday, August 27th, 1939, Woody Brown and John Robinson decided to attempt soaring inside huge cumulus clouds and thunderstorms that are frequent to the mountains and desert east of San Diego during the summertime. Launches were made at Blair Dry Lake by auto tow. Brown used the R.S.-1 sailplane while John flew his trusty *Robin #4*.

On his first auto tow, Robinson encountered a thermal at 150 feet and circled in the light lift hoping that Brown could join him. Try as he might, Brown could not find the core of the light lift and Robinson continued to battle the thermal for a good 30 minutes before he had reached 1,000 feet of altitude over the dry lake. Suddenly, the rate of climb increased.

At 2,000 feet, a large buzzard joined Robinson as he climbed higher. Soon enough, another buzzard joined, and yet a third bird arrived. Robinson recognized the latter as a large eagle. After coming close to hitting the eagle in a turn, the eagle maintained a safe distance.

At 7,000 feet, the birds left Robinson as he continued to climb even higher. At 9,000 feet, he entered the base of a developing altocumulus cloud, and at 10,000 feet, while still inside the cloud, the lift ceased altogether. The air in the cloud was smooth, suggesting it would not continue to develop, and Robinson set out to find a more active cloud in which to fly in.

Finding a suitable cloud on his way back to the dry lake, very heavy rain started to fall to the south of his position. Entering the cloudbase, the lift increased from 10 feet per second to 30 feet per second and the air became very turbulent. Soon, the air speed indicator ceased to function due to water clogging his venturi; his cowling frosted over; and the temperature dropped below freezing. While looking at the thermometer registering 22°F, one of the panels in the nose suddenly broke and blew out, allowing the cold air into the cockpit in a similar manner to his previous high-altitude flights. Dressed for the high heat on the desert floor, Robinson was ill-equipped to maintain warmth under these conditions. He decided to leave the cloud as soon as possible, leveling off at an altitude of 15,500 feet above the dry lake, an estimated 17,500 feet above sea level. After exiting and upon looking back at the cloud, he noted that it covered half of the sky. A thunderstorm of quite large dimensions had developed while he was inside.

With so much altitude to spare, Robinson continued west over the Laguna Mountains and reached the El Cajon Valley at 3,000 above sea level. His landing was made at the Walz Ranch to the east of the Linda Vista Airport. Robinson's exploits with the *Robin #4* sailplane also landed him on the front cover of *Soaring* magazine for November, 1939.

By September, 1939, Great Britain and France were preparing to declare war on Germany. At Torrey Pines, members of the Associated Glider Clubs of Southern California continued training in the Grunau 8 two-place training sailplane. New glider enthusiasts were recruited from Consolidated Aircraft Corporation as a result of Jerry Litell's numerous glider articles in *Consolidator* magazine. These included: Mr. McCreight, Mr. Palsulich, Mr. Wallace, Mr. Craig, and Mr. Kennedy of the Engineering Department; Scott Royce (past President of the University of Michigan Glider Club); Harry and Ray Parker of the Wood Shop; Ed True of the Tool Shop (a former worker with the Bowlus Sailplane Company); Paul Madsen, Matt Wielopolski, and Jim Conniry of the Machine Shop; Tom Eccles of the Hull Department; and Russ Kern.

A strong westerly breeze had developed early in the morning of October 3rd, with unstable air and associated puffy cumulus clouds coming into San Diego from the Pacific Ocean. Ed True and Woody Brown met at 6:00 a.m. at the Torrey Pines Gliderport and set up Brown's newly refurbished R.S.-1. Launching at 6:30 a.m., Brown found several weak thermals under the cumulus clouds, even at this early hour of the morning. By 8:00 a.m., the thermals were much stronger, and he could occasionally drift inland about 1 mile with an altitude of 1,200 feet. By 2:00 p.m., he landed to greet Dick Essery who had arrived on the scene with the Grunau 8. Brown helped set up the ship and make a quick hop to take an interested friend for a ride. By 3:00 p.m., Woody was off again in the R.S.-1 and found that after using thermal lift to get to cloud base, he could fly directly out to sea about three miles and could manage to hold zero sink under the puffy cumulus clouds. After more experimentation, Brown turned east once again and soared with the thermal lift to Clarence Prescott's Airport, ten miles east of Torrey Pines. He landed at 5:00 p.m., giving him ten hours of nearly continuous soaring.

On the very next day, similar weather conditions developed. Not one to rest when the flying was good, Brown was up early in the morning and took off at Torrey Pines at 6:30 a.m. Two hours into the flight, he was at cloud base between 2,000 to 4,000 feet. Turning to head east using thermal lift, he soared once again over Clarence Prescott's Airport. Brown recognized that the United States Navy was conducting dive bombing practice in the nearby area. The bombing was too close for comfort. Instead of lingering in the area, he flew south towards downtown San Diego:

> *The rest of the flight over the city was one of the greatest pleasures of my life. I flew down long corridors between the different shaded clouds into rooms of clear air surrounded completely by silvery mist, with a floor of buildings and a roof of blue sky.*

He was forced to land at Lindbergh Field, as the lift died in an expended cumulus cloud. His landing at 11:30 a.m. caused quite a stir at the nearby United States Navy Training Facility.

> *Some thought it was a pontoon job; others, someone who had forgotten to lower their retractable landing gear; then finally in desperation they thought possibly it was a man from Mars.*

The Associated Glider Clubs of Southern California made plans for the 2nd annual glider meet to be held in February, 1940, at the Torrey Pines Gliderport. Scott Royce became a club instructor and replaced Frank Graham, who moved to Pensacola, Florida. Associated Glider Clubs of Southern California member, Lieutenant Tennes, left San Diego while on duty (he was reported to have taken his Bowlus Baby Albatross with him on the aircraft carrier Enterprise to Hawaii). Woody Brown was discouraged in the fact that his distance record was broken by a Russian pilot shortly after his 280-mile flight. Brown practiced in the R.S.-1 in preparation for another distance attempt in 1940. Dick Essery started construction on his *Baby Bomber*, a two-place side-by-side sailplane of his own design. Steve Kesckes and Jerry Litell had finished remodeling the *Swift* sailplane. It now carried a midwing with 50 more square feet of wing area and spoilers were added. Test flights by Brown were successful.

*Above Left: Woody Brown standing in front of the graceful R.S.-1 "Zanonia" sailplane. At the time, the "Zanonia" was considered to be the most efficient aircraft in the United States.*

*Below Left: Woody Brown (r) and friend Patricia Moore (l) with the "Zanonia."*

*Above: John Robinson with the "Zanonia" at the Torrey Pines Gliderport in 1939 or 1940. Robinson and the "Zanonia" became synonymous in the years to come.*

During December, 1939, John Robinson purchased the R.S.-1 sailplane from Woody Brown, following the tragic passing of Brown's wife, Betty. Brown had brought the sailplane back from the Wichita Falls meet, and with the willing help of the original designer, Harland Ross (who had moved back to California and was living in the Los Angeles area), Brown and Ross reworked the R.S.-1 sailplane at Brown's home in La Jolla until it was in flying condition. Shortly after making a few flights in the San Diego area with the sailplane, Brown sold the ship to Robinson with the understanding that Robinson was well suited to flying such a high-performance ship and capable of guiding the aircraft to soaring records. Robinson immediately advertised his *Robin #4* in the December issue of *Soaring* magazine for $850, or $750 without the trailer, and renamed the R.S.-1 the *Zanonia.*

## *A Midwinter Glider Party*

The Southern California Soaring Association in Los Angeles staged a glider meet January 27th and 28th, 1940, at the ranch of Clarence Brown, motion picture director for Metro Goldwyn Meyer Studios. Clarence Brown loaned the use of his private ranch airport in the Santa Monica Mountains for the event. The site was located in Stokes Canyon between Calabasas Peak and Brent's Crag, about five miles north of Ventura Boulevard. Three trial flights at the site were made by Frank Kelsey, flying a Bowlus Baby Albatross towed to 750 feet by Jay Buxton's winch.

A good relationship between the Southern California Soaring Association (Los Angeles) and the Associated Glider Clubs of Southern California (San Diego) was fully developed, and as a result, 12 sailplanes, 6 powered planes, and many pilots combined for a fun time. More than 40 flights were made and many of the regions' best pilots were in attendance, including Bob Bailey, Hawley Bowlus, Gus Briegleb, Harold Huber, Doug Hugill, Volmer Jensen, Paul Mantz, Jack O'Meara, John Robinson, Harvey Stephens, and Don Stevens. Robinson flew the R.S.-1 *Zanonia* on several occasions, but the lift was too weak for thermaling. O'Meara made the only soaring flight of the meet on a very weak thermal.

## *Activities at the Torrey Pines Gliderport*

Plans for a "Torrey Pines Glider Meet" were made in late 1939. By February, 1940, a total of 10 to 12 sailplanes were expected for the meet. Of these sailplanes, at least three two-place sailplanes were expected. The meet was held on March 2nd and 3rd, 1940 at the gliderport. Several glider pilots from Los Angeles had been driving south to Torrey Pines to fly on the weekends and many were looking forward to the meet.

*Above: A collection of Bowlus sailplanes at the 1940 Torrey Pines Glider Meet preparing for launch.*

*Below: At least two sailplanes were forced to land on the beach during a lull in the prevailing westerly wind.*

On March 2nd and 3rd, 1940, a large contingent of eight pilots from Los Angeles arrived for the glider meet, including Hawley Bowlus. John Robinson scored the most points in the duration and altitude contests, with Hal Huber placing second and Woody Brown placing third.

Soaring conditions were poor at best, especially on March 3rd. In order to keep the 2,000 spectators entertained, a minimum of 2 sailplanes were kept aloft at the same time. Many pilots were unable to remain soaring for longer than 20 minutes. Robinson's best flight was for a duration of 2 hours, 30 minutes. He reached an altitude of 200 feet above the cliff. Meet officials included William Van Dusen, Dick Essery, and Jerry Litell.

Major Reuben H. Fleet, who had moved the Consolidated Aircraft Company from New York to San Diego, demonstrated a keen interest in the activities and donated the three first prizes. Highlights of the meet included a flight by Hank Stiglmeier, who soared in a Bowlus Baby Albatross. Scratching for any available lift, Stiglmeier flew back and forth below the edge of the cliff. He was finally forced to duck into a canyon along the cliff face, come up the side, and land in the sagebrush near the top without damaging the sailplane.

A variety of sailplanes could be found at the meet, including Frank Wolcott's Briegleb secondary glider, a two-place Bowlus Baby Albatross, John Robinson's R.S.-1 *Zanonia*, a newly finished two-place sailplane by George Palmer, and a Bowlus Super Albatross. Harvey Stephens and Victor Korski also attended the meet. In February, 1940, Jerry Litell wrote:

> *The thrill of sailing lightly around in the sky, defying nature's law of gravity, not by expenditure of throbbing, roaring power, but by using his own skill and knowledge of the nature of unstable air--balancing its energy with the force of gravity--that thrill is reserved for the soaring pilot alone. That sense of achievement is worth all the hours of work spent constructing and grooming his ship, and the waiting for wind...And where would be that wonderful sense of achievement? Soaring is flying for sport, not for transport. That is primarily the purpose of the airplane. The transition from sailplane to airplane, if desired, is easy and the future transport pilot will have that fundamental understanding of his element which only comes from riding the winds.*

Perhaps one of Littel's greatest contributions to the sport of soaring was made through his pen and the attraction that it gave others to his favorite sport. At the time, Littel was soaring a new sailplane, the *Whitecap*, with help from Steve Kecskes and Harry Comer.

*Woody Brown in the cockpit of the Bowlus Super Albatross at the 1940 Western Soaring Championships.*

## San Diegans at National Contests in 1940

The annual meet at Arvin was held April 13th to April 21st, 1940. On Sunday, April 14th, the event was marred by tragedy when two sailplanes collided on the main ridge. Paul "Sandy" Sanderson had been in the air for just over 30 minutes in one sailplane (identification mark 21741). San Diegan George Palmer had been soaring for about seven minutes in the Yates/Palmer YP-1 sailplane (identification mark 25662). There were only three planes soaring on the ridge at the time. Sanderson and Palmer were soaring in close proximity and were most likely not aware of each other. Their planes collided and fell to the ground, fatally injuring both pilots. It was a shock to all

*Dick Essery (r) and an unknown passenger ready for takeoff in the "Baby Bomber" two-place sailplane.*

of the participants of the meet. Palmer was employed by the Ryan Aeronautical Company and was a pilot of considerable experience. Sanderson was Stress Analysis Engineer at Lockheed and had served as chairman of the Technical Committee of the Southern California Soaring Association. Additionally, he was a former instructor in the University of Michigan Glider Club and had trained in the Navy flight course at Pensacola, Florida.

Oddly that same day, the soaring conditions were spectacular. All but one of the 27 sailplanes at the meet were scattered in all directions high in the sky. San Diegan Ray Parker hooked a group of thermals and landed 28 miles to the northwest at the Kern County Airport just beyond Bakersfield. He soared for four hours on April 15th in cloudy and overcast conditions. Jerry Litell attended the event, but spent much of the time on the ground working on his sailplane to satisfy licensing requirements. Harry Comer and Victor Korski took turns as navigator and co-pilot in Dick Essery's two-place *Baby Bomber* sailplane. Essery and Comer flew to Lebec, 35 miles to the south, and collected $35 for a goal prize. On a different occasion, Essery and Korski flew to McFarland, five miles short of their goal.

*Towing the "Baby Bomber" by car to another winch launch at the 1940 Western Soaring Championships at Arvin, California.*

The greatest distance of the meet was 170 miles, made by Woody Brown in the Bowlus Super Albatross and John Robinson in the R.S.-1 *Zanonia*. Their paired flight was to the east of Arvin, over Bear Mountain, across the Mojave Desert to Twentynine Palms. A storm front helped push them along. During the trip, both pilots got low over a dry lake and searched separately for lift. Each rose once again to 5,000 feet, and resumed their paired flight to Twentynine Palms.

In the end, Brown successfully repeated as meet champion, making many flights in the Bowlus Super Albatross. Robinson came in second, followed by Harland Ross, Henry Stiglmeier, Harold Huber, Dick Essery, Ray Parker, Gus Briegleb, Don Stevens, and Max Archer. Robinson was awarded $25 for the first flight to Gorman, and Essery was the recipient of the Aircraft Owners and Pilots Association Trophy for the design and construction of the *Baby Bomber* two-place sailplane, in combination with his exploration of the difficult Tejon Pass region. The *Baby Bomber* was the sensation of the contest and Essery finished in sixth place, despite the fact that he took a full day out to make private tests on the ship. The sailplane was unusual in that the pilots sat side-by-side in the cockpit. The wings were fashioned essentially from standard Bowlus Baby Albatross wings. Ernie Stout helped Essery design the ship, while both worked at Consolidated Aircraft Corporation in San Diego. In total, over 427 flights were made over the duration of the contest.

Following their performances at the 1940 Arvin meet, San Diego glider pilots turned in commendable performances at the annual Southwestern Soaring Meet in Wichita Falls, Texas. Fifteen pilots entered the meet, accumulating 3,114 miles of soaring flights. Harland Ross flew 143 miles in the Bowlus Super Albatross. Dick Essery soared 107 miles to a landing at Bridgeport, Oklahoma. Flying in the R.S.-1 *Zanonia*, John Robinson flew to 8,200 feet on a flight to Enid, Oklahoma. But, Randy Chapman of Michigan was awarded top honors for distance with a flight of 176 miles on a flight to Aline, Oklahoma. Essery and Vic Korski made a goal flight of 123 miles from Wichita Falls to a landing at Love Field in Dallas, Texas. Their greatest altitude was approximately 3,000 feet, and on several occasions, the ship was within 600 feet of the ground. Brown flew the *Screamin' Weiner*, a sailplane designed and built by the members of the Crown City Glider Club near Pasadena. Woody Brown had an unfortunate ground loop during takeoff, when the wing tip caught on the grass, spinning the sailplane around and cracking a wing spar.

John Robinson was awarded the meet championship (including the *Popular Aviation* Championship Pilot Trophy and *Western Flying* Altitude Trophy), Dick Essery followed in second place, and Harland Ross of Los Angeles came in third. Later, Robinson remembered:

> *...in June of 1940, Wichita Falls, Texas had a contest with wonderful thunderstorm weather on four days of the eight day meet. With cloud bases at 700 to 800 feet above ground level, I was spiralling up to 15,000 feet and running for the next storm at 80 to 100 miles per hour indicated. There were no thermals between the storms. The rest of the pilots were climbing only to cloud base, and then falling short of the next storm, as each was about 30 miles apart. My distances ranged from 121 miles to 170 miles each day. This resulted in a soaring contest score never seen before or since. I ended the contest with twice the points of the second place pilot.*
>
> *Jay Buxton, the 'Grand Old Man of Soaring' of those early days, was contest manager of both the Wichita Falls meet and the Elmira National Soaring Contest. He cornered me after the Wichita Falls contest and told me that I should reconsider my idea of not going to Elmira. He insisted that I should be able to win the National Contest at Elmira, judging from my performance in Texas. Since I couldn't think of a good rebuttal to this 'logic,' I did go...*

At the 11th annual United States Soaring Nationals held at Elmira, New York, John Robinson soared 92 miles to Danville airport, 12 miles southeast of Scranton, Pennsylvania, gaining an altitude of 10,000 feet along the way.

> *When I arrived at Elmira, New York, I had also become proficient at flying in very weak thermals. On weekends, Woody Brown's wife would auto-launch*

*Woody and me over the cliffs at Torrey Pines in two sailplanes. She would go home in a third car, and we would land and de-rig each other. Ridge lift there was good, and we could easily fly all day and longer. During these long flights, I discovered I could break the monotony by circling away from the cliffs in very weak, narrow thermals of 0 to 100 feet per minute. These thermals had developed over the ocean and were convected over the cliffs and inland by the shore breeze, allowing me to soar inland one to two miles. I had learned to locate, sustain and climb in these weak ocean thermals which was very good practice for the Elmira, New York contests.*

On the last Saturday of competition at the 1940 Nationals, using his "instrument soaring techniques," Robinson flew south across Pennsylvania and Maryland. He was so far south that he was no longer on his maps. His final glide to a landing in a field in central Virginia, a total of 290 miles, set a new American distance record for sailplanes. This flight also exceeded Woody Brown's distance record set at the 1939 Wichita Falls contest. A description of the events was captured later in Soaring magazine:

*As the day wore on and all but two pilots had reported in, great tension was felt at headquarters. John Robinson and Robert Stanley were still unreported. Officials, pilots and crew members were busily computing speeds and distances against time and as the hours rolled by, it became more and more apparent that two pilots were either lost or had established new American records. As dusk was settling on Harris Hill, two phone calls came in rapid succession. The first to report was Robert Stanley and passenger, Ernest Schweizer, who had landed at Washington D.C., and distance of 216 miles. This established a new American distance record for 2-place sailplane with passenger. The second call, a few minutes later, was from John Robinson who had landed his 'Zanonia' at Mineral, Virginia, a distance of 290 air miles. Robinson's flight established a new American distance record.*

Robinson was awarded the Edward S. Evans National Championship Trophy, with a total of 2,415 points versus 2,052 for the second-place pilot Chester Decker, who until the last Saturday of the meet, was leading the competition.

Following the National Soaring Contest, Lewin Barringer of Orange, New Jersey, and John Robinson made the first soaring flights in Sun Valley, Idaho. On August 1st, Robinson took off in the afternoon from Hailey, Idaho, and climbed to an altitude of 10,000 feet (almost 16,000 feet above sea level). He headed north, circling over Sun Valley, Idaho, and eventually landed on the Sun Valley golf course after a total flight time of 2 hours and 50 minutes. Two days later on August 3rd, Robinson and Barringer climbed to 10,400 feet for a new United States official altitude record, surpassing Barringer's official mark of 6,535 feet. On August 8th, Robinson teamed up with national downhill ski champion Dick Durrance as a passenger, and set a new

*National Soaring Champion John Robinson with the Zanonia sailplane at Harris Hill, Elmira, New York.*

unofficial two-place United States altitude record of 12,600 feet above his point of takeoff in a Schweizer SGS 2-8 (later designated as TG-2). Unfortunately, although Durrance was able to photograph the altimeter when the record altitude was reached, Robinson carried no barograph onboard. On August 12th, Barringer and passenger Sepp Froelich soared to 13,700 feet above release for a new world's record for two-place sailplanes. Jay Buxton also participated in the flights at Sun Valley, Idaho, flying a Haller Hawk, Jr. sailplane.

Attending the 1940 American Open Soaring Contest in Lockport, Illinois, John Robinson hoped for more exciting soaring flights. On August 29th, Robinson and passenger Bob Blaine managed to make a flight of over 50 miles to Crisman, Indiana, in a Schweizer TG-2. By August 31st, the weather had improved considerably, and Robinson took the day's honors by flying from Lockport to La Porte, Indiana, on an occluded cold front. During the flight, he flew solo for over two hours on instruments alone and soared to 12,700 feet in a two-place Schweizer TG-2. Reports in the *San Diego Union* kept local pilots informed of Robinson's success. Robinson commented:

> *I was fascinated watching the ice grow thicker on the leading edges of the wings and struts. The rudder started to stick in neutral position, and I knew from previous experiences of icing up with my sailplane Zanonia, that the ice was starting to build across the gap between the leading edge of the vertical fin and the counter balance on the rudder itself. If this continued, the rudder would freeze solid, and I would be deprived of the use of this very necessary control surface. Therefore, I began a continual 'fanning' of the rudder keeping it moving all the time and thus preventing its freezing solid.*
>
> *I flew through considerable hail off and on. it was always less than the size of a large pea, and therefore did no harm, although making a terrific noise.*

On Labor Day, Robinson and Miss Dede Pawley flew in a two-place sailplane to Kouts, Indiana, for a distance of 60 miles. For this flight, Robinson was given meet honors for greatest distance flown with a passenger, greatest duration with a passenger, and greatest altitude reached with a passenger. He placed third overall, behind J. Shelly Charles and Stan Corcoran.

## *Activities in San Diego*

At the August, 1940 meeting of the Associated Glider Clubs of Southern California, members discussed the possibility of obtaining a single-place sailplane for solo pilot training. Several pilots had already completed training in the two-seat Grunau 8 sail-

*John Robinson soaring in the R.S.-1 "Zanonia" above the beach at Torrey Pines.*

plane and were eager for solo wings of their own. Harry Comer, Ray Parker, and Josh Wilbur attempted to convince other club members of the necessity for such a sailplane.

Within a month, on August 20th, the club purchased a single-place Bowlus Baby Albatross as their second club ship. Ernie Stout, Scott Royce, and Jerry Littell were responsible for obtaining the ship. This was not just any Baby Albatross, rather it was the *Thunder Bird*, the same ship used, built, and flown by Woody Brown to his United States distance record flight at the 1939 Southwestern Soaring Championships at Wichita Falls, Texas. The *Thunder Bird* had finally returned to roost in San Diego.

The members of the Associated Glider Clubs of Southern California built a clubhouse at the Torrey Pines Gliderport to store glider-related equipment. Paint brush in hand, Comer single-handedly painted the "hangar/clubhouse" green. Following a complete overhaul of the Grunau 8 by Woody Brown, Harry Comer, Ray and Harry

Parker, the sailplane was painted red and cream by Vic Korski, Ray Robin, Harry Comer, and Ray Parker. Brown upholstered the front and rear cockpit with green leatherette and trim. Dick Essery was flying virtually every weekend at Torrey Pines with his *Baby Bomber*, making approximately 10 passenger flights of about 20 minutes each in an attempt to introduce newcomers into soaring.

On August 28th, 1940, Tom Hammond, Jr. launched a rubber-band-powered free-flight model airplane into the sky near Point Loma High School. Surprisingly, the plane climbed to a height of approximately 1,000 feet and crossed out over San Diego Bay. Officials at the North Island Naval Air Station watched in amazement as the model circled at an altitude of 300 feet or higher for over 1 hour, in what appears to have been thermal lift. The circles continued one after the next, directly over the airport, suspending flight activities at the Naval Air Station. Finally, the model made a graceful three-point landing directly in the center of the facility, ending the flight that reportedly lasted more than two hours. The plane was recovered by a tractor operator, S. M. Prodanovich, and officials at the Naval base found Hammond's name on the aircraft following inspection. The model had a wingspan of 40 inches, a length of 32 inches, and was constructed of balsa and wax paper. The following morning, a lead article in the *San Diego Union* suggested that naval officers suspected that the model plane was flown skillfully by radio control, a rumor that was never confirmed nor denied.

Members of the Associated Glider Clubs of Southern California honored National Soaring Champion John Robinson with a dinner on October 11th, 1940. Robinson gave a brief account of his championships at both the Southwestern and National soaring meets. Ernie Stout spoke of the growing interest in gliding and soaring across the United States. Ray Parker had already test flown the *Thunder Bird* and Scott Royce gave an account of the test flights and the ship in general.

# *CHAPTER 5*

# *1941-1945*
# *The War Years*

## *United States Army Camp Callan*

The original lease, signed on December 31st, 1937 by the City of San Diego and the Associated Glider Clubs of Southern California for 20 acres of land in Pueblo Lot 1324, was set to expire on December 31st, 1942. At the request of the City Attorney on October 23rd, 1940, the Associated Glider Clubs of Southern California surrendered and terminated the lease. The United States Government had requested the land from the City of San Diego for the purposes of building a United States Army training center. America was becoming more involved in World War II and the empty lands north of La Jolla provided the military with ample room to practice.

Members of the Associated Glider Clubs of Southern California gave up their flying site so that America could become better prepared for war. Club Secretary Edward F. True signed the paperwork certifying the transfer on behalf of the club Board of Directors. A unanimous vote by the City Council on December 10th, 1940, passed an adopted resolution 72901, officially giving the land to the United States Government in the interests of national defense. By the end of October, it was disclosed that a United States Army training camp would be built on the Torrey Pines land, with 7,500 draftees instructed in modern warfare.

Antiaircraft Replacement Training Center Camp Callan was officially first cleared for construction late in 1940, and received its first soldiers in the latter part of February, 1941. Camp Callan was named in deference to the memory of Major General Robert A. Callan (1874-1936), a veteran of 2 wars with 40 years of continuous service. Callan was a graduate of the United States Military Academy at West Point in 1892, and was involved in the Spanish-American War and World War I. During the last months of World War I, he commanded the 33rd Artillery Brigade and the Orga-

*Above: Soldiers training on the obstacle course at U.S. Army Camp Callan. An obstacle course was situated at the far east end of the east-west glider runway at the Torrey Pines Gliderport.*

*Right: The famous Oozlefinch, the mascot of the Coast Artillery Corps.*

nization and Training Center for Tractor Artillery, with authority over approximately 12,000 officers and enlisted men.

During the first year of Camp Callan's history, approximately 40,000 troops past through its gates. Training included courses in handling gunnery equipment, such as rifles, bayonets, anti-aircraft and machine guns. Troops were conditioned on a variety of obstacle courses, hazards, and hikes. In its first year of operation, Camp Callan was known as a Coast Artillery replacement training center, with batteries assigned to both anti-aircraft, and seacoast artillery training missions. With the established gun firing positions, one purpose of the camp was to teach trainees how to fire long-range weaponry in the event that the Japanese fleet tried to attack the West Coast. Due to the damage inflicted on Great Britain by the Luftwaffe in the spring of 1942, Camp Callan's training program was altered to place full emphasis on the anti-aircraft weaponry. Ranges existed for training with hand-held guns to 155mm howitzers. Camp Callan was also featured in a *National Geographic* article on the military build up in San Diego which included photos of the large guns.

Not only did Camp Callan have training facilities, but it also had a large outdoor parade ground, two motion picture theatres, an outdoor theatre (with a 5,000 person capacity), three chapels, and a service club where the Camp Callan Swing Band would play for dances. Although the training was rigorous, there was a chance for occasional rest and relaxation.

During this turbulent time in world history, the Torrey Pines Gliderport and surrounding terrain was transformed rapidly into an anti-aircraft training facility. Out of this transformation came the "Oozlefinch," the mascot of the Coast Artillery Corps. The Oozlefinch was the subject of legend. Reportedly, it flew backwards in order to keep the dust out of its eyes. Swiftly, the Oozlefinch became the "guardian angel of the men who fire the big guns." The origin of the bird is mysterious. The first description was credited to Captain H. M. Merriam, who, while stationed at Ft. Monroe, Virginia, made references to a bird and its "oddly logical habit" of flying backwards to avoid dust in his eyes. Without knowing it at the time, the Oozlefinch was a perfect ironic description for the way local glider pilots felt about not being able to soar on the updrafts at Torrey Pines during the war. Civilian aircraft were banned from flying within 15 miles of the coastline, and the war forced a hiatus to the majority of local gliding activity.

## *Local Soaring Clubs*

In April, 1941, members of the Consair Soaring Club ("Consair" was the acronym for the union of the Convair and Consolidator Aircraft Companies) purchased its first ship, a Haller Hawk sailplane under the guidance of Jim Spurgeon. The "first group" of soaring pilots consisted of Mr. Crouch, Mr. Hanscom, Mr. Harrington, Mr. Holman, Mr. James, Mr. Redwine, Mr. Scott, Mr. Todd, the Korn brothers, Wally Wiberg, and Jim Spurgeon. By December, 1941, so many employees were interested in the soaring club that "Associate Membership" was offered instead of full membership. Club membership was limited due to insufficient resources, training ability, and locations to soar. Employees at the Ryan Aeronautical Company also started a Ryan Glider Club. Wade Stienruck, Pete Girard, as well as several others, were involved in the club.

## *San Diegans at National Competitions in 1941*

At the annual Western Soaring Championships at Arvin, Dick Essery was awarded the meet championship after some tremendous flights with the *Baby Bomber.* He flew the greatest total distance (417 miles) and established a new record for goal and return of 42 miles. He took home two trophies as well as cash awards. Nearing the last day of the meet, Essery and Howard Morrison of San Fernando were deadlocked for first place. Morrison finished second, flying a Bowlus Baby Albatross, Harold Huber of San Fernando was third, flying the Bowlus Super Albatross, and Henry Stiglmeier placed fourth with a Bowlus Baby Albatross. San Diegan Ray Parker placed fifth overall.

Neither Woody Brown (previous Arvin champion) nor John Robinson (national champion) were on hand to defend their honors. Richard Johnson had quite a flight in his Bowlus Baby Albatross flying over the mountains near Grapevine and Lebec, to a landing near Saugus, a distance of 65 miles. The American goal and return distance records were broken both for single and two-place sailplanes. Morrison flew from Arvin to Maricopa, and returned in a Bowlus Baby Albatross, a distance of 42 miles. Essery soared in the *Baby Bomber* with a passenger over nearly the same route to establish the record for two-place sailplanes. Stiglmeier made a remarkable flight by soaring into a thunderhead with his Bowlus Baby Albatross, reaching an estimated altitude of more than 20,000 feet over the point of takeoff. Unfortunately, Stiglmeier's barograph needle had been set too low and the needle ran off the chart at 16,800 feet, rendering the flight unofficial.

> *Although Stiglmeier opened his spoilers to hold down the rate of climb, he found the rate of climb showing 30 feet per second up. Soon all of his instruments except the turn and bank indicator iced up and about half an inch of ice formed on the leading edges of the wings and struts. His controls froze in the spiral condition and ice formed on his cockpit enclosure. As he had no oxygen equipment and was not warmly dressed he suffered from both cold and altitude. Flying by feel, ear, and with the help of his turn and bank, which continued to function, Stiglmeier managed to spiral back down through the storm and make a safe landing, the ice having been dissipated when he dropped below the 15,000 foot level.*

*Dick Essery (r) and an unknown passenger in the "Baby Bomber." Essery was awarded the 1941 Western Soaring Championship.*

At the National Soaring Contest, pilots gathered at Elmira, New York once again, despite the war efforts. John Robinson recollected:

*Early soaring contests were mostly friendly get-togethers for soaring fun and cross-country attempts by entrants. A few of the pilots had flown beyond 20 miles from the home field. Some pilots only flew in the summer time, mostly at a contest, while some of us flew every weekend, which allowed us to feel very much at home in the cockpit. At this time, there were no glider classifications. Each competition was an open class contest, with only one champion at each Regional contest, and only one National Champion.*

*Rules and regulations were composed by the 'contest committee' at each contest site each year. In 1939 and 1940, I had to memorize four and five different sets of rules and remember the differences. One had to be a 'Philadelphia Lawyer' to be successful. Points were awarded each day for distance, altitude and duration. Speed replaced the latter criteria in the 1941 Nationals, when the committee realized it took more pilot skill to fly 200 miles in five hours, than it did to do it in six hours! The pilots who chose to showboat for the spectators by sitting on the ridge at Harris Hill had been getting 'duration' points, but in my mind this was not really a valid test for choosing a National Soaring Champion. Soon, bonus points were awarded for goal, goal and return, and flying two-place ships. Goal points were a variable which became important when the pilots arrived at this goal with 5,000 to 8,000 feel above ground level, and enough daylight to glide more miles than the 'goal points' would compute.*

*Goal and return flights were used very little, because of the necessity of sending an observer ahead to the turnpoint for visual identification. The pilot who had to fly low enough for a visual identification was often faced with climbing back up again. Photographic proof of turnpoints came many years later.*

*Air to ground radio communication was not used. A telephone retrieve system was utilized for outlanding. The downed pilot would usually walk to a farm house which might or might not have a telephone. If not, a drive into town was necessary to phone the contest headquarters and leave directions for the retrieve.*

Following his flights in the R.S.-1 *Zanonia*, Robinson was awarded the Edward S. Evans Trophy for the national championship for the second consecutive year. At the closing banquet, Major General Henry H. Arnold, Chief of the Army Air Forces spoke on the importance of gliders in the war. He declared:

*We must know how to use them and learn to train others to use them...we in the Army air forces have never denied, never have failed to appreciate the military possibilities of the glider. Because of our geographical situation we have made power-driven airplanes our first consideration, with particular reference to the long-range, heavy bomber this is made mandatory by our policy of hemispheric defense. That does not mean that our plans contemplated ignoring the glider. Far from it.*

It was a "call to arms" for the participants of the National Soaring Contest, and many pitched in to aid the military in glider design, manufacture, and with the training of glider pilots.

## *Glider Schools*

In 1941, John Robinson started a glider school at Elmira, in conjunction with the Elmira Area Soaring Corporation (the forerunner to the Harris Hill Soaring Corporation). During the summer, he started the first military glider training school in the United States at Elmira. In October, when bad weather and snow threatened to close the training facility for the winter, he and other instructors were transferred to Twentynine Palms, California, where the glider training continued.

In November of 1941, the United States Army made plans to open a glider school at Twentynine Palms, 50 miles northeast of Palm Springs. The "Twenty-Nine Palms Air Academy" was the second of its type in the United States. Classes began on January 5th, 1942, and the first class graduated during the latter part of February. The Air Forces soon discovered that the average pilot could learn gliding in four weeks (30 hours of flying time). Shortly thereafter, admission was opened to any Army officer or enlisted man aged 18 to 32 (later changed to 35) with some amount of previous interest or understanding of aviation. During the spring of 1942, Wilmott Ragsdale, a columnist for *Time* magazine, stopped by the glider school and took a ride.

*Time's Wilmott Ragsdale wasn't sure you could do a loop in an Army glider until he went up in one at the new glider school at Twentynine Palms, California--suddenly felt his safety belt tighten and saw the desert above him.*

*He wasn't sure how you get down, either--until his pilot banked the wings almost vertical, fell off into swooping circles and came out at 90 m.p.h., 400 feet above the ground.*

For the first class of glider students, launches were made by auto tow, auto-pulley tow, winch, and aerotow. Later in the program, aerotow became the primary means of launch, using either a single, double, or even triple tow of sailplanes behind a single towplane. Frankfort TG-1 and Schweizer TG-2 sailplanes were used. Glider enthusiasts who worked at the Twentynine Palms school included John Robinson, Ray Parker, Larry Creighton, Paul Fletcher, Dave Stacey, Harvey Stephens, Wally Neugent, Bud Kimball, Howard Morrison, Frank Wolcott, Lyle Maxey, Ed Laine, Chuck Cohls, Warren Merboth, Don Sanford, John Novak, Volmer Jensen, R. E. Franklin, and Dick Johnson. Twenty-two students and glider pilots associated with the Twentynine Palms glider school attained their "C" certificate during 1942. Another 19 students and glider pilots attained their "C" certificates in 1943. The school closed that year. Several students, including Carl Gwartney, later piloted glider-led invasions at Normandy and in the Netherlands.

While instructing at the Twentynine Palms Glider School, Richard Johnson made an attempt for his Golden "C" altitude requirement in his Bowlus Baby Albatross. On June 12th, 1942, Warren Merboth, Bill Tracy, Paul Fletcher and Richard Johnson drove to Deadman Dry Lake and set up the Baby Albatross. Following launch, Johnson was carried to a cloud base at 12,000 feet; he entered the cloud and continued higher into the sky. At 14,700 feet, the lift died out and Johnson went searching for another cloud with the hope of perhaps setting a new altitude record over 17,474 feet. But at such high altitudes, ice soon began forming on the leading edge of the wings and also began to clog sensors for his instruments. Airspeed began to increase as the sailplane went into a left spiral dive; Johnson was unable to properly orient the sailplane due to the faulty instrument readings. After diving back through the cloud base, Johnson escaped via parachute just prior to the collapse of the sailplane. From the ground Bill Tracy recalled:

> *We had long since given up trying to keep our eyes on Dick (a sailplane at 12,000 feet is a small article) and were loafing on the roof of the flight shack. The three of us were suddenly startled by a noise that sounded very much like thunder but was considerably louder than average thunder. It seemed to come from a large cumulus almost directly above the field. Warren yelled, 'It's busted up on him.' We saw the ship in a steep spiral dive with one wing off, then the other wing disappeared and we saw the chute open. To put it moderately, this was quite a spectacle. One wing floated down lazily, the wingless pod screamed down like a bomb, and there was fabric and plywood in the air for the following twenty minutes.*

Dick Johnson was later found walking across the desert back to Deadman Dry Lake and was picked up by car soon thereafter.

## *H. Grafton Chapman*

By late October of 1942, Capt. H. Grafton Chapman (financier of Elmore E. Shoudy's glider in 1928, and developer of the hydro-primary glider school near Coronado in 1930) was called to active duty and assigned to the United States Army Air Corps. Prior to this time, Chapman had served for many years in the cavalry reserve and fought in World War I with the Canadian, British, and American expeditionary forces. In November, 1914, he enlisted as a private in the 21st battery, sixth brigade of the second Canadian division, and later was commissioned in the British army and assigned to trench mortar battery No. Y-1, which saw extended service on the battlefront between Ypres and Loos in what is now Belgium. When the United States entered the war, Chapman resigned his commission with the British, returned to America, and became an instructor in bombing, hand grenades, and trench mortars. Following his move to the San Diego area after World War I, he was a member of the American Legion and commander of San Diego Post 6 in 1932. Before his call to duty for World War II, he was on the police force at the Rohr Aircraft Corporation.

## *Robinson Soars Over Mount Whitney*

Following the closing of the Twentynine Palms Glider School in 1943, Robinson soon turned his attention back to soaring in the R.S.-1 *Zanonia*. At 2:45 p.m. on September 4th, 1943, Robinson was towed to approximately 1,000 feet at the airport near Bishop, California by auto tow with 2,500 feet of wire with a predetermined goal of Lone Pine. Soon, Robinson was climbing between three and five feet per second in a rising thermal. This carried him to an altitude of 7,000 feet (2,000 feet above release altitude). Another thermal presented itself and carried him to 8,000 feet. He soon topped Black Mountain at 9,075 feet and it was not long before the altimeter read 15,000 feet in yet another thermal. Reaching behind his head with his left hand, Robinson moved a lever to turn on his barograph, which he realized had not been turned on prior to takeoff. All of this was done while continuing to circle in a thermal.

He continued south down the valley, cruising between 15,000 and 18,000 feet. His highest altitude recorded was 19,200 feet.

> *While revelling in this wonderful type of soaring, I was also admiring the beautiful scenery from this high vantage point. The trackless deserts form an interesting contrast with the mountains which are heavily forested in some spots and barren in others. To the west beyond the Owens Valley was the High Sierra Nevada Mountain Range with its white snow fields and blue lakes. Over these several large thunder storms were building up and dumping their loads of rain on the western slopes.*

Arriving at Lone Pine with plenty of altitude to spare, Robinson decided to make a journey towards Mount Whitney.

*Desiring a closer view, I glided down past the highest-peaks into the steep canyons where snow banks and jagged pinnacles of rock reached out within 100 feet of my wingtip. Exploring several canyons in this manner, I passed over many small crystal-clear lakes in which the sunken logs were plainly visible.*

Robinson's landing at Lone Pine came at 6:10 p.m., three hours after his takeoff 56 miles away. Robinson made a flight to 18,000 feet the following day, on a route to the north over the White Mountains.

# *CHAPTER 6*

# *1946-1950*
# *Post War Soaring*

## *Interest in Gliding Stirs Again*

Activities of the Associated Glider Clubs of Southern California were paralyzed during the war effort, due to the United States Navy order prohibiting civilian aircraft flights within 150 miles of the Pacific coastline. With the end of the war, surplus United States Army sailplanes became available in government surplus sales, and this provided the necessary spark to rekindle interest in local motorless aviation.

At least four surplus sailplanes were purchased by San Diegans before March of 1946. Ray Parker became President of the Associated Glider Clubs of Southern California and others, including Robert "Bob" Fronius, Steve and Henrietta Kecskes, and Wallace "Wally" and June Wiberg, helped establish San Diego as a superior soaring location.

In late February, 1946, an informal glider meet was held between local Southern Californian clubs at the former Twentynine Palms Glider School. San Diegans Mr. and Mrs. David Boone, Mr. and Mrs. Max Breitenbach, Steve and Henrietta Kecskes, and former San Diegan John Robinson all shared honors at the meet. Robinson had the longest flight of the meet with a flight of 4 hours, 8 minutes in the *Zanonia.*

On March 15, 1946, Bob Fronius and Wally Wiberg attempted to set a new record for a two-place sailplane endurance over the cliffs at Torrey Pines. The standing record was set at 9 hours, 12 minutes. Takeoff occurred by auto tow at 6:06 a.m. from the gliderport. They landed 8 hours, 37 minutes later on the beach below Camp Callan after the wind died. Wally Wiberg was quoted as saying:

> *The storm which was forecast to bring winds of 45 miles an hour simply did not materialize. We would not have been able to stay up as long as we did*

*over any other area I know of. All we proved was that Torrey Pines is one of the world's best spots to fly sailplanes.*

It was estimated that the pair flew 430 miles during their nearly nine-hour flight back and forth on the cliffs between the Scripps Institution of Oceanography and Del Mar in a Laister-Kauffman LK-10. On a separate occasion, Wiberg's LK-10A two-place sailplane was aerotowed behind a war surplus Stearman biplane from Bill Gibbs' Airport (now known as Montgomery Field). With Wiberg and Fronius inside, the sailplane released over the cliffs at Torrey Pines for some soaring. After soaring on the cliffs in the prevailing westerly seabreeze, Fronius suggested that they fly south to Mount Soledad to continue soaring in that area. *En route* to Mount Soledad, the lift became less apparent, and they turned west over La Jolla, coming low over the La Jolla Country Club. Turning once again to the northeast, they continued out over the flats at the La Jolla Beach and Tennis Club and La Jolla Shores but were too low to gain substantial lift from the north side of Mount Soledad. They headed to the northeast where they made a landing on a ridge southeast of the Scripps Institution of Oceanography.

The towplane soon returned on schedule to pick up the sailplane, but the tow pilot reasoned that the landing area was so small that the sailplane must be damaged in some way. He returned to the airport to come back with the sailplane trailer behind his car.

On the ridge, Fronius and Wiberg decided to relaunch the undamaged sailplane. The LK-10 was pointed into the wind. The slope below the sailplane was at about 45° down directly into the wind. Wiberg jumped in the front seat and Fronius pushed on the tail. Two boys who happened to be in the area were enlisted to help keep the wingtips level. After a short roll down the hill, the sailplane hit a bump and bounced into the air with sufficient airspeed for flight. It was the first sailplane hand launch of its kind. Soon thereafter, Wiberg gained enough altitude to continue north over the Scripps Institute of Oceanography to the main section of the cliffs. He continued soaring until dusk, making a landing on the top of the cliffs, avoiding the United States Army obstacles at Camp Callan along the way. Fronius was forced to walk to towards Camp Callan and hitched a ride in a car along the way.

Members of the Associated Glider Clubs of Southern California went to the San Diego City Council in an effort to once again lease the Torrey Pines Gliderport property. On June 25, 1946, Ordinance No. 3209 authorized the glider club to lease the property for $100 per year for a period of five years, ending on June 30th, 1951. The lease was officially entered into on July 27th, 1946, formally reestablishing soaring at the Torrey Pines Gliderport.

Following a takeoff from the Sweetwater Airport by winch launch on September 28th, 1946, Henrietta Kecskes became the first woman member of the newly resurrected Associated Glider Clubs of Southern California to solo. She was believed to be the first woman to solo in a glider in San Diego since mid-1930. That same day, Steve Kecskes attained a commercial glider license. Henrietta Kecskes was soon elected president of the Associated Glider Clubs of Southern California, with Harry Parker as vice president, George Underhill as secretary, and David Boone as treasurer.

## *San Diegans at National Competitions in 1946*

Eager to bring a soaring contest back to the region, the Southern California Soaring Association hosted the Fifth Western Soaring Championship on July 13th to the 26th, 1946. United States Navy gave permission to hold the contest at Condor Field near Twentynine Palms, California. Condor Field was used by the United States Army for glider training, and was turned over to the United States Navy following the end of World War II. Permission was also granted for the use of one of the military hangars, which provided some necessary shade for both pilots and planes in the summer heat.

John Robinson, who had relocated to Altadena, California, was the meet champion in the R.S.-1 *Zanonia*. Ray Parker of San Diego took second place and made the longest flight of the meet by flying 207 miles to Wickenburg, Arizona. For this distance flight, Ray Parker made the only Golden "C" of the meet, the sixth awarded in the United States. Merchandise prices and monetary awards were handed out at a special banquet on July 29th at Scully's Cafe in Leimert Park.

The thirteenth annual National Soaring Contest was held at Elmira, New York, from August 3rd to 18th. Following the war, many military surplus gliders showed up at the Nationals. John Robinson and Ray Parker came from Southern California to attend the meet, soaring in the R.S.-1 *Zanonia* and the *Screamin' Weiner*, respectively. By the end of the contest, Robinson retained his National Soaring Championship, and was given the Edward S. Evans Trophy on a permanent basis for his three consecutive championships. Ray Parker placed sixth in the *Screamin' Weiner*.

## *First Annual Pacific Coast Midwinter Championships*

Members of the Associated Glider Clubs of Southern California worked hard to plan a soaring meet akin to the type that was held at Torrey Pines prior to World War II. It was hoped such a meet would stimulate enthusiasm in gliding and result in some members.

As a prelude to the "First Annual Pacific Coast Midwinter Championships," Harry Parker and David Boone made several flights for the press on January 11th, 1947, using a United States Army surplus winch for launch. Parker was first to take to the air in a Frankfort TG-1. Boone followed with a quick flight over the cliffs and returned for a landing. The weather conditions were less than favorable for soaring,

*John Robinson and the "Zanonia" in 1946 at Elmira, New York following a third consecutive National Soaring Championship.*

but it gave everyone a "dress rehearsal" for the main event, which was scheduled for February 1st. Invitations were sent to pilots in 11 states.

Two 2,000-foot runways were "cleared" in roughly the same positions as in the years preceding the war. Instead of using the flat gliderport as a parade ground, the United States Army installed an obstacle course, complete with water barriers, two-foot culverts, earthen trenches, etc. With a good amount of effort, the runways were flattened once again and the contest site was prepared.

Henrietta Kecskes and James M. Fitzhugh of the San Diego Junior Chamber of Commerce were placed in charge of the meet. Fitzhugh was a member of both the Associated Glider Clubs of Southern California and the San Diego Junior Chamber of Commerce and was a necessary sparkplug for the success of the event. Trophies and cash awards were contributed by local aircraft companies, including the John J. Montgomery Memorial Championship trophy which was to be awarded to the meet champion. The 23 members of the Associated Glider Clubs of Southern California were ready to assist with the competition. The public was invited to attend for free. An estimated 8,000 people watched the weekend activities. According to Herman Stiglmeier:

> *In 1947, I had lots of surplus gliders, an aftermath of the previous war years. Because duration, altitude, spot landing, and distance counted in winning, I selected a Bowlus Baby Albatross glider for the competition. My chief rival at this meet was Gus Briegleb, flying a BG-7. Airplane tow was available only for exhibition flying. This meant that all competition flights started from the release point of the winch tow. To win in the distance event, I needed to get 400-500 feet altitude off the winch and to fly north or south as far as I could. On my last tow, five minutes before closing time, I was successful in getting enough altitude and headed south towards La Jolla, I landed on the farthest possible piece of sand at the southern end of La Jolla Beach. And so this anxious competitor won the first John J. Montogmery Memorial Trophy.*

By June, 1947, Mrs. Max J. Breitenbach joined Henrietta Kecskes as the second woman in the Associated Glider Clubs of Southern California to make a solo glider flight.

After his 17th dual glider flight with instruction, student member Bill Ivans took his first solo glider flight in a Schweizer TG-2 at Torrey Pines on September 6th, 1947. By October 5th, Ivans had made 50 solo flights and commemorated the occasion with a solo flight at Torrey Pines in a Schweizer TG-2. As was the case with others that had preceded him, his instruction and training at Torrey Pines was an instrumental first step toward a long and exciting life in soaring.

## *San Diegans at National Competitions in 1947*

Over Memorial Day weekend, 1947, 26 pilots gathered at Elmira, New York for a three-day soaring meet. More than 100 hours of soaring were completed by the competitors. John Robinson in the R.S.-1 *Zanonia* took first place in altitude, with a flight to 8,200 feet, and accumulated duration, soaring for a total of 15 hours and 31 minutes. On one flight, he stayed aloft 8 hours, 5 minutes, reaching 7,000 feet. The following day, he flew for 7 hours and 26 minutes to attain an altitude of 8,200 feet.

From June 14th to 21st, the Annual Western Championships were held at Bishop, California. Reports of conditions aloft were provided by Robert Symons and Herman Stiglmeier, who both had radios in their sailplanes. Harland Ross made reconnaissance flights in the Bishop Flying Service's Cessna 140 with reports to the pilots on the ground. On June 16th, Ross investigated some lenticular clouds to the east of the Sierras. At 10,000 feet, he encountered a wave, and soon reached 19,600 feet (5,000 feet above the service ceiling for the Cessna 140). This occurred with a passenger on board, a full tank of gas, and three barographs on board to record the happenings.

On the first day of the meet, Symons exceeded the American record for goal and return distance by soaring from Bishop to Lone Pine and back, a distance of 112 miles. On the same day, Symons, Ross, Herman Stiglmeier, and Myron Wells made flights in excess of 10,000 feet, securing the requirements for their Golden 'C" awards. Over the following days, Wells and Ross had flights over five hours in duration, satisfying their duration requirements for the Golden "C". Robert Symons released from tow near Black Mountain and reached Las Vegas (a distance of 192 miles) nearly six hours later on a goal flight, completing the requirements for his Golden "C".

The Western Glider Champion was selected as the pilot holding the highest number of first place awards amassed in western contests held during 1947. These contests included the Torrey Pines meet held in February, the Twentynine Palms Soaring Contest held March 22nd and 23rd, the El Mirage Soaring Festival held on May 30th through June 1st, and the Sixth Annual Western Soaring Championship held at Bishop. Although not all of the local pilots flew in all of these meets, it was believed by members of the Southern California Soaring Association and the Associated Glider Clubs of Southern California that Ray Parker should be awarded the title of Western Glider Champion of 1947 by winning five events out of two contests entered.

The first year that the National Soaring Contest moved to location away from Elmira, New York was 1947. This gave much pleasure to pilots on the West Coast, who were no longer required on an annual basis to make a transcontinental drive with their glider in tow to compete in the National Soaring Contest. On July 4th, when the competition began at Wichita Falls, Texas, 54 sailplanes, piloted by 60 pilots, were on hand. Hawley Bowlus was one of the officials at the meet.

By the last day of the contest, Paul MacCready, Ray Parker, John Robinson, Don Pollard, and Dick Comey were all close in terms of total points. Robinson recalled:

*Ray Parker in the cockpit of the "Rigid Midget" sailplane. After a start in the Associated Glider Clubs of Southern California, Ray became well-known at many soaring contests.*

*Anything can happen at a National Soaring Contest--even on the last day. That I learned on July 19th, 1947, the last day of cross-country competition at the Fourteenth National, Wichita Falls, Texas.*

*The weather was clear; there was a light north-northeast wind and the sun beamed down warmly upon the Texas countryside. Already many sailplanes were circling in thermals in the vicinity of the contest site.*

*It was 11:33 a.m. when the Stearman PT-17 towed me aloft in Zanonia, my small single-place high performance sailplane. Releasing the towline 2,000 feet over the airport, I joined a group of sailplanes circling in a thermal. Round and round, up and up we went, like a flock of buzzards, each one trying to outdo the other.*

*Presently the rate-of-climb slowed, and I glided down to the west to join Ray Parker in the Rigid Midget and Paul MacCready in the Screamin' Wiener, who were circling in another thermal slightly below. Their thermal wasn't producing much climb, and soon we scattered in search of greener air. Since my pre-announced goal was Big Spring, Texas, more than 200 miles away, my course lay to the southwest.*

*I had dropped back down to tow-release altitude before another thermal indicated itself on the variometer. As I turned to spiral, a sailplane piloted by one of the French contestants came into view below. He stayed with me dur-*

*Robinson and crew preparing the "Zanonia" for a flight during the 1947 Soaring Nationals at Wichita Falls, Texas.*

*ing several thermals, dropping a bit farther behind in each until he disappeared. That was shortly after noon. From then on I was alone in the Lone Star state.*

Following highways, one after the other, Robinson reached cloudbase at 10,000 feet and glided as fast as he could across the sky. He reached Colorado City by 5 p.m. and, at 5:40 p.m., he was soaring over his preannounced goal of Big Spring, Texas, 210 miles from Wichita Falls, at an altitude of 5,500 feet. Deciding to press on rather than land and achieve his goal flight, he hooked a tremendous thermal just west of Big Spring, taking him to 11,000 feet.

*...the fact that it was after 6 p.m. made it imperative to stretch the glide as far as possible. I would be able to pass Midland, but sadly enough, the Dallas section of my aeronautical chart ended there. I had an Austin section, a Roswell section, and Albuquerque section, and an Oklahoma City section, but my course lay into the El Paso section which I did not have. However, I was carrying a Texas road map, and the course was now over highway 80, so it seemed logical to continue.*

While circling in a thermal just before Midland, Robinson observed a column of smoke on the horizon directly ahead. The column was coming from a carbon plant near Penwell, 15 miles southwest of Odessa. Soaring in the smoke cloud, Robinson continued up to 8,000 feet at 7:05 p.m. Continuing on, he saw yet another smoke cloud on the horizon, and circled again in the smoke until 7:57 p.m,. at which time it was nearly dark on the ground below.

*Mileage suddenly assumed an urgent importance. A check of distance back to Wichita Falls showed it to be over 300 miles. The single-place Official American Distance Record was 290 miles. 'Zanonia' and I had set the record in 1940. maybe we could break it again. Another pressure point was the fact that the French competition had made the best distance so far during the contest (310 miles). There was no alternative. The glide had to be continued until a landing was absolutely necessary.*

*At 2900 feet on the altimeter, the highway was less than 200 feet below. Soon the tops of the telephone poles began whizzing by the wing tips. Then I was looking up at the telephone poles, but gliding on!*

*The terrain seemed to be slightly downhill. Suddenly, as I made contact with the pavement, a building loomed into view in the semi-darkness. With a controlled landing run, turned off the pavement onto the gravel to stop directly in front of the C & B Cafe and Service Station just three miles short of Barstow, Texas at 8:10 p.m. A dog began to bark, and Mr. and Mrs. C. W. Swafford, owners of the cafe, came out to investigate the apparition. Requesting*

*Paul MacCready at the "Screamin' Wiener" at the start of his world goal and return single-place record flight of 230 miles at the 1947 National Soaring Contest.*

*use of their telephone, I explained that I was a contestant in the glider contest at Wichita Falls, over 320 miles away. Mrs. Swafford was very congenial and knew quite a bit about the contest. 'By the way,' she said, 'have they raffled off that Ford yet? I have a ticket on it!' It could only happen in Texas!*

For this flight of 333 miles as measured on a map, Robinson set a new official American distance record of 325 miles, using the radius of the earth's surface as a means of computing the distance. His was the first American soaring flight to exceed 500 kilometers (310.7 miles). For his flight, he received the Governor's Trophy, a wrist watch from Zales Jewelers, two $5.00 steak dinners, and one $15.00 Stetson hat from Bill Warren's Village Inn. Even Robinson's crew chief, John Olley, won the Douglas Trophy, a model of a Douglas DC-6, for being the most efficient crew chief as judged by the Field Operations staff.

MacCready finished second in the *Screamin' Wiener*, setting a world goal and return single-place record of 230 miles. This flight exceeded the world record of 212 miles held by the Soviet Union. The day before his record-setting flight, MacCready took off at 11:15 a.m. with a goal and return flight to Buzz Field near Roaring Springs. Although the thermals were small and turbulent, the *Screamin' Wiener* was particularly suited to tight circling in narrow lift.

*By 3 o'clock Buzz Field appeared but the thermal in the locality seemed to be dying, the clouds dissipating, and my altitude decreasing. At 1000 feet altitude and two miles from the field I noticed a hawk doing very well nearby. Any thermal a hawk can soar in is a thermal that a sailplane can generally soar in better, so I borrowed the bird's thermal and soon outclimbed my feathered variometer. At 2000 feet I swooped over the field, circled, and saw my trailer below and a plane taking off to identify me.*

*I tossed out the two rolls of toilet paper I carry on goal and return flights for identification, and they unraveled in the sky. My ground crew had told the observers that this was going to happen, and it definitely identified me since I was the only one to toss out two rolls of toilet paper over Buzz Field on July 15, 1947. Spectators always had quizzical looks on their faces when I loaded up with the paper before takeoff--they wondered how complete a sailplane the 'Wiener' could be.*

The larger afternoon thermals and cumulus clouds carried MacCready home at altitudes of 11,000 feet. The following day, MacCready set out on what would become his world record. His declared goal of Anson, Texas was to the southwest of Wichita Falls. At 3:45 p.m., MacCready was over Anson Airport, dropping two more rolls of toilet paper out the side of the *Wiener.* Directly over the field, he caught a thermal to 8,000 feet and continued back to Sheppard Field, his point of departure. The flight took a total of 6 hours and 25 minutes.

At the end of the contest, Ray Parker was third in the *Rigid Midget*, and Robinson placed fourth in the *Zanonia*. With his Schweizer 1-21, Dick Comey took the meet Championship, with two flights over 10,000 feet, three flights between 200 and 300 miles, and one flight exceeding 300 miles.

## *The Second Annual Pacific Coast Midwinter Championships*

The Associated Glider Clubs of Southern California once again cosponsored the Second Annual Pacific Coast Midwinter Championships with the San Diego Junior Chamber of Commerce at Torrey Pines on February 28th and 29th, 1948. Entrants included Paul MacCready with his Polish *Orilk* sailplane. MacCready received a lot of press because of his recent accomplishments, including his world goal and return distance record.

At least 16 sailplanes and approximately 60 pilots preregistered for the meet. Grading and resurfacing of three runways was completed prior to the meet. The main east-west takeoff runway was lengthened, a special landing runway was built to the side of the main east-west takeoff runway, and a runway for powered aircraft was lengthened and improved. At the time of the meet, 15 sailplanes were assembled for the activities.

Contestants competed in a number of categories, including bomb drop, distance, duration, altitude, and spot landing. Harry Parker of the Associated Glider Clubs of Southern California and Jerry Matsen of the San Diego Junior Chamber of Commerce were co-chairmen of the meet. Trophies included the Consolidated-Vultee Trophy for altitude, the Ryan Aeronautical Company Trophy for duration, a trophy for aerobatics, the Rohr Aircraft Trophy for spot landing, the Saron Trophy for bomb drop, and the Essery Trophy for two-place distance. During the meet, three types of launching methods were used: auto tow, winch, and aerotow.

On the first day of the contest, John Robinson was launched from Torrey Pines at 11:37 a.m. in the R.S.-1 *Zanonia*. He soared back and forth on the exceptional sea breeze and then soared out over the ocean. After several circles and figure eights, Robinson hooked a strong thermal and disappeared into a cumulus cloud. When the sailplane was not sighted in the vicinity of Torrey Pines, observers notified the local police, sheriff, and forest service officials to watch for the missing plane. Meet officials did not hear from Robinson until 2:30 that afternoon, when he telephoned contest officials that he had landed safely on Highway 80 (now Interstate 8) near Alpine.

Gus Briegleb was runner-up in the single-place distance category for a flight along the cliffs north to a landing on the beach near Del Mar. John Stasneck of Santa Monica, California, led in the duration category with a flight of 3 hours and 36 minutes, closely followed by Donald Ratty of San Diego, with a duration of 3 hours and 31 minutes. MacCready led the field in altitude, with a flight of 5,000 feet, by soaring

*Above: Wally Wiberg in the cockpit of the Bowlus Baby Albatross "Thunder Bird" at the Torrey Pines Gliderport following World War II.*

*Below and Right: John Robinson riding the cliff edge in the R.S.-1 "Zanonia" at Torrey Pines.*

away from Torrey Pines to the east over the mountains and returning for a spot landing at the gliderport.

Herman Stiglmeier set the nose of his Bowlus Baby Albatross 7.25 inches from a white mark in the center of a ring 50 feet in diameter to lead in the spot landing category. More than 3,000 spectators lined the gliderport and cliffs during the first day alone. The weather was perfect for soaring, but by 3:00 p.m., the breeze slackened and rain started to fall. At this time, many of the airborne contestants attempted to land simultaneously, creating several tense moments, but no serious accidents occurred. James E. Sands of Corona, California blew out the tire on his Schweizer TG-3A when making a quick landing.

On Sunday, Dick Johnson took off in a Schweizer TG-2 at 12:24 p.m. and cruised back and forth along the ridge. Encountering thermal lift, he soared from Torrey Pines inland over Miramar. Continuing to the south, he came down to 600 feet above La Mesa before catching another thermal to reach over 4,000 feet. From there, he soared towards the southeast and, although he attempted to stay on the American side of the border, he was forced to land in Tecate, Mexico, after a flight of 3 hours and 1 minute. This was believed to be the first time that a sailplane had flown from a contest site to a destination outside the boundary of the United States. The cross-country flight put Johnson over the top in terms of points and he was declared meet champion.

With free admission, more than 12,000 spectators crammed the cliff edge and launching area over the weekend. Newsreelmen from Fox Movietone Newsreels drove south from Hollywood to capture the meet on film for all of the country to see and enjoy on the silver screen. Portions of the meet were also carried on local television. Paul Tuntland, flying a Pratt-Read sailplane, put on an incredible aerobatic demonstration for the spectators. One observer was quoted as saying, "It was plenty to see everything in the book performed by others. But, to see the book done upside down--well, that's something for a revised edition." Newspaper reports stated that Tuntland completed a 360° turn in the Pratt-Read while flying upside down. Completing the turn, he did an inverted stall, followed by an inverted loop. Second place in the aerobatics competition went to Ray Parker, who completed a series of slow rolls. Robinson placed third in aerobatics with a dizzying 12-turn spin.

Three years after the end of the war and the reestablishment of soaring activities in San Diego, the Associated Glider Clubs of Southern California had over 60 members, along with over 100 associate members. Club equipment included a V-8 Mercury powered winch with tow speeds up to 80 m.p.h., two Schweizer TG-2s, a Frankfort TG-1A, a Briegleb BG-7, and a Pratt-Read. The club leased five former United States Army buildings at the Torrey Pines Gliderport, which were used for equipment storage and for meetings. Every weekend, Torrey Pines was bustling with soaring activities, with new pilots being trained directly at the site in the two-place sailplanes. Instruction was free and the fee for equipment use was $3.00 per hour. The club had eight commercial pilots, five private pilots, and the majority of the rest of the membership were student pilots. Between the end of the war and summer of 1948, a total of 2,023 flights were made in the club sailplanes, totalling 186 hours of soaring.

## *San Diegans at National Competitions in 1948*

Between June 30th and July 11th, 1948, 70 contestants brought 50 sailplanes to the National Soaring Contest at Elmira, New York. The best flight of the meet was made by Paul MacCready. He flew the *Orlik* sailplane from Elmira, New York, to Middlefield, Ohio, a distance of 222 miles. This represented the first long-distance cross-country soaring flight to the west of the Elmira area and it was believed to be the longest soaring flight made anywhere in the world in 1948. MacCready also made a goal flight of 167 miles to Trenton, New Jersey, to win a prize of $250 offered by the President of the Chase Aircraft Corporation. MacCready's flight to Middlefield clinched the championship. Not one of MacCready's first five flights were under a distance of 140 miles.

John Robinson flew 178 miles from Elmira to New Midway, Maryland, in the famous Air-100 sailplane loaned to him by the French Embassy. Don Pollard of Roanoke, Virginia placed third after a flight of 142 miles to Altoona, Pennsylvania. Ray Parker also had a flight of 146 miles at the contest, in the *Rigid Midget*, securing fourth place. Dick Johnson flew the *Tiny Mite*, while Wally Wiberg flew the *Screamin' Weiner*. MacCready was awarded the Richard C. duPont Memorial Trophy for his national soaring championship, John Robinson placed second, and Donald Pollard third.

From July 24th to August 1st, 1948, the annual Southwest Soaring Contest was held at Grand Prairie, Texas. July 24th proved to be the best soaring day and John Robinson made the longest flight of the meet, flying 209 miles to Kirkland, three miles short of his goal of Childress. During the rest of the meet, however, weather conditions did not permit thermal activity until late each day, and pilots could not takeoff very early in the morning for cross-country flights. Robinson made the best altitude gained during the meet to win the $50 cash prize donated by the First National Bank of Grand Prairie. He gained 12,850 feet with a maximum of 14,500 feet above takeoff. For his flights, Robinson placed first at the meet, and fellow Californians Ray Parker, Richard Lyon, and Richard Johnson placed second through fourth.

## *El Mirage Dry Lake*

Members of the Southern California Soaring Association held a contest at the El Mirage Gliderport between September 4th through 6th, 1948. 20 gliders were entered by 25 pilots and a total of 102 flights were made over the three-day period. The festival was co-sponsored by the Adelanto, Victorville, Apple Valley, and San Bernardino County Chambers of Commerce. Dick Lyon, Gus Briegleb, and John Ludowitz finished first through third, respectively. John Robinson finished sixth, and Bob Fronius eighth. San Diegan Dave Boone and his wife brought a TG-1A to the event and placed 12th. Jim Spurgeon helped provide entertainment at the watermelon feed and weenie roast.

During the fall in 1948, Bill Ivans took a "soaring safari" to El Mirage Dry Lake to fly with the Briegleb's and gain instruction in thermal techniques at the Briegleb Soaring School. In a TG-1A, Ivans and his instructor, Doc Smith, climbed to 10,300 feet in an afternoon's soaring. The following afternoon, Ivans took off in the Frankfort TG-1A by auto tow across the six-mile dry lake. He released at 1,000 feet, worked some light lift for a while until he suddenly entered a region of uniform lift at about 400 feet per minute. Climbing and climbing, he soared to over 12,000 feet where the lift gave out.

> *Though somewhat dazed by my unexpected success, I was able to relax still further and to take stock of the situation. One of my first impressions was that of being chilly; the light sport shirt which was appropriate enough in the 110°F heat on the surface of the dry lake now proved to be somewhat scant attire. However, I dismissed this as being a trivial matter.*

Continuing on, he climbed higher in another thermal, where he reached cloud base at 16,000 feet. With the lack of oxygen, slight icing on the leading edge of the wing, and numbing cold, Ivans made a final check of the altimeter, which read 16,050 feet, and started in a decent for a landing at El Mirage. In approximately 3 hours of soaring, he had gained 12,450 feet, more than enough to fulfill the altitude requirements for the Silver "C" and Golden "C" badges.

The following day, Ivans and Gus Breigleb thought that it would be a good day for a cross-country attempt. Breigleb suggested a goal flight to Daggett, 48 miles to the northeast of El Mirage. Flying in the Frankfort TG-1A, Ivans soon found his way across the desert at altitudes of 12,000 to 13,000 feet, and arrived at Daggett at 7,500 feet, 50 minutes after leaving El Mirage.

Later in the week, Ivans satisfied the duration requirement for the Silver "C" with a flight over El Mirage of over five hours in a Briegleb BG-7. It brought an end to a remarkable vacation in the desert, from Ivans' first thermaling attempts to his Silver "C" award.

## *Bishop and the Sierra Wave*

At the end of 1948, an expedition of sorts was held at Bishop, California. In attendance were Fred Walters, Carl Walters, and Dick Lyon with the Walters LK-10; John MacDonald and Bob Symons with the Inyo-Mono Soaring Association Schweizer TG-3; Dick Johnson with the *Tiny Mite*; John Robinson with the R.S.-1 *Zanonia*; and

*Bill Ivans in front of a Frankfort TG-1 at the Briegleb Glider School at El Mirage Dry Lake in 1948.*

Paul MacCready with the *Orlik*. Lew Mass and John Olley crewed for the *Orlik* and the R.S.-1 *Zanonia*, respectively. Harland Ross helped with towing, crewing, officiating, etc.

On December 31st, 1948, MacCready soared in his *Orlik* to an amazing 29,500 feet above sea level, setting a new official United States altitude record. Takeoff was made by aerotow behind a BT-13 at 11:45 a.m., with the ground temperature registering a very chilly 39°F. A large lenticular cloud could be seen just east of the White Mountains about twenty miles to the north of the field. At 12,000 feet, they passed over the Whites, and a quick check of the lenticular revealed that there were three layers to the standing wave. MacCready released at 13,000 feet at 12:26 p.m. Gliding west toward the Sierra Mountains, he encountered gusts both up and down of 2,000 feet per minute. Despite these gusts, he entered a standing wave 30 miles south of Bishop and was soon flying at 27,500 feet. The outside air temperature of -36°F was so cold that ice began to form on the inside of the canopy from the condensation of his breath. After scraping patches of ice free from the canopy, Paul changed directions, heading north along the Sierras, gradually losing altitude to 17,000 feet above sea level. Noticing another lenticular wave to the south down the Owens Valley over Independence, he headed south and climbed to a best altitude of 29,500 feet. Over two and a half hours of his 5-hour flight were spent at altitudes over 27,000 feet.

MacCready's altitude record was official in every way, but his record would be rapidly surpassed. On January 1st, 1949, Robinson in the R.S.-1 *Zanonia* and Paul MacCready in the *Orlik* were towed to 10,000 feet behind a BT-13 tow plane piloted by Dick Lyon. Northwest of their takeoff location from Bishop, California, in the Owens Valley, were a series of lenticular clouds...evidence of a standing wave. Shortly after release, Robinson's variometer was reading 1,000 feet per minute of climb, and MacCready and Robinson chose different directions, each hoping to use the lift from the standing wave to set a new record for absolute altitude in a sailplane. Flying through the turbulent air surrounding the wave, Robinson later recalled:

> *The up and down drafts had such sharp edges that the ship would pitch or dive violently to exaggerated attitudes. Once, while indicating 60 miles per hour airspeed, the nose pitched up past 80°, nearly vertical, standing the plane on its tail, then levelling it out again without stalling... Seconds later I was thrown into a vertical nose down position because my tail was still in an updraft while my wing had entered a downdraft. Airspeed changed only from 60 to 70 miles per hour in this maneuver as I pulled the control stick back while hanging in the safety belt. The glider had been literally slapped down from beneath me.*

Frost soon coated the inside of the canopy as the sailplane rose higher into the sky. Flying south, he arrived at Independence around 2 p.m., and re-entered the Sierra Wave.

*Paul MacCready soaring high above the Sierra Nevada Mountains in the Orlik II sailplane in 1948.*

*I had reached a new low point of 9,300 feet and was back up to 10,000, gliding southwest toward the gap between the roll cloud and the mountain range. This was where I expected to find the area of lift. Through a disgustingly small clear spot which I had rubbed in the frosted canopy, I strained my eyes in an effort to find the Independence airport.*

*Suddenly, with shuddering violence, the plane was jerked out from under me. The already tight safety belt yanked me down with it, but not before my head hit the rear portion of the canopy with a resounding whack that broke the panel. One of the barographs tore loose from its moorings, and the thermos bottle bounced on top of my shoulder instead of under my arm. I grabbed the thermos as the ship kicked me in the seat, hard, going up--and then tried to leave me going down again.*

Shortly thereafter, the air became eerily smooth and the variometer pegged at 2,000 feet per minute of climb. After a quick drink of lemonade from his thermos, Robinson turned on the oxygen tank and mask at 16,000 feet and continued his rapid ascent past 20,000 feet, where the climb slowed to approximately 1,000 feet per minute. By 3:15 p.m., he plateaued at 29,000 feet and the temperature inside the cockpit had dropped to 10°F. Clearing the frost from his canopy, Robinson was able to see the San Joaquin Valley to the west and even Mount Baldy to the south near Los Angeles (over 160 miles away).

Robinson continued to slowly drift south along the Sierra, eventually spotting Mount Whitney (14,496 feet), the highest point in, what was then, the 48 United States. Just north of Mount Whitney, Robinson started to climb once again and plateaued at 33,500 feet above sea level, establishing a new American altitude record.

By this time, it was 4:20 p.m. and Robinson was cold and thirsty (as he did not care to remove his oxygen mask at these altitudes). It was 10°F in the cockpit and it was a much colder -40°F outside. With the record in hand, it was imperative that he land in a place where there were would be witnesses.

Throughout the afternoon, the Owens Valley below had been filling with clouds. By looking through an opening in the clouds, Robinson spotted Owens Lake. He turned south toward the familiar Mojave Desert with its many airfields, dry lakes, and usual lack of cloud cover. At 5 p.m., Robinson was down to only 20,000 feet and quickly realized his predicament. The sun was setting to the west and, in a very short time, he would not be able to recognize any landmarks at all on the Earth below, especially the tall mountains that were nearby. Suddenly, through a hole in the clouds, Robinson spotted runways on a dry lake bed.

*It was just dark enough that I didn't care whose airport it was, or where it was. I just wanted to be on it.*

In order to lose the required altitude in a rapid fashion, Robinson initiated a spin doing five turns per 1,000 feet. His rate of descent was 2,000 feet per minute in a completely stalled configuration, with an airspeed of about 30 miles per hour. Recovering at 10,000 feet after 50 turns, he flew west to make up for the 5 miles he had drifted east from the airport during the spin. But attempts to locate the airport for a second time were unsuccessful.

> *The altimeter read 9,500 as I dove against the wind getting back to the airport. The next time I looked at it the reading was 10,500. The rate-of-climb showed 1,000 feet per minute UP!*

Continuing to the west, he arrived at where the airport should have been at 11,000 feet. A quick glance to the ground showed that the lights of the runways were on and Robinson entered into another long spin, recovering with 2,800 feet to spare. Lighted runways and hangars were clearly visible. He entered a final approach and made a controlled landing into the gusty 40 mile per hour wind, stopping 50 feet from a set of hangar doors. The altimeter read 2,100 feet and it was 5:22 p.m.

As Robinson prepared to exit *Zanonia*, a sergeant in a jeep rolled up and helped push the sailplane into the hanger next to a series of jet aircraft. The Officer of the Day met Robinson in the Officers' Mess, and after hearing of the tale, permitted Robinson to phone back to his takeoff location in Bishop.

> *At this point, almost an hour after landing, I still knew only that I was on a military installation. Finally I asked which one. The answer, 'Muroc Air Force Base,' amazed me. I didn't know that I was that far south. There are several military fields in this area, some of them not even on the maps. Later review of the flight statistics revealed that the 110 miles between Owens Lake and the point over Muroc was covered in 40 minutes, an average of 165 miles per hour ground speed with an 85 mile per hour cross tailwind.*
>
> *When the call went through, three telephones on the Bishop airport were answered simultaneously. Everyone had been waiting anxiously except John Olley, my crew chief, who undoubtedly, was just relaxing. When I mentioned my highest altitude of over 24,000 feet gained above low point, and 33,400 feet above sea level, everyone whooped with joy--for these were both new American altitude records in gliding.*

Robinson's flight also qualified as a world record for absolute altitude above sea level in a sailplane. He was also awarded the highly prestigious Lillienthal Medal of the Fédération Aéronautique Internationale for his record soaring performance, the first American to receive this distinction.

For their work in discovering the Sierra Wave, Harland Ross and Robert F. Symons were awarded the Warren E. Eaton Memorial Trophy for their outstanding contribution to the art, sport, or science of soaring flight in the United States.

## *The Third Annual Pacific Coast Midwinter Championships*

In preparation for the Third Annual Pacific Coast Midwinter Championships held in 1949, club member Jim Spurgeon related his experiences with gliding to the local press:

> *Gliding teaches you the inherent ability to fly. There is a science to it, but it is mostly art. Before you have been in it very long, you fly by touch. You become a part of your plane just as you become a part of a bicycle. I have a license for flying power planes but I don't believe that you can ever feel as much a part of a power plane as you can a glider. You find a seagull flying along beside you and know that you and the seagull are akin.*

At least 22 sailplanes were entered in the contest, piloted by some of the nation's best pilots. Roman Benn served as meet director. On the first day, the contestants were soaring happily back and forth for over two hours. Suddenly, there was a lull in the wind. Among the six sailplanes that remained in the air, there was a contest to see who could stay up; contest rules specified that a beach landing disqualified the associated flight. Slowly, Milton Kuntz in his Schweizer TG-3, Bob Fronius in the *Robin*, and Dick Johnson in a Schweizer TG-2 were seen soaring below the cliff edge on their way to the beach. John Robinson in the R.S.-1 *Zanonia*, Paul MacCready in the *Orlik*, and Harold Huber in the Bowlus Senior Albatross continued on just above. Kuntz landed on the beach first, followed by Fronius and Johnson. Robinson squeaked in over the edge for landing on top and, then all of a sudden, the winds came back up again. Soon all the ships were relaunching to join MacCready and Huber, who had duration locked up for the day.

Robinson was aerotowed aloft in the R.S.-1 *Zanonia* for an aerobatic flight. After completing a series of stunts, he realized that the wind was at its peak. Refusing to use an aerotow for the start of a cross-country competitive flight, he landed and waited on a long takeoff line for a winch tow. Finally, he took off from Torrey Pines on the winch and turned north along the cliffs. Pushing the light breeze for all it was worth, he landed 21 miles up the coast on the beach near Oceanside, giving him first place in the distance category and also setting a new local record for longest cross-country flight along the shoreline cliffs north of Torrey Pines. Later, he recalled:

*After losing out on duration, I elected to go cross-country from winch tow, via the slope wind. For many years soaring pilots have talked about trying to slope soar north along the cliffs from Torrey Pines, going as far as possible, but no one had ever tried it.*

*There are several qualifications for such an enterprise: low tide, giving the pilot a wide beach on which to land, sufficient slope wind out of the southwest, a crew for retrieving, a 'do it now' incentive. All the above conditions existed at 4:00 p.m. on Saturday. A winch tow netted about 600 feet altitude, which I increased a little over the high cliffs as I started north. Altitude above the beach was 1,050 feet.*

*The first break in the cliffs at Torrey Pines wasn't too noticeable, but the next gap north of Del Mar let me down to about 300 feet. The slope wind would maintain my altitude over the cliffs, but normal sink developed while gliding along the beach in the gaps where there were no cliffs. I was letting down in steps between succeeding rows of cliffs, without ever regaining my lost altitude. The cliffs became progressively lower. So did I.*

*Leaving Solana Beach I was only fifty feet above the edge, and the cliffs are less than 100 feet. I stretched the glide past 'George's Place' in what I considered a hopeless attempt to reach the next bluff, which couldn't have been more than forty or fifty feet high. Most of the time there was a good beach down below. When I reached the bluff, the lift area of the slope wind was so narrow I could feel it only on my right wing. It was sustaining, however, and I gained perhaps twenty or thirty feet while passing cars on the highway, bound in the opposite direction. Some of the drivers looked worried; others stopped and climbed out.*

*Over a cove where several seagulls were soaring, I managed a couple of figure 8's and eked out a gain of forty feet. This sounds silly compared with altitude gains for most cross-country soaring, however, this bit of gain made the continuance of the flight possible. I passed Encinitas so low I felt I was intruding on the privacy of many homes with swimming pools.*

*It was an amazing feeling to soar silently mile after mile, less than 100 feet above the beach. Soon it was only fifty, but I continued, expecting to land at any moment. Scanning the beach for obstructions now required almost constant attention. I thought I could avoid rocks by steering with the rudder, but fishermen standing with their poles presented a much greater problem. They might move at the wrong moment. Several did not even see me as I passed silently fifty feet over their heads.*

*Above: A gaggle of sailplanes making a high speed pass in formation at the 1949 Pacific Coast Midwinter Soaring Championships. From left to right: a Briegleb BG-7, a Bowlus Super Albatross, Paul MacCready in the Orlik II, and John Robinson in the R.S.-1 "Zanonia."*

*Above Right: A Schweizer 1-19 soaring the ridge at Torrey Pines on a windy day.*

*Below Right: The Bowlus Super Albatross below cliff level at Torrey Pines.*

NC
91818

*South of Oceanside even the twenty to thirty foot cliffs flattened out into the beach and I knew that I must land. A southbound car on the highway ahead stopped. Several figures jumped out waving wildly. As they passed below me I recognized Mia Klemperer and her daughter. As ten feet was hardly enough altitude, I slid to a stop on a very clear section of the beach below the cliffs. Happily the Klemperers were contest-bound and took me back with them to contact John Olley, who was with my car and trailer.*

*This flight, which required twenty-two minutes to cover 21.3 miles, is not much compared with thermal flights. But it will always be outstanding in my memory for the extremely low altitude at which it was accomplished.*

MacCready launched and made a 14-mile cross-country flight to San Marcos. This was good enough for second place in the distance category. Herman Stiglmeier placed third in distance with a six-mile flight to Del Mar along the coast. A wide variety of sailplanes flew in the meet, including a Frankfort TG-1 (NX 90620), Briegleb BG-7, a Bowlus Super Albatross flown by Myron Wells, a Pratt-Read flown by Herman Stiglmeier, a Schweizer TG-2 flown by Dick Johnson, the *Rigid Midget*, the *Orlik* flown by MacCready, and the R.S.-1 *Zanonia* piloted by Robinson. During the meet, Wells skimmed the edge of the cliff in the Bowlus Super Albatross, attempting to hook a handkerchief held high in the air on a stick by Paul Tuntland. This was a real crowd pleaser.

In the two-place distance category, Johnson captured first place with a flight of ten miles to a landing at Poway. Second in this category was Tuntland of Los Angeles, followed by Richard Lyon, also of Los Angeles. Lyon won the spot landing contest by stopping the nose of his sailplane two and three-quarter inches from the target. Tuntland placed second with a distance of 4 inches and V. L. Atkins of Santa Barbara placed third with a distance of 5 inches. Bomb-dropping honors went to Joe Stasneck of Santa Monica, who dropped his bag of sand within 9 feet, 5 inches of the bull's eye. Bill Ivans placed second with a distance of 10 feet, 5 inches and Dick Johnson and Fred W. Walters of Hawthorne tied for third place with identical scores of 17 feet, 2 inches. In the duration category, MacCready spent 5 hours and 15 minutes on his cross-country flight to San Marcos, earning him first place.

Sunday's lift was so unfavorable that soaring flights were nearly impossible to achieve. Acrobatic prizes went to Ray Parker of Twentynine Palms flying the *Rigid Midget*. Robinson placed second and Tuntland was third. Pilots used a biplane flown by Pete Girard to tow them to a sufficient height prior to their acrobatic flying routines. Harold Huber of Glendale, flew the Bowlus Super Albatross to 1,250 feet, giving him the Convair Altitude Trophy, and enough points for third place. The John J. Montgomery Club won the Peterson Club Participation Trophy.

At the end of the meet, MacCready was declared meet champion with 78.8 points flying in the *Orlik*. Robinson placed second in the R.S.-1 *Zanonia* with 75.8 points. At one time, there were 14 sailplanes soaring together up and down the coastline, giving the newspaper photographers quite a field day. Cameramen from four newsreel companies, one television station, and one national magazine were on hand for the event. It was not only good publicity for the local glider enthusiasts, but good publicity for the sport of soaring across the nation.

During the midst of the competition, Mrs. G. S. Dale, a 59-year-old grandmother was taken aloft for her first glider flight by Stan Hall of Los Angeles. Mrs. Dale was the wife of Commander Dale, holder of United States glider license number 85. Hall and Mrs. Dale stayed in the air for 20 minutes and, after landing, Mrs. Dale was quoted as saying,

> *It was a wonderful experience, I don't know when I have done anything that gave me so much pleasure. I'll go again whenever Mr. Hall will take me.*

Soon after the end of the contest at 4 p.m., Bob Fronius demonstrated the use of a parachute to save a "disabled" sailplane. Starting at 3,500 feet via aerotow, Fronius put the *Robin* (the sailplane previously owned by Robinson) into a 75 m.p.h. slip, at which point the "Ship-Chute" was released. The parachute had a 30-foot canopy with special vents. Shroud lines were packed into a sleeve to prevent contact with the control surfaces. Fronius designed and built the parachute system. Following several minutes of deployment, the parachute was released prior to a successful landing at the gliderport. It was a technical advancement as well as a crowd pleaser.

## *Nation's Youngest Glider Pilot*

Don Matson, age 14 and Kearney High School freshman, successfully soloed in a Schweizer TG-2 at the Torrey Pines Gliderport on April 23rd, 1949. Steve Kecskes served as soaring instructor and Matson's father, Steward, was a local flight instructor in powered aircraft at Gibbs' Field (Montgomery Field). Don Matson's solo flight made him the youngest glider pilot in the United States at that time. C.A.A. representative W. H. Grevemeyer was at Torrey Pines to hand Matson his student's permit just before his solo flight. Matson had 15 hours power dual instruction and about 35 glider instruction flights. 14-year-old Irving Gere was also preparing to attain his glider license.

Following the end of the war, members of the Associated Glider Clubs of Southern California depended on Ray Parker's Army surplus winch to boost them into the sky at Torrey Pines. However, as the winch launches continued, the amount of surplus winch wire began to decrease. Members of the club placed a note in *Soaring* magazine asking for ideas on where to obtain more winch wire, and what type was the best for this purpose. Don Peterson was in charge of tallying information from other clubs across the country, using winches so that the comments could be re-published in a future issue of the club newsletter, *Wind and Wings*.

Of his experience in the Associated Glider Clubs of Southern California, Harold Fawcett recalled:

> *In the middle of 1950, I came to United States Naval Air Station, Miramar for duty; took a ride in a beautiful TG-3 at Elsinore, my first in California... Shortly thereafter I attended a meeting of the Associated Glider Clubs of Southern California and became a member. In those days, the meetings were held underground (literally) at Torrey Pines, approximately the area of the south end of the power plane landing strip, in the remains of an ammunition storage area from Camp Callan. All new members were present for their first meeting. You were initiated with quite a ceremony. An interesting fact, club participation was nearly 100% even though gasoline lanterns were used and if I remember right, a kerosene stove donated by a club member was used to keep us warm.*

## *The Sierra Mountain Wave Project*

John Robinson, Larry Edgar, and Ray Parker, were selected as pilots for the Mountain Wave Project to investigate the nature of the high-altitude standing waves over the Owens Valley. The Southern California Soaring Association, University of California, Los Angeles, the Air Force Cambridge Research Center, and the Naval Ordinance Test Station were all involved with the project. By flying sailplanes high into the atmosphere, the structure of the standing wave was described. Downdrafts as strong as 4,000 to 5,000 feet per minute existed near the leeward-side of some of the mountains.

At Bishop, strong wave conditions on January 27th, 1950, enabled Harland Ross and George Deibert to set two world two-place sailplane altitude records. Their absolute altitude of 36,000 feet was achieved after a gain of 24,300 feet, while flying in a modified Schweizer TG-3A. The reported temperature outside the cockpit at 36,000 feet was -69° F.

## *The Fourth Annual Pacific Coast Midwinter Soaring Championships*

With local gliding activities rekindled past their prewar status, members of the Associated Glider Clubs of Southern California decided to officially rededicate the Torrey Pines Gliderport at the Fourth Annual Pacific Coast Midwinter Championships. In combination with the San Diego Junior Chamber of Commerce, cacheted glider mail was carried aloft during the event.

On February 25th, 1950, 22 glider pilots showed up at Torrey Pines, only to find the entire site shrouded in a blanket of fog. Bill Ivans, Chairman of the meet for the Associated Glider Clubs of Southern California, took off from Gillespie Field just before 2 p.m., towed behind a plane flown by Dean Moorehead. Over the Torrey Pines Gliderport, Ivans found the fog bank too thick to make a release and subsequent landing. He released closer to Del Mar and came to a landing in an empty field. Bob Fronius helped Ivans tow the plane back to Gillespie Field by car.

A large crowd spent the time inspecting the various sailplanes that were on display at the gliderport, including the Nelson Hummingbird, a new type of motorglider owned by Ted Nelson of San Leandro, California. Harry Perl of San Diego and Don Mitchell had helped develop the plane that sported a retractable motor. Unfortunately, due to heavy fog, the meet was postponed to March 11th and 12th.

Over 5,000 people were on hand on Saturday March 11th and a record crowd of 12,000 witnessed the event on March 12th. Bill Beuby managed to stay aloft 5 hours and 48 minutes in his modified Schweizer TG-2. John Loufek flew 14 miles with a passenger in his sailplane and captured the longest distance of the meet at the Montgomery Trophy for meet champion. Dave Boone placed second, and John Robinson third. Young Irving Gere took the trophy for the closest bomb drop, missing the mark by only 9 feet, 6 inches. Bill Ivans edged out John Robinson for the aerobatic championship by demonstrating an inverted precision circle in his Schweizer 1-23.

## *A Night Flight at Torrey Pines*

After work one windy day, Bob Brown and a friend drove out to Torrey Pines and set up a Schweizer TG-2 for a quick flight by auto tow. Small position lights were taped on the wingtips and tail as a safety precaution in case the flight continued into dusk. A strong 18- knot sea breeze set in and within minutes after launch, Brown was lifted to an altitude of 1,300 feet above sea level. Brown wrote:

> *It seemed only a short time until is was almost dark and time for me to land. The wind was too strong to allow a normal downwind landing. I would have to land into the wind along the same strip I had been launched from by the car. The downwind leg was covered so fast I found myself too high on the final leg. To complicate matters, an updraft from the tall eucalyptus at the end of the runway tossed me another 200 feet higher.*
>
> *The air was so turbulent I decided to go 'round again, but I lost so much time regaining position for another try that it became too dark to land. A real gale was blowing now. It gave plenty of altitude and I knew I would be safe until the moon came out to give me light for a landing when the wind died. Meanwhile, my friend gathered flare pots from a road-repair tool shed, lit*

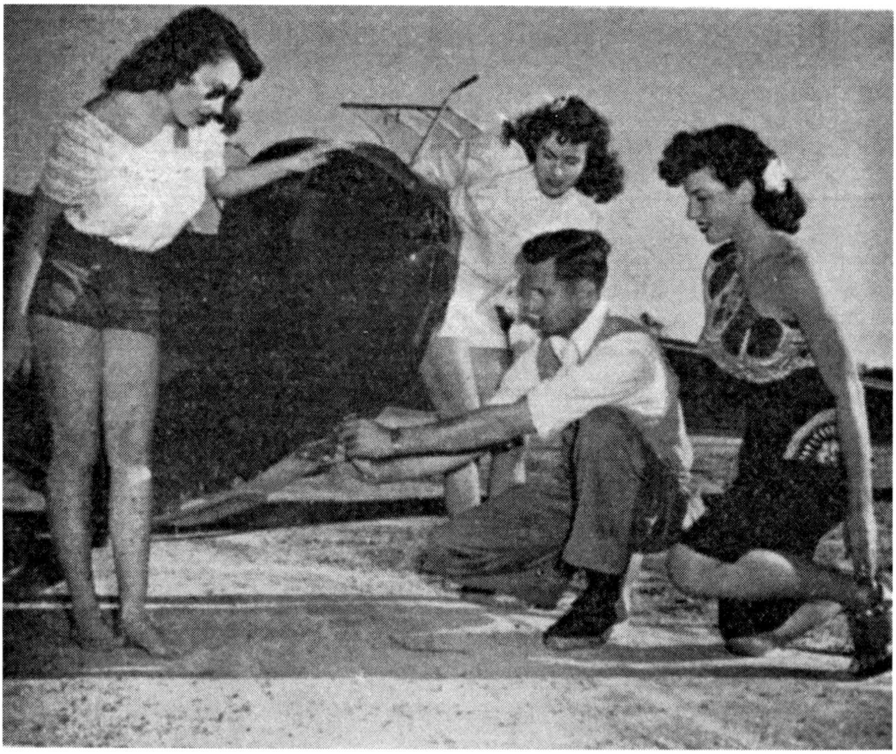

*Above: The Associated Glider Clubs of Southern California Schweizer TG-2 on winch launch to open the 1950 Pacific Coast Midwinter Soaring Championships.*

*Below: Three young ladies learn the proper technique to hook a winch line to the Schweizer TG-2. At the annual contests, a "Queen" would be crowned for the duration of the event and helped attract additional news coverage by the local press.*

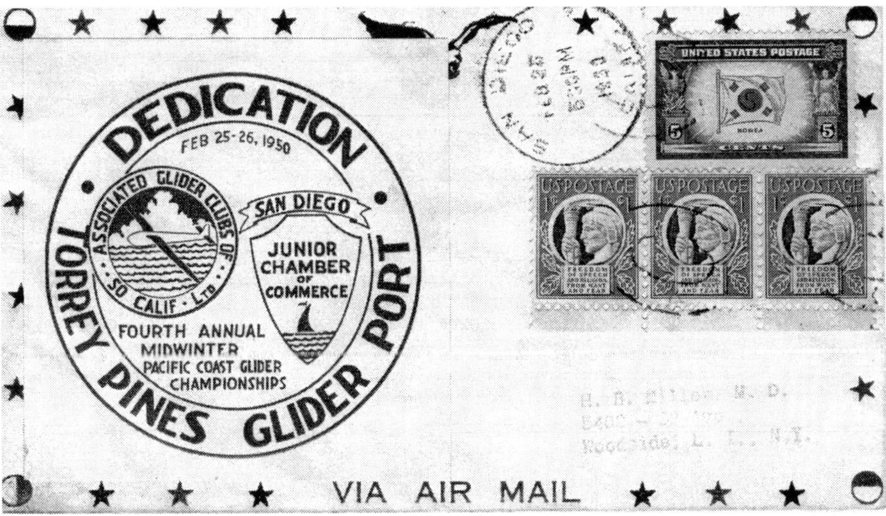


*Two varieties of glider mail from the 1950 Pacific Coast Midwinter Soaring Championships as a re-dedication of the Torrey Pines Gliderport.*

*Looking north at the 1950 Pacific Coast Midwinter Soaring Championships, an event that continued annually to the mid-1980s at Torrey Pines.*

*Looking south at the 1950 midwinter meet. A large crowd stands on the cliff tops where hang gliders and model sailplanes are launched presently.*

*them, and placed them along the cliff-top to outline the runway. This was a great help since it was now pitch black and I needed a reference point on the ground very badly.*

*I was quite comfortable and began to enjoy night flying. After two hours the moon came out. I was enjoying the sight until I looked out to sea and saw a huge, ominously dark cloud mass moving toward the cliffs. From its location and the wind direction I had a small hope it might pass to the north. In a half-hour, it hung directly overhead, blanketing the moonlight.*

*Abruptly, without warning, the wind died. The ship started to sink in the blackness. 700...600...500...400 feet... Beads of perspiration dropped off my forehead while I strained to see the feeble light of the flares lining the runway.*

*Then all of the devils of the sky reached down and threw the TG-2 upward into a turbulent mass of air. The rate-of-climb indicator raced to, and passed, 1000 feet per minute. Airspeed was 80 miles per hour, and it didn't slow much when I came back on the stick. The drumming of hail on the canopy made me pray it would get no larger.*

*I lost all contact with the ground. Someone had told me, 'If you ever get in trouble in a cloud with the TG-2, let the ship fly itself.' I took my hands from the controls and let the old ship go where it would. At times the airspeed would go to 85, drop to 50, and sometimes I would be thrown against the safety belt. The cloud had us by the nape of the neck--throwing us up and shaking us at the same time. The ship seemed to enjoy its new freedom, bucking like a colt just let out to pasture. I said to the cloud, 'You've had your fun -- how about letting us out of here?' As though it heard me, everything became calm. I saw moonlight and took control of the ship, coming out of the cloud near the very top.*

*It was a magic moment. There I sat on a huge section of cloud, bathed in moonlight, surrounded by other white mountains of vapor. For the next two hours I soared up the face of one cloud after another, eventually spiraling down through an opening and returning to the cliff. The moon was shining and the wind was blowing again.*

*I stayed aloft until 4:30 a.m., and then landed on the beach to end the most exciting flight of my life.*

## Montgomery Field

On May 20th, 1950, Gibbs Field was officially rededicated as Montgomery Field in honor of the "first American to fly," John J. Montgomery. Aircraft manufacturers displayed several new private planes, and members of the Associated Glider Clubs of Southern California displayed many modern sailplanes. Six members of the Montgomery family arrived in San Diego for the dedication ceremonies, and James Montgomery (John's brother) was towed aloft in the John J. Montgomery Soaring Club's Schweizer TG-2 piloted by Dave Boone. The club purchased the TG-2 from Dick Lyons.

## John Robinson, First Diamond "C" in the World

The Diamond "C" badge was established by officials of the Fédération Aéronautique Internationale as soaring's highest achievement award (following the Silver "C" and Gold "C" awards). Requirements included a distance flight of over 310.7 miles, an altitude gain of more than 16,405 feet, and a predetermined goal distance flight of over 186.42 miles. At the time, such achievements were at the cutting edge of sailplane technology. Only the very best pilots in the world could accomplish parts of this award. No one had successfully completed all three tasks for the first Diamond "C."

On July 1st, 1950, John Robinson took off in the R.S.-1 *Zanonia* from El Mirage Gliderport in the Mojave Desert, north of Los Angeles. His declared goal of Overton, Nevada, was over 221 miles away. R.S.-1 *Zanonia* faithfully carried him over desert to his declared goal and to the first Diamond "C" in the world. Robinson satisfied the first Diamond requirement in July, 1947, with a 325-mile distance flight from Wichita Falls, Texas, to Barstow, Texas. The second requirement was satisfied in January of 1949, with his 33,500 foot altitude record flight over Bishop, California. It was yet another international accomplishment for the former San Diegan.

## Bill Ivans

Soaring in his new Schweizer 1-23 over Bishop on December 30, 1950, Associated Glider Clubs of Southern California member Bill Ivans set two new world records for altitude. He reached an absolute altitude of 42,100 feet, with a gain of over 30,100 feet. On the way down, he celebrated with a series of loops and rolls. This record held for another 11 years to follow.

Ivans was awarded the prestigious Lillienthal Medal in 1950, as a recognition for his particularly remarkable sporting performance in soaring flight. Later, in 1951,

Ivans was awarded the Warren E. Eaton Memorial Trophy for his contributions to the art, sport, or science of soaring flight in the United States.

# *Epilogue*

Of the first ten pilots to satisfy the requirements for the first-class glider license in the United States, nine were trained in San Diego. These included William Hawley Bowlus (#2), William Van Dusen (#3), James Allison Moore (#4), Earle R. Mitchell (#5), Albert E. Hastings (#6), John C. Barstow (#7), Roy H. Pemberton (#8), Charles A. Lindbergh (#9), and Anne M. Lindbergh (#10). Anne Lindbergh was the first woman to receive a first-class glider license in the United States.

Of the first 23 to hold a second-class glider license, 19 were trained in San Diego. These included William Hawley Bowlus (#3), William Van Dusen (#5), James Allison Moore (#6), Albert E. Hastings (#7), John C. Barstow (#8), Fred H. Rohr (#9), Roy H. Pemberton (#10), Earle R. Mitchell (#11), Letain Kittredge (#12), Charles A. Lindbergh (#13), Anne M. Lindbergh (#14), E. M. Lacey (#16), E. Lowell Bullen (#17), Ruth Alexander (#18), Peaches Wallace (#19), Forrest H. Hieatt (#20), Bud Perl (#21), Alan R. Essery (#22), and Guinivere Kotter (#23).

Of the first 86 pilots to hold a third-class glider license, 30 were trained in San Diego (35%), including William Hawley Bowlus (#17), William Van Dusen (#18), John C. Barstow (#20), Douglas T. Kelley (#21), Earle R. Mitchell (#22), Fred H. Rohr (#23), E. M. Lacey, Jr. (#24), A. J. Coles (#25), I. N. Lawson, Jr. (#26), George L. McLeod (#28), James A. Moore (#29), Albert E. Hastings (#32), Bud Perl (#34), Roy H. Pemberton (#35), Letain Kittredge (#37), Charles A. Lindbergh (#40), Peaches Wallace (#42), Anne M. Lindbergh (#43), E. Lowell Bullen (#45), Ruth B. Alexander (#46), Forrest H. Hieatt (#47), Morris Charles Tombler (#48), Carl Blair Rogers (#49), Lloyd William Standley (#50), William Stanley Saville (#51), Alan R. Essery (#52), Guinivere Kotter (#53), Val F. Schmohl (#77), George S. Dale (#78), and Albert Austin Gabbs (#86).

San Diegans took to the sport of gliding and soaring in the late 1920s and 1930s at a rate equal to or faster than any other portion of the country. This was largely due to the efforts of one individual, William Hawley Bowlus, and his dedication to soaring.

The history of gliding and soaring in San Diego certainly did not end with the efforts of Hawley Bowlus, John Robinson, Woody Brown, Harland Ross, and Bill Ivans prior to 1951. In fact, one might claim that the history was starting. The annual Pacific Coast Midwinter Soaring Championships became a mainstay of the soaring competition circuit between 1951 and 1985, with an additional meet held in 1991. On an annual basis, the best American sailplane pilots would travel to San Diego specifically for this meet. The event generated incredible interest in soaring; tens of thousands of spectators attended the meet at Torrey Pines over one weekend (similar to the turnout at the annual Buick Invitational Golf Tournament held at the nearby Torrey Pines Golf Course). Many of the spectators became interested in soaring and as a result, the Associated Glider Clubs of Southern California gained in popularity.

In the late 1950s and early 1960s, much of the land surrounding the Torrey Pines gliderport was given by the citizens of San Diego to the University of California for the construction of a campus in La Jolla. A San Diego City-wide vote approved this land transfer. Included in the package was the eastern half of the Torrey Pines Gliderport and members of the Associated Glider Clubs of Southern California were confused and frustrated by this action. In conversation with University officials and the City of San Diego, club members attempted to preserve the site as a soaring park, but these efforts fell on deaf ears. Recognizing the importance of the site to the community, officials at the University suggested that they would keep the site open as a gliding area for as long as possible, until the land was needed for another academic purpose. Members of the University of California San Diego Glider Club began flight operations at Torrey Pines in conjunction with the Associated Glider Clubs of Southern California.

In the mid-1950s, radio-controlled model sailplanes first started to appear at the Torrey Pines Gliderport. A world record for radio-controlled sailplane endurance was set at Torrey Pines in 1956. Pilots from the many local aircraft companies became interested in radio-controlled modeling, and Torrey Pines slowly became known as a locale for both full scale soaring and model soaring. By 1969, the Torrey Pines Gulls Radio-Controlled Soaring Society, Inc. became the second officially chartered soaring club of the Academy of Model Aeronautics. At first glance, members of the Associated Glider Clubs of Southern California were hesitant to let the modelers share the same airspace with the full scale sailplanes at Torrey Pines. But after many attempts by Kelly Pike (the first president of the Torrey Pines Gulls) and other Gulls, local modelers convinced the full scale sailplane pilots that they were respectful of the rather unusual airspace restrictions at Torrey Pines. The modelers helped with crowd control and conducted model demonstrations at the annual Pacific Coast Midwinter meets. Many members of the Torrey Pines Gulls became championship-quality pilots. Mark Smith, who was a member of both the Torrey Pines Gulls and the Harbor Slope

Soaring Society in Costa Mesa, captured four national titles and set a world endurance record for radio-controlled model sailplanes while soaring in Maui. Smith's radio-controlled seagulls were used in the filming of the movie Jonathan Livingston Seagull. Other members such as Don Edberg, and Steve Neu represented the United States in World Championships. David Fogel became Junior National Champion of the National Soaring Society in 1977 and Gary Fogel set a declared distance record for Class A radio-controlled sailplanes at Torrey Pines in 1995. New designs and equipment were designed and tested at Torrey Pines, and as a result, Torrey Pines became known as an "outdoor wind tunnel" for the testing of new gliders. The Torrey Pines Gulls club is currently known as one of the oldest and largest radio-controlled soaring clubs in the world. Other radio-controlled sailplane clubs such as a the Torrey Pines Scale Soaring Society organized in later years and continue to share the cliffs.

In the late 1960s, hang gliding experienced a "revival." No longer were the hang gliders as fragile and flimsy as in the early 1900s. Designs were patterned after the famous Rogallo flexible wing. In December of 1969, Australian Bill Bennett was the first to launch in a hang glider from the top of the cliff at the Torrey Pines Gliderport, landing on the beach below. Soon thereafter, Bob Wills became the first to launch, soar, and land a hang glider on the tops of the cliffs at Torrey Pines. Four world endurance records for hang gliders were set at Torrey Pines between 1972 and 1973. Taras Kiceniuk, Jr. (1 hour, 11 minutes; 2 hours and 26 minutes), Bob Wills (3 hours, 3 minutes), and Mike Mitchell (3 hours, 45 minutes) each set records. These pilots recognized the superb soaring conditions offered near San Diego. In the early 1970s, Torrey Pines was recognized as a hang glider mecca and since that time, numerous flight tests with new hang glider designs have been made at Torrey Pines. The site is internationally regarded as a focal point in the development of modern hang gliding.

By the late 1980s, paragliding was developing rapidly into an organized sport in Europe. Torrey Pines was one of the first sites in the United States where paragliding became as popular. Yet again, another new form of motorless flight called Torrey Pines home, and yet again, there was more confusion on how to handle all of the air traffic control in the name of safety. The Torrey Pines Soaring Council formed to help organize the flight activities. Each club was represented by one member on the Council and the Council acted as an advisory board to the City Parks and Recreation Department. The gliderport was still listed as an official landing facility with an airport identifier (CA84) and one paved runway (runway 9-27, 1,500 feet x 30 feet). The unpaved southeast-northwest cross runway was used as an emergency landing strip for sailplanes during winch launches.

Largely through the efforts of Larry and Gary Fogel, on June 6th, 1992, the National Soaring Museum dedicated the Torrey Pines Gliderport as a National Soaring Landmark by the National Soaring Museum. Torrey Pines was the fifth such designation in the United States and was the first site to receive this honor west of the Mississippi River. Pioneer glider pilots including Woody Brown, John Robinson, Bud Perl and many other San Diegan glider pilots attended the ceremonies. The city-owned portion of the gliderport was later dedicated as a City Historical Site (#315) in

1993. Letters of support from City Councilmember Abbe Wolfsheimer, Mayor Maureen O'Conner, Mayor Susan Golding, Governor Pete Wilson, Congressman Randy "Duke" Cunningham, Congressman Bill Lowery, Congressman Lynn Schenk, Senator Dianne Feinstein, and President Bill Clinton follow in Appendix 1.

Following the recommendation of the Historical Site Board on April 13th, 1993, the Council of the City of San Diego adopted resolution R-281753. This resolution recommended that the city-owned portion of the Torrey Pines Gliderport should be listed on the National Register of Historic Places. The City Council also resolved that the City Manager was directed to work with "appropriate persons from the University of California, San Diego...and the Torrey Pines Soaring Council to see if a compromise can be reached regarding any future development of the thirty (30) acres of the Torrey Pines Gliderport owned by the University of California, San Diego, that takes into account the needs of the University of California, San Diego but is compatible with the historic preservation of the site." With assistance from State and National historical agencies, eventually the entire Torrey Pines Gliderport was listed on both the California Register and National Register of Historic Places. Torrey Pines became the first gliderport to receive such designations in America.

Other former local soaring sites have received similar recognition. In the mid-1990s, through a push led by Bob Fronius, June Wiberg, and Dr. Donald Hunsaker, a plaque was placed above the ridge at Point Loma commemorating the early pioneers that flew American-designed and manufactured sailplanes in San Diego and Point Loma. In 1996, Point Loma was dedicated as the seventh National Soaring Landmark of the National Soaring Museum honoring specifically William Hawley Bowlus and John C. Barstow for their milestone flights in soaring history. In 2000, the Arvin-Sierra Gliderport was similarly established as the tenth National Soaring Landmark.

For more information on the various local clubs and organizations that promote the history of soaring in San Diego County, contact: the Associated Glider Clubs of Southern California (www.AGCSC.org), Torrey Pines Gulls Radio Controlled Soaring Club (www.TorreyPinesGulls.org), San Diego Hang Glider and Paraglider Association (http://home.san.rr.com/sdhgpa/), the Torrey Pines Flight Park (www.flytorrey.com), The Wing Is The Thing (http://members.home.net/twitt/), the San Diego Aerospace Museum (www.aerospacemuseum.org), the San Diego Historical Society (www.sandiegohistory.org), and the Torrey Pines Gliderport Historical Society (www.tpghs.org).

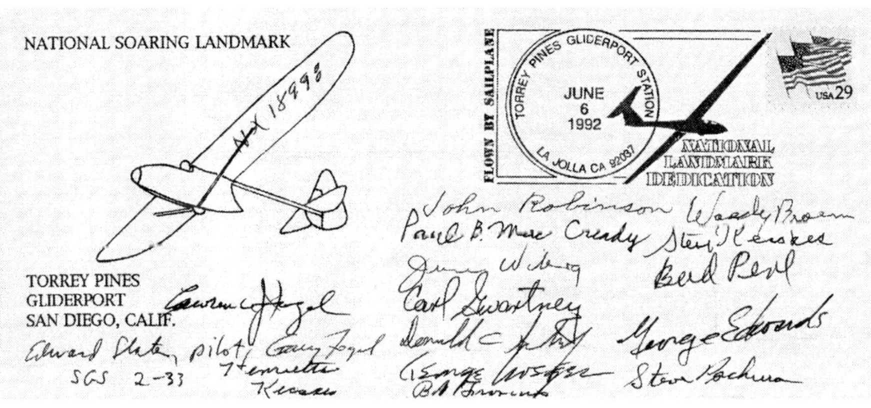


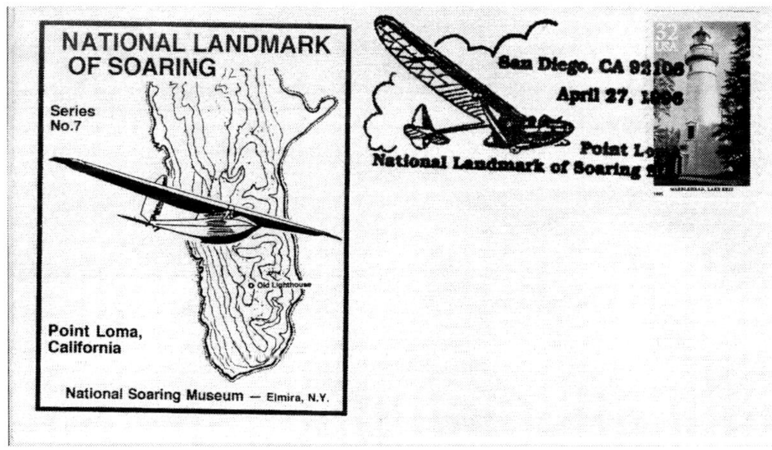


*Glider mail from the dedication of the National Soaring Landmark at Torrey Pines (top) and at Point Loma (bottom).*

# *Appendix 1*

## *Letters of Support*

Following the various historical designations of the Torrey Pines Gliderport, numerous letters and special resolutions were generated at the local, state, and federal levels. Nine of the more important letters and resolutions are shown in Appendix 1 and serve as a reminder that the historic value of the Torrey Pines Gliderport is firmly established and recognized.

# City Council of San Diego

# Special Commendation

## presented to

**TORREY PINES GLIDERPORT**

WHEREAS, the Torrey Pines Gliderport has served as a unique soaring site for over 60 years; and

WHEREAS, the beauty of such flight remains inspiring, but with recent developments near the Gliderport, the long term future of all soaring activities is in considerable jeopardy; and

WHEREAS, the National Soaring Museum's Landmark Program can help to preserve soaring at this unique and historic site; NOW, THEREFORE

BE IT PROCLAIMED, that I, Abbe Wolfsheimer, Councilmember for the First District of the City of San Diego, do hereby commend the Torrey Pines Gliderport, San Diego, California, for its role in furthering the history of soaring.

Abbe Wolfsheimer
Abbe Wolfsheimer
Councilmember
District 1

June 4, 1992
Date

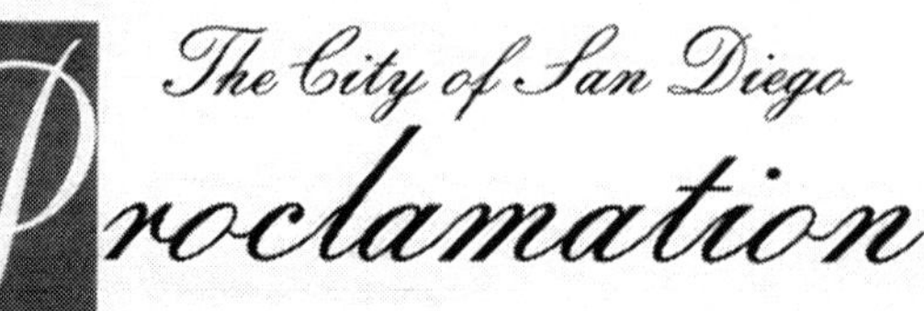


Presented By
The Office Of
The Mayor

**WHEREAS**. the Torrey Pines Gliderport has contributed greatly to the history of motorless flight; and

**WHEREAS**, on February 24, 1930, Charles A. Lindbergh flew in the lift at Torrey Pines on a flight from Mt. Soledad in La Jolla to Del Mar; and

**WHEREAS**, in the 1930's there were flights by Hawley Bowlus, Bud Perl, Richard Benbough, Woody Brown and John Robinson whose activities are well documented through years of soaring; and

**WHEREAS**, many well respected pilots including Bill Ivans and Paul MacCready developed their skills at Torrey Pines; and

**WHEREAS**, in the late 1960's the Torrey Pines Gulls Radio Controlled Soaring Society began operations chartered by the Academy of Model Aeronautics; and

**WHEREAS**, in the mid 1970's the Torrey Pines Hang Gliding Association began operations chartered by the U.S. Hang Gliding Association; and

**WHEREAS**, the Torrey Pines Soaring Council was established in the mid-1980s to regulate and ensure flight safety; and

**WHEREAS**, the Torrey Pines Paragliding Association and the Torrey Pines Scale Soaring Society began operations; and

**WHEREAS**, the National Soaring Museum, Soaring Society of America recently recognized Torrey Pines Gliderport as a National Landmark; and

**WHEREAS**, the University of California at San Diego Soaring Society join in the dedication ceremonials at which many of the early pioneers are expected to be present;

**NOW, THEREFORE, I MAUREEN O'CONNOR**, the Thirty-first Mayor of the City of San Diego, do hereby proclaim June 6, 1992 to be **"TORREY PINES GLIDERPORT DAY"** in San Diego.

IN WITNESS WHEREOF, I HAVE HEREUNTO SET MY HAND, THIS DAY, AND HAVE CAUSED THE SEAL TO BE AFFIXED HERETO:

Maureen O'Connor
MAUREEN O'CONNOR
MAYOR

June 3, 1992
DATE

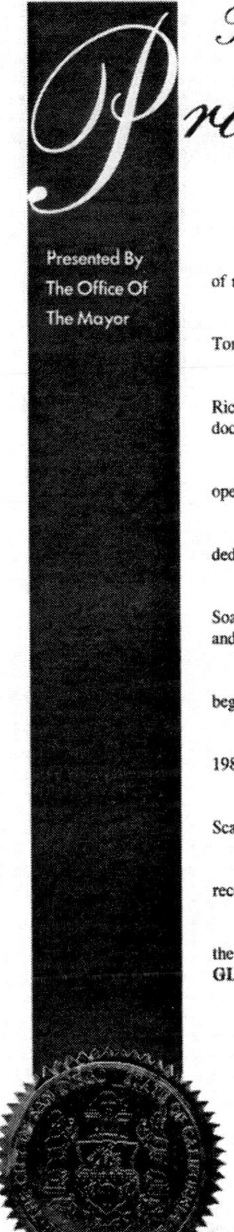


The City of San Diego

# Proclamation

## TORREY PINES GLIDERPORT

**WHEREAS,** the Torrey Pines Gliderport has contributed greatly to the history of motorless flight; and

**WHEREAS,** on February 24, 1930, Charles A. Lindbergh flew in the lift at Torrey Pines on a flight from Mt. Soledad in La Jolla to Del Mar; and

**WHEREAS,** in the 1930's there were flights by Hawley Bowlus, Bud Perl, Richard Benbough, Woody Brown and John Robinson whose activities are well documented through years of soaring; and

**WHEREAS,** the Associated Glider Clubs of Southern California have operated at Torrey Pines since 1937; and

**WHEREAS,** on January 1, 1939, the Mayor of San Diego, P.J. Benbough, dedicated the Torrey Pines Gliderport to the youth of California; and

**WHEREAS,** in the late 1960's the Torrey Pines Gulls Radio Controlled Soaring Society began operations chartered by the Academy of Model Aeronautics; and

**WHEREAS,** in the mid 1970's the Torrey Pines Hang Gliding Association began operations chartered by the U.S. Hang Gliding Association; and

**WHEREAS,** the Torrey Pines Soaring Council was established in the mid-1980s to regulate and ensure flight safety; and

**WHEREAS,** the Torrey Pines Paragliding Association and the Torrey Pines Scale Soaring Society began operations; and

**WHEREAS,** the National Soaring Museum, Soaring Society of America recognized Torrey Pines Gliderport as a National Landmark;

**NOW, THEREFORE, I, SUSAN GOLDING** the Thirty-second Mayor of the City of San Diego, do hereby proclaim March 21, 1993 to be **"TORREY PINES GLIDERPORT DAY"** in San Diego.

IN WITNESS WHEREOF, I HAVE HEREUNTO SET MY HAND, THIS DAY, AND HAVE CAUSED THE SEAL TO BE AFFIXED HERETO:

Susan Golding
SUSAN GOLDING
MAYOR

March 21, 1993
DATE

OFFICE OF THE GOVERNOR
State of California

March 21, 1993

I am delighted to join all gathered today to celebrate the dedication of the Torrey Pines Gliderport Historical Site #315 by the City of San Diego Historical Site Board.

This is indeed a momentous occasion for the people of San Diego and glider enthusiasts everywhere. For more than six decades, Torrey Pines has been a focal point for important motorless flight operations.

San Diegans are justifiably proud of the remarkable history of this site. It was the jumping off point for air pioneers like Bud Perl, Charles Lindbergh, and Woody Brown. It has also been the location of many important glider championships and films.

Torrey Pines is a beautiful place. It and its glider port add to the color and uniqueness of our great state.

To all attending, please accept my very best wishes for a most enjoyable and memorable event and every continued joy and success with Torrey Pines Gliderport in the years ahead.

Sincerely,

Pete Wilson

PETE WILSON

# RESOLUTION

**IN HONOR OF**
**TORREY PINES GLIDERPORT**
**June 6, 1992**

**WHEREAS**, during the 1920's and 1930's, the pioneers of motorless flight struggled to develop and test new and innovative designs of gliders; and

**WHEREAS**, throughout the twentieth century, numerous leaders and legends of aviation and glider history utilized the Torrey Pines area, including Charles Lindbergh, Hawley Bowlus, Bud Pearl, Richard Benbough, Woody Brown, John Robinson, Bill Ivans, Paul MacCredy and Richard Johnson; and

**WHEREAS**, the Torrey Pines Gliderport is under authority of the City of San Diego Parks & Recreation Department, with the advisory direction of the Torrey Pines Soaring Council and shared with the Torrey Pines Scale Soaring Society; and

**WHEREAS**, the Torrey Pines Gliderport has today been designated as a National Landmark by the National Soaring Museum of the Soaring Society of America; now therefore be it

**RESOLVED**, that in honor of the spirit, ingenuity and enthusiasm of the pioneers who flew at Torrey Pines and the future pilots who will share this gliderport and continue this tradition of motorless flight, Saturday, June 6, 1992 is hereby declared **"TORREY PINES GLIDERPORT DAY"** in the cities and communities of California's 44th Congressional District.

**IN WITNESS THEREOF, I HAVE HEREUNTO SET MY HAND THIS DAY, AND HAVE CAUSED THE GREAT SEAL OF THE UNITED STATES HOUSE OF REPRESENTATIVES TO BE AFFIXED HERETO:**

HOUSE OF REPRESENTATIVES
UNITED STATES

**RANDY "DUKE" CUNNINGHAM**
**Member of Congress**

WHEREAS, this day marks the dedication of a San Diego landmark which has served as a launching point for countless innovations in motorless flight, and has endured as the home for the pioneering and development of aviation as we know it today; and,

WHEREAS, San Diegans and flight enthusiasts from throughout the world have come to the Torrey Pines Gliderport to enjoy the many activities made possible by the warm westerly winds of the pacific, from homemade gliders towed off Black's Beach in the late 1920's, to today's high-tech hang gliders, paragliders and radio controlled model gliders; and,

WHEREAS, while it was the likes of Charles Lindbergh, Woody Brown, and John Robinson whose accomplishments made history at this famous site, this day would not be possible without the many people who have worked so hard through the years to maintain the grounds, ensure safety, and promote the events that made each daring feat so spectacular,

NOW THEREFORE, I, BILL LOWERY, Member of the United States House of Representatives and Representative of the People of the Forty-First Congressional District of the Great State of California, do hereby resolve that Saturday, June 6th, 1992 shall officially recognize the historical significance the **Torrey Pines Gliderport** as a landmark in the Forty-First Congressional District.

IN WITNESS WHEREOF, I have hereunto set my hand this the Sixth day of June, in the Year of Our Lord Nineteen Hundred and Ninety Two, and the Independence of the United States of America, the Two Hundred Sixteenth.

Bill Lowery

MEMBER OF CONGRESS

LYNN SCHENK
49TH DISTRICT, CALIFORNIA

Congress of the United States
House of Representatives
Washington, DC 20515-0549

March 21, 1993

**TO: THE TORREY PINES SOARING COUNCIL**
**On The Occasion of the Dedication of The Torrey Pines Glider Port as an Historic Site by the City of San Diego.**

Dear Friends:

On this occasion of the dedication of the Torrey Pines Glider Port as an Historic Site, I would like to offer my congratulations to the **TORREY PINES SOARING COUNCIL** for their hard work and perseverance in making this day possible.

Today, in celebrating the spirit and freedom of flight, we are reminded of those pioneers who have dared to soar. We mindful of their contributions and what their bravery and dedication has meant from generation to generation. Today, we salute these pioneers; individuals such as Hawley Bowlus, who supervised the building of the "Spirit of St. Louis", John Robinson who soared as a champion from these high, dangerous cliffs and Woody Brown who made the first launch and landing on top of the cliff. This afternoon, we are in the company of another such pioneer, **Bud Perl**, who flew from these cliffs in the late twenties. We are proud of the contributions they make to our community and to the history of flight.

We owe our appreciation to the **TORREY PINES SOARING COUNCIL** for their tireless work and dedication to the preservation of this site. In the words of the author*:

***"Oh Wind of heaven, by Thy might,***
***Save all who dare the Eagle's flight".***

Sincerely,

Lynn Schenk

Lynn Schenk
Member of Congress

* John Bacchus Dykes, 1861.

PRINTED ON RECYCLED PAPER

DIANNE FEINSTEIN
CALIFORNIA

# United States Senate

WASHINGTON, DC 20510-0504

March 21, 1993

The Torrey Pines Soaring Council

Dear Friends:

It is with great pleasure that I join the Torrey Pines Soaring Council and the citizens of San Diego in dedicating the Torrey Gliderport as the City of San Diego's Historical Site Number 315.

This site has contributed to the history of motorless flight. We remember the historic voyage by the famous aviator Charles A. Lindbergh on February 24, 1930, when he flew in a lift at Torrey Pines on a flight from Mt. Soledad to Del Mar.

It is most fitting that the National Soaring Museum of the Soaring Society of America has recognized the Torrey Pines Gliderport as a National Landmark.

I commend the Torrey Pines Soaring Council for their success in preserving this site as a national treasure for everyone to enjoy.

Sincerely Yours,

Dianne Feinstein
United States Senator

THE WHITE HOUSE

WASHINGTON

May 14, 1993

I am delighted that the Torrey Pines Gliderport has been designated a historic site by the City of San Diego.

Torrey Pines is part of a rich aviation tradition in Southern California. Since Professor John Montgomery's pioneer flight in 1884, thousands of Americans have enjoyed Torrey Pines' famous bluffs and stunning ocean views. Torrey Pines has played an important role in the development of new technology -- from the Robinson variometer to the Dead-man pulley take-off system -- and its natural beauty and serendipitous location have greatly advanced the sport of soaring.

As the only remaining gliderport in America that is directly adjacent to the Pacific Ocean, Torrey Pines serves as an extraordinary site for the enjoyment of all Americans who are interested in the wonders of human flight.

Bill Clinton

# *Appendix 2*

## *Photograph Credits*

### ***Organizations:***

National Soaring Museum: 2, 4, 70(a), 99(a), 136(a), 159, 166(b)-167, 187, 196, 198, 213, 217, 222(b).
Soaring Society of America: cover, 136(b,c)-137(b), 143, 150, 152(b)-153, 169, 178, 216, 227, 240, 242-243.
Associated Glider Clubs of Southern California: back cover, 234.
Vintage Sailplane Association, 235.

### ***Personal Collections:***

Collection of Richard H. Benbough: 21, 26-28, 32-33, 36-37, 41, 43, 45, 62, 64-65, 67-68, 76-77, 81, 88-92, 98, 104(a), 111, 117, 126, 146-147, 189(a), 192, 204, 223.
Collection of Blair Burkhardt: 132.
Collection of Gary Fogel: 99(b), 165, 241, 253-261.
Collection of Robert Fronius and June Wiberg: 152(a), 222(a).

Collection of Paul MacCready: 219, 229.
Collection of Patricia Moore: 174, 186, 191.
Collection of the Van Dusen family: 60, 118, 137(a).
Collection of A. M. O. Smith: 30, 48.
Collection of Lloyd Standley: 47, 73, 122-123.

## ***Books, Magazines, and Reviews:***

Edwin Way Teale, The Book of Gliders, E. P. Dutton and Co., Inc., New York, 1930: 70(b), 104(b).
Percival White and Mat White, Gliding and Soaring, Whittlesey House, McGraw-Hill Book Co., Inc., New York, 1931: 56(a), 57.
Emanuele Steiri, Gliders and Glider Training, Essential Books, Duell, Sloan, and Pearce, New York, 1943: 166(a), 172, 193.
The Callander: Camp Callan's Pictoral Review, Camp Callan, San Diego, California, August, 1943: 201.
Consolidator magazine: 144, 189(b).

## ***Three-view Drawings:***

Three-view drawings provided by David Sanders: 3 (derived from drawings by Herb Kelley as published in W.W.1 Aero magazine, May, 1989), 10 (derived from drawings of the Chanute-type hang glider published in *Popular Science* magazine, April, 1909 and from photos in Waldo: Pioneer Aviator by Waldo Dean Waterman and Jack Carpenter, Arsdalen, Bosch, and Co., Carlisle, MA, 1988), 13, 25, 50, 100, 133 (derived from drawings by Bob Marshall), 148 (derived from drawings by Charles Freel), 173 (derived from information provided by Martin Simons).

# *References*

## *Chapter 1-The Glider Pioneers, 1883-1927*

**John Montgomery**: Martin, Robert E., "American-Unknown to Fame First Man on Record to Leave Earth on Wings," *Popular Science*, Vol. 117, No. 4, October, 1930; Josselyn, Winsor, "He Flew in 1883," *Harper's Magazine*, Vol. 181, June, 1940; Montgomery, John J., "Some Early Gliding Experiments in America," *Aeronautics*, Vol. 4, No. 1, 1909; Siposs, George, *Hang Gliding Handbook-Fly Like A Bird*, Tab Books, PA, 1975; Spearman, Arthur D., *John Joseph Montgomery: Father of Basic Flying*, University of Santa Clara, Santa Clara, pg. 6, 7, 1967; Leitzell, Ted, "Sailboats in the Sky", *Esquire*, June, 1941; Leitzell, Ted, "Sailboats in the Sky," *Esquire*, June, 1941; McDonald, Jr., E. F., *Youth Must Fly*, Harper and Bros. Pub., New York, 1942; Hettich, John, "Montgomery and the Birds," *AeroDigest*, Vol. 52, No. 1, 1946; "The Montgomery Aeroplane," *Scientific American*, May 20, 1905; Crouch, Tom D., *The Bishop's Boys: A Life of Wilbur and Orville Wright*, W. W. Norton and Company, New York, 1989; Spearman, Arthur D., "John Joseph Montgomery, Father of Basic Flying," *Soaring*, March, 1968; Kelly, Fred C., "Montgomery's Great Glide," *Science Digest*, Vol. 27, No. 4, p. 81-83, April, 1950; Larson, O. H., "Montgomery Glider-1883," from the collection of the Southern California Historical Aviation Foundation, Apr. 30, 1985; *Los Angeles Daily Times*, August 29, 1883; Rhodes, W. T., "Montgomery Freeway Will Relieve Traffic in South San Diego," *California Highways*, Jan.-Feb., 1951; Short, Simine, *Glider Mail: An Aerophilatlic Handbook*, American Air Mail Society, 1987; "Kin of Montgomery Due in S. D. Today," *San Diego Union*, May 19, 1950; "First Glider Tower Takes Initial Flight," *San Diego Union*, May 21, 1950; Chanute, O., "Progress in Flying Machines," Lorenz and Herweg Pub., Long Beach, California, Facsimile of the 1894 ed., 1976. **Donald H. Gordon**: Hallert, Major George V. N. "Donald H. Gordon--Pioneer Flyer and Inventor", Historical Committee, San Diego Aerospace Museum; Scott, Mary *San Diego: Air Capital of the West*, The San Diego Aerospace Museum, 1991; *San Diego Union*, May 3, 1964; *Aeronautics*, Oct., 1910, p. 125. **Waldo D. Waterman**: Waterman, W. D. and Carpenter, J. *Waldo: Pioneer Aviator. A Personal History of American Aviation, 1910-1944,* Arsdalen, Bosch, and Co. 1988; Dewey, J. "Jonathan Livingston Seagull, Move Over!" *San Diego Magazine*, Vol. 25, No. 6, April 1973; Scott, Mary *San Diego: Air Capital of the West*, The San Diego Aerospace Museum, 1991; *San Diego Union*, newsclipping from July, 1959, San Diego Historical Society collection. **Frazier Curtis**: Breder, M. "Nostalgia Lane," *La Jolla Journal*, Nov. 14, 1963. **Halfway to Oz on a Magic Umbrella**: Personal Communication, Dr. Bard C. Cosman; Baum, L.

Frank, *Sky Island*, Books of Wonder, New York, 1912. **A. Clare Rand**: Hidden Valley Heritage-Escondido's First 100 Years 1888-1988 by Alan McGrew, p196; Autobiography of A. Clare Rand, Escondido Historical Society.

## *Chapter 2-Glider Fever in San Diego, 1928-1929*

**Max Shemer and Maury Tombler**: Personal collections of R. Benbough and G. Fogel. **Elmore E. Shoudy**: Various San Diego newspaper clippings, G. Fogel collection. **William Hawley Bowlus**: Teale, Edwin Way *The Book of Gliders*, Dutton and Co., Inc., New York, 1930. **Bowlus Sailplane #16 (493)**: Records of the United States Department of Commerce, G. Fogel collection; Benbough, R. "The Paper-wing Bowlus Sailplane" *Soaring*, May, 1982, pp.85-90. **Bowlus Sailplane #17 (599M)**: Records of the United States Department of Commerce, G. Fogel collection. **Dale Drake**: *Los Angeles Times*, April 7, 1929; *Los Angeles Times*, April 8, 1929; *San Francisco Chronicle*, April 8, 1929; Pierce, John *How to Build and Fly Gliders*, Popular Book Corporation, New York, 1930. **The Meysenburg Sailplane (3051)**: Records of the United States Department of Commerce, G.Fogel collection. **The Pacific Beach Glider Meets**: *San Diego Union*, July 2, 4-6, 1929; *San Diego Tribune*, July 2 and 5, 1929; *San Diego Sun*, July 2 and 5, 1929; Entrance form for the Pacific Coast Glider Meet, Aug. 31, Sept. 1st and 2nd, from the collection of R. Benbough; *San Diego Union*, Sept. 1-3, 1929; *San Diego Sun*, Aug. 30, Sept. 3, 1929; *Aviation*, Sept. 28, 1929; *Pacific Beach Society Newsletter*, Vol XII, No. 11, Nov. 1990. *San Diego Union*, Mar. 18, 1979; Pierce, John *Science, Art, and Communication*, Clarkson N. Potter, Inc., New York, 1968; Pierce, John *How to Build and Fly Gliders*, Popular Book Corporation, New York, 1930. **Contestants at the Pacific Beach Glider Meets**: Personal communication, David Park, 1999; *Model Airplane News*, Jan., 1979; Cebeci, Tuncer *Legacy of a Gentle Genius: the Life of A.M.O. Smith*, Horizons Publishing, Long Beach, 1999; *The Thermal*, June 1939. **The Evans Prize**: *AeroDigest*, June 1929. **Bowlus Establishes United States Glider Records**: *San Diego Union*, October 6, 1929; *Los Angeles Times*, October 6, 1929; *San Diego Evening Tribune*, October 7, 1929; *San Diego Sun*, October 7, 1929; *San Diego Sun*, October 19, 1929; *San Diego Union*, October 20, 1929; *San Francisco Chronicle*, Oct 20, 1929; *Newark Ledger*, October 29, 1929; Minutes of the Board of Directors and National Council-National Glider Association, November 23, 1929; *Popular Mechanics*, Oct, 1929; Teale, Edwin Way *The Book of Gliders*, 1930. **Stocks Fall While Gliders Soar**: *New York Times*, 1929. **Training New Glider Pilots**: *Aviation*, November 2, 1929; *San Diego Sun*, Nov 6, 1929. William F. Crawford's Motorglider: *Aviation*, Nov 23, 1929; *Popular Aviation*, August, 1930; "Glider to Go Over Oceanside" *Oceanside Blade-Tribune*, Nov. 27, 1929; Personal communication, Richard Benbough. **Cimmino and Leonard Primary Glider (593V)**: United States Department of Commerce records, G. Fogel collection. **McLean Northrup Primary Glider (594V)**: United States Department of Commerce records, G. Fogel collection. **Pacific Beach Glider Club**: Personal Communication, Lloyd Standley; United States Department of Commerce records, G. Fogel collection. **The Redondo Beach Glider Meet**: *Los Angeles Times*, Dec. 1, 1929; *Los Angeles Times*, Dec 2, 1929; *Redondo Reflex*, Dec 2, 1929; *Redondo Reflex* Nov 29, 1929; *Daily Breeze*, Dec 6, 1929; *Aviation*, December 14, 1929. **Bowlus Sailplane #18 (586V)**: *San Diego Sun*, December 4, 1929; *San Fernando Daily News*, December 4, 1929; *Los Angeles Times*, December 4, 1929; *San Diego Union*, December 4, 1929; *Aviation*, December 14, 1929; *Los Angeles Times*, Dec 11, 1929; *San Diego Union*, Dec 11, 1929; *Aviation*, Dec 21, 1929; *San Diego Union*, Dec 11, 1929. **Western Flyers Primary Glider (372V)**: United States Department of Commerce records, G. Fogel collection. **Robert Goebel Primary Glider (39W)**: United States Department of Commerce records, G. Fogel collection.

## *Chapter 3-The Golden Year, 1930*

**Soaring Records for Bowlus**: *San Diego Sun*, January 6, 1930; *San Diego Union*, January 7, 1930; Teale, Edwin Way *The Book of Gliders*, 1930; *Aviation*, January 18, 1930; *San Diego Sun*, January 12, 1930; *San Diego Union*, January 12, 1930; United States Department of Commerce Bureau of Standards Official Report, January 12, 1930; *San Diego Sun*, January 13, 1930; Clippings from various San Diego area newspapers, date unknown. G. Fogel Collection; *San Diego Union*, January 14, 1930; Press Release from the Aero Club of San Diego, January, 1930; *San Diego Union*, January 12, 1930; *San Diego Union*, January 15, 1930. **Bowlus Sailplane #20 (584V)**: United States Department of Commerce records, G. Fogel collection; *San Diego Union*, March 3, 1978. **Several Clubs Join to Form the Associated Glider Clubs of Southern California**: Scrapbook of Etta Mae Wallace, member of the Anne Lindbergh Gliders Club. **Charles Lindbergh Soars at Point Loma**: *San Francisco Examiner*, January 24, 1930; Bowlus, William Hawley "Lindbergh Learns to Glide," *Popular Mechanics Magazine* 53(4):529-530. April, 1930; *San Diego Union*, January 23, 1930; Newspaper clippings from various San Diego area newspapers, dates unknown. Collection of G. Fogel; *San Diego Union*, January 20, 1930; Van Dusen, William "Charles Lindbergh - Glider Pilot," *Western Flying*, May, 1930; Page, Victor W. *Henley's ABC of Gliding and Sailflying*, Norman W. Henley Pub. Co., New York, 1930; *San Diego Union*, January 22, 1930. **Bowlus Primary Glider G-1 (598M)**: Personal communication, Richard Benbough; United States Department of Commerce records, G. Fogel collection; Personal communication, Albert Gabbs. **Bowlus Primary Glider T-2 (365V)**: United States Department of Commerce records, G. Fogel collection. **Peaches Wallace**: *San Diego Union*, January 27, 1930; *San Diego Tribune*, January 27, 1930. **Mount Soledad**: *La Jolla Journal*, January 23, 1930; *La Jolla Light*, January 28, 1930. **Anne Morrow Lindbergh**: *San Francisco Chronicle*, January 30, 1930; *San Diego Union*, January 30, 1930; *Washington Post*, February 2, 1930; Lindbergh, Anne Morrow *Hour of Gold, Hour of Lead*; Teale, Edwin Way "It's the Newest Thing to Fly Like a Bird," *Popular Science Monthly*, May 1930; "Making America Glider Conscious" *The Literary Digest*, Feb 22, 1930; Van Dusen, Helen "Anne Flies a Home Product," *The Modern Clubwoman*, May, 1930; *La Jolla Light*, February 4, 1930; Personal communication, Bud Perl. **The Anne Lindbergh Gliders Club**: *San Diego Tribune*, January 27, 1930; *San Diego Sun*, January 31, 1930; *San Diego Union*, February 15, 1930; *San Diego Union*, February 16, 1930; *San Diego Tribune*, February 17, 1930; Records of the National Glider Association; Records of the Anne Lindbergh Gliders of San Diego. G. Fogel collection; Logbook of Helen Van Dusen; *San Diego Union*-Tribune, October 25, 1994; *San Diego Union*, February 18, 1930; United States Department of Commerce Records, G. Fogel collection; *San Diego History*, "Women in San Diego...a history in photographs," Volume 24, Number 3, 1978. **Glider Operations at Lebec, California**: *Los Angeles Times*, February 4, 1930; *Washington Post*, February 4, 1930; *Newark Star-Eagle*, February 8, 1930; *New York Times*, February 16, 1930; *Los Angeles Times*, February 6, 1930; *Los Angeles Times*, February 7, 1930; *Los Angeles Times*, February 9, 1930; *Oceanside Breeze*, November 23, 1988. **The Barr-Batzloff Sailplane (58W)**: United States Department of Commerce records, G. Fogel collection. **Gliders in La Jolla**: *La Jolla Light*, February 7, 1930; *La Jolla Light*, February 13, 1930; Personal communication, Lloyd Standley, 1997; Records of the Associated Glider Clubs of Southern California. G. Fogel collection; *La Jolla Light*, February 21, 1930; *San Diego Union*, February 24, 1930; *San Diego Sun*, February 24, 1930; *La Jolla Light*, February 25, 1930; *La Jolla Light*, April 15, 1930. **Bowlus Sets Another Record and Charles Lindbergh Soars on the Lift at Torrey Pines**: United States Department of Commerce Bureau of Standards Report of Glider Endurance Flight made by W. Hawley Bowlus at San Diego, California of February 23, 1930. G. Fogel collection; Newspaper clippings from San Diego area newspapers, date unknown. G. Fogel collection; *San Diego Sun*, February 25, 1930; *La Jolla Light*, February 28, 1930; *La Jolla Journal*, February 23, 1930; *La Jolla Journal*, February 27, 1930; *New York Times*, March 9, 1930; *Time*, March 10, 1930. **A Model Sailplane Meet**: *La Jolla Light*, February 28, 1930; *La Jolla Journal*, February 27, 1930; Newspaper clipping from San Diego area newspapers, date unknown. G. Fogel collection; *La Jolla Light*, March 4, 1930. **New Glider Rules Established**: Newspaper clipping from San Diego area newspapers, date unknown. G. Fogel collection; *Aviation*, April 26, 1930; *La Jolla Journal*, March 30, 1930; *La Jolla Light*, April 1, 1930; *La Jolla Journal*, April 3, 1930. **The South Bay Glider Club**: Newspaper clipping from San Diego area newspapers, date unknown. **The Girls' Division of the Mount Soledad Glider Club**:

*La Jolla Light*, March 7, 1930; *La Jolla Journal*, March 4, 1930; *La Jolla Light*, March 4, 1930; *La Jolla Light*, March 11, 1930; *La Jolla Journal*, March 13, 1930; *La Jolla Light*, March 25, 1930; *La Jolla Journal*, April 3, 1930. **Glider Flights Near Oceanside**: "Glider Flights From Bluff This Sunday, July 4" *Oceanside Blade-Tribune*, Jun. 27, 1930; "Glider Flights Create Interest" *Oceanside Blade-Tribune*, Jun. 30, 1930; "Glider to Fly Off the Bluff" *Oceanside Blade-Tribune*, Jul. 3, 1930; Records of the Oceanside Historical Society Meeting, Tuesday, April 26, 1994. **Bowlus Sailplane #19 (587V)**: United States Department of Commerce records, G. Fogel collection. **San Diego Senior High School Primary Gliders**: Newspaper clipping from San Diego area newspapers, date unknown. G. Fogel collection; *San Diego Tribune* clipping, G. Fogel collection. United States Department of Commerce records, G. Fogel collection. **Lindbergh Soars at Carmel, California**: *San Francisco Chronicle*, March 5, 1930; *San Francisco Chronicle*, March 6, 1930; *San Francisco Chronicle*, March 7, 1930; *San Francisco Chronicle*, March 8, 1930; *San Francisco Chronicle*, March 9, 1930; *New York Times*, March 9, 1930; *San Francisco Chronicle*, March 10, 1930; *San Francisco Chronicle*, March 14, 1930; *San Francisco Chronicle*, March 15, 1930; *San Francisco Chronicle*, March 16, 1930; Personal Communication, Bud Perl. **Harland Ross**: Logbook of Harland C. Ross. **The Y.M.C.A. "Y" Triangle Club**: United States Department of Commerce records, G. Fogel collection; *San Diego Union*, March 30, 1930. **Dedication of the Emerald Hills Golf Course**: *San Diego Union*, March 22, 1930; Photo of amphibian primary glider in Germany. G. Fogel collection; *San Diego Union*, March 23, 1930; Personal communication, Lloyd Standley, 1997; *San Diego Sun*, March 26, 1930; Van Dusen, Helen, Records of the Anne Lindbergh Gliders Club, 1930. **A Formation Glider Flight**: Newspaper clippings from various San Diego area newspapers. G. Fogel collection; *San Diego Union*, Mar 20, 1949. **Maurice Collins**: Newspaper clippings from the G. Fogel collection. **The Escondido Glider Club**: *San Diego Union*, March 31, 1930. **A Transcontinental Glider Tow**: The tow pilot's name has been recorded in books and newspapers as both "Jernigin" and "Jernigan." Since Frank Hawks adopted "Jernigin" for his book *Speed*, similar nomenclature has also been adopted in this book; Hawks, Frank. Speed. 1931; Bowers, Peter M. "Interesting Gliders," *Soaring*, July-August, 1954, pg. 22; *San Diego Tribune-Sun*, February 21, 1949; *Los Angeles Times*, March 28, 1930, Part II; *Los Angeles Times*, March 30, 1930; *New York Times*, March 30 through April 7, 1930; *New York Times*, April 13, 1930. **Public Relations and Glider Lessons**: Clippings from various San Diego area newspapers, date unknown. G. Fogel collection; *La Jolla Journal*, April 10, 1930; Log book of Helen Van Dusen; *La Jolla Journal*, April 17, 1930. **A Trip to the East Coast**: *Aviation*, April 12, 1930; "Planes, Engines, and Accessories at the Detroit Show," *Aviation*, April 19, 1930; *San Diego Sun*, April 29, 1930; *Aviation*, May 3, 1930; *Aviation*, May 10, 1930; Teale, Edwin Way, "How to Get Into Gliding," *Popular Science*, April 1930; Jordanoff, Assen, "Gliding Made My Flying Better," *Popular Science Monthly*, September, 1930. **Bowlus Sailplanes #22 (589V) and #23 (590V)**: United States Department of Commerce records, G. Fogel collection. **An Unofficial World Record**: *San Diego Sun*, April 29, 1930; Barstow, Jack, "How I Broke the World's Glider Record," *Popular Mechanics Magazine*, 54:1-3, July, 1930; *Aviation*, May 10, 1930; Barstow, Jack, "How I Broke the World's Glider Record," *Popular Mechanics Magazine*, 54:1-3, July, 1930; *San Diego Union*, June 17, 1930; Letter from D. F. Walker to W. Van Dusen dated May 3, 1930; *San Diego Union*, Mar 20, 1949. **Glider Activities in San Diego**: Clippings from various San Diego newspapers, date unknown. G. Fogel collection; Logbook of Helen Van Dusen; *San Diego Union*, May 21, 1930; *Hi-Tide Newsletter of the La Jolla Junior-Senior High School*, May 29, 1930; Personal communication, Lloyd Standley; *San Francisco Chronicle*, June 12, 1930; United States Department of Commerce records, G. Fogel collection. **Sterling Owen and Robert Goebel**: United States Department of Commerce records, G. Fogel collection; Photo, San Diego Historical Society collection; Logbook of Harland C. Ross. **Bowlus Sailplane #24 (315W)**: United States Department of Commerce records, G. Fogel collection. **Bowlus Sailplane #25 (316W)**: United States Department of Commerce records, G. Fogel collection; *Soaring* January, 1937. **Bowlus Sailplane #26 (317W)**: United States Department of Commerce records, G. Fogel collection. **Bowlus Sailplane #27 (318W)**: United States Department of Commerce records, G. Fogel collection. **Bowlus Sailplane #28 (319W)**: United States Department of Commerce records, G. Fogel collection. **Bowlus Sailplane #29 (320W)**: *Aviation*, June 28, 1930; Benbough, Richard "The Convertible Albatross," *Soaring*, May, 1984. **Bowlus Sailplane #30 (321W)**: United States Department of Commerce records, G. Fogel collection. **Bowlus Sailplane #31 (10144)**: United States Department of Commerce records, G. Fogel collection. **H. Grafton Chapman Flies a Hydro-Glider**: Clippings from various San Diego newspapers, date unknown. G. Fogel collection. **Exhibition Glider Flights at Morena**: *San Diego Union*, July 2, 1930; Logbook of Helen Van Dusen. **Dedication of the Peaches Wallace Gliderport**: Wallace, Peaches "Activities of the Anne Lindbergh Glider Club for Girls," *Aviation Mechanics*, July-August, 1930; *Popular Mechanics*, June 1930; *San Diego Sun*, July 1930; *San Diego Sun*, July 24, 1930; *San Diego Union*, July 28, 1930; Letter from J. H. Rainwater to Mrs. H. K. W. Kumm dated July 28, 1930. G. Fogel collection; Logbook of Harland C. Ross. **Western Flyers Club Gliders #4 (681W) and #5 (682W)**: United States Department of Commerce, records, G. Fogel collection. **Essery, Dickenson, Freedman Glider #2 (683W)**: United States Department of Commerce, records, G. Fogel collection. **Gliding Activities in Fall, 1930**: *San Diego Union*, August 3, 1930; Letter to Etta May Wallace from Mrs. H. K. W. Kumm dated August 8, 1930; Report of the National Glider Association, August 23, 1930; Perl, Bud "I Learn to Fly a Glider," *Popular Mechanics*, August, 1930; Personal communication, Richard Benbough; *San Diego Union*, August 4, 1930; United States Department of Commerce records, G. Fogel collection. Personal communication, Albert Gabbs. **Dr. H. Karl William Kumm**: *San Diego Union*, August 23, 1930. **Ruth Alexander**: Clippings from various San Diego newspapers, date unknown. G. Fogel collection; Personal communication, Helen Van Dusen. **Bowlus Sailplane Company Closes**: Personal communication, Bud Perl. **Bowlus Leaves San Diego**: Personal communication, Richard Benbough. **Aerial Shows at Lindbergh Field and Ryan Airport**: *San Diego Union*, October 12, 1930; *San Diego Union*, November 9, 1930. **Harland Ross and the "Silver King" (908Y)**: Santille, Alcide "Harland, the Man I Knew," *Soaring*, May, 1982; Logbook of Harland C. Ross. **Primary Gliders at Torrey Pines**: Personal communication, Richard Benbough; Personal communication, John Robinson; Archives of the National Soaring Museum; *San Diego Union*, December 18, 1930; *San Diego Union*, December 19, 1930.

## *Chapter 4-From Point Loma to Torrey Pines and Beyond, 1931-1940*

**Glider Activities in 1931-1933**: Logbook of Harland C. Ross; Letter from Van Dusen to D. Walker, G. Fogel collection; Progress report of the National Glider Association, March 1931; *San Diego Union*, March 14, 1931; Records of the La Jolla High School Alumni Association; *Los Angeles Times*, August 27, 1931; *San Diego Union*, April 3, 1932; *San Diego Sun*, May 7, 1933; various San Diego newspapers, May 21, 1933. **A Connection to San Diego**: *San Francisco Chronicle*, March 9, 1931; *Soaring*, January, 1937; *Soaring*, January, 1938; Blacksten, R. *Soaring* Dec., 1991; *Los Angeles Times*, July 27, 1931; *New York Times*, November 22, 1931; *New York Times*, November 28, 1931; *San Diego Union*, December 3, 1931; *Los Angeles Times*, December 18, 1931; *Los Angeles Times*, December 19, 1931. **Gliding Activities in 1934-1935**: National Soaring Museum archives; *The Gliding and Soaring Bulletin*, May 1, 1935; *Consolidator*, May, 1939; *The Surfer's Journal* 5(3), 1996; Personal communication, Woody Brown (care of Nicole Dods), John Robinson, and Steve Kesckes; *San Diego Union*, November 8, 1935. **1935-1936 California Pacific International Exposition**: *San Diego Union*, March 15, 1936; *San Diego Union* March 16, 1938; *San Diego Union*, August 31, 1936. **Carl Goller**: *San Diego Sun*, September 18, 1936. **Glider Badges**: Schweizer, P. *Wings Like Eagles: The Story of Soaring in the United States*, Smithsonian Institution, 1988. **The Robin #3 Sailplane**: Personal communication, John Robinson; *Soaring*, July, 1938. **The Ross-Stephens R.S.-1 "Zanonia"**: *Soaring*, October, 1937; *Soaring*, April, 1938; *The Thermal*, January, 1939. **Jerry Litell**: *Consolidator*, July, 1937. **The Freel Flying Wing (18131)**: *Parade of Youth*, July 25, 1937; Hilbert, C. L. *Consolidator*, 1937; Maloney, E. T. *Northrop Flying Wings*, Planes of Fame Publishers, Inc., 1975. **Soaring at the Salton Sea**: Brown, W. P. "Hunting Thermals by a Sea in the Desert," *Soaring*, December, 1937. **The Associated Glider Clubs of Southern California**: *Consolidator*, November, 1937; *Soaring*, March, 1938; *Soaring*, December, 1938; Personal communication, John Robinson. **The Auto Tow Pulley Takeoff System**: Barringer, L. *Flight Without Power*, p.90 Pitman Pub. Co., New York, 1942; Personal communication, John Robinson. **A Regional Competition**: *Soaring*, September, 1937; *Soaring*, November, 1937. **A Lease for Torrey Pines**: San Diego City records; San Diego City Ordinance 1285;

Lease to the Associated Glider Clubs of Southern California for the Torrey Pines Gliderport, G. Fogel collection; *Soaring*, July, 1938. **The Robinson Variometer**: Personal communication, John Robinson. **The Bowlus Baby Albatross**: *Aviation*, March, 1938; *Soaring*, April, 1938; *San Diego Union*, Feb 11, 1940; *American Aviation*, February 15, 1940; *Soaring*, Feb.-Mar., 1940; *Soaring*, Jan. 1983. **Glider Meets at Arvin**: *Soaring*, June, 1938; *Soaring*, July, 1938; *Soaring*, October, 1938. **Desert Thermals**: *San Diego Sun*, May 12, 1938; *Soaring*, October, 1938; Vosbaugh, F. G. "Men-Birds Soar on Boiling Air," *National Geographic* July, 1938; *Soaring*, July, 1938; *The Surfer's Journal* 5(3), 1996; Personal communication, Steve Kesckes and John Robinson. **Robert Stanley**: *Soaring*, January, 1938; *Soaring*, March, 1938; *Soaring*, August, 1938; *Soaring*, September, 1938; Records on Robert Stanley care of the National Soaring Museum archives. **Thermals for Harland Ross**: *Soaring*, November, 1938. **San Diego Soaring Activities**: *Soaring*, November, 1938; Personal communication, John Robinson; *San Diego Sun*, December 31, 1938; Clippings from various San Diego newspapers, dates unknown. G. Fogel collection. **Dedication of the Torrey Pines Gliderport**: *Soaring*, February, 1939; Personal communication, John Robinson; Clippings from various San Diego newspapers, date unknown. G. Fogel collection. **Thermals from Torrey Pines**: *Soaring*, December, 1939; Personal communication, John Robinson. **A Club Grunau 8**: *Consolidator*, March, 1939; *Consolidator*, May, 1939; *Soaring*, August, 1939; Spurgeon, J. "San Diego Gliding History," Collection of the Vintage Sailplane Association (the reader should note that this latter document has several inconsistencies, many of which were corrected in the development of this book). **The Thunder Bird**: Personal communication, John Robinson; *Soaring*, July, 1939. **The Dedication of the Arvin-Sierra Soaring Site and the Third Annual Western Soaring Championships**: *Soaring*, May, 1939. **Blair Dry Lake**: *San Diego Union*, May 8, 1939; *Soaring*, June, 1939. **San Diegans at National Contests in 1939**: *Soaring*, July, 1939; *San Diego Union*, June 6, 1939; *Soaring*, September, 1939; *Soaring*, Jan 1940; *Soaring, Jan-Feb, 1941. Wichita Daily Times*, June 7, 1939; Personal communication, John Robinson. **Soaring in San Diego**: Personal communication Woody Brown; *Soaring*, August, 1939; *Soaring*, October, 1939; *Soaring*, November, 1939; *Consolidator*, September, 1939; *Soaring*, December, 1939. **A Midwinter Glider Party**: *Soaring*, February-March, 1940; *Western Flying*, March, 1940. **Activities at the Torrey Pines Gliderport**: *Consolidator*, February, 1940; *San Diego Union*, March 4, 1940; *Consolidator*, March, 1940. **San Diegans at National Contests in 1941**: *Soaring*, April-May, 1940; Consolidator, May, 1940; Personal communication, Woody Brown; McReynolds, C. "Soaring on the West Coast" *Aviation*, June 1940; *Soaring*, June-July, 1940; *San Diego Union*, June 8, 1940; *Consolidator*, August, 1940; *San Diego Union*, Jun 16, 1940; Robinson, J. "Early Days," *Soaring*, June, 1987; *San Diego Union*, July 2, 1940; Soaring, August-September, 1940; *San Diego Union*, Aug 1, 1940; *San Diego Union*, Aug. 2, 1940; *San Diego Union*, Aug. 9., 1940; *The Thermal*, Sept., 1940; *San Diego Union*, Sept 1, 1940; *Soaring*, March-April, 1941. **Activities in San Diego**: *Consolidator*, August, 1940; *Consolidator*, September, 1940; *The Thermal*, September, 1940; *San Diego Union*, Aug, 29, 1940; *Consolidator*, November, 1940.

## *Chapter 5-The War Years*

**United States Army Camp Callan**: Resolution 72901, records of the City Clerk, G. Fogel collection; San Diego Tribune-Sun, Oct. 31, 1940; The Oozlefinsh: Camp Callan's Pictoral Review, Third Ed. May, 1943, Public Relations OFfice of Anti-aircraft Replacement Training Center Camp Callan; Schulman, J. P. "WWII triggers weapons training center" Traditions, July, 1994; Simpich, F. "San Diego Can't Believe It" National Geographic, January, 1942. **Local Soaring Clubs**: Consolidator, April 1941; Personal communication, Doug Fronius. **San Diegans at National Competitions in 1941**: San Diego Union, April 26, 1941; San Diego Union, April 29, 1941; Aviation, June, 1941; Robinson, John "Early Days" Soaring, June, 1987; San Francisco Chronicle, July 14, 1941. **Glider Schools**: San Francisco Chronicle, November 29, 1941; Jackson, H.E. "Sailplane Seminary" Flying, 31:22-24, 1942; Time, June, 29, 1942; Soaring, Mar-Apr. 1942; Soaring, Jan-Feb., 1946. **H. Grafton Chapman**: San Diego Union, December 12, 1928; San Diego Union, Oct 31, 1942. **Robinson Soars Over Mount Whitney**: *Soaring*, Mar.-Apr., 1944.

## *Chapter 6-Post War Soaring 1946-1950*

**Interest in Gliding Stirs Again**: *San Diego Union*, March 4, 1946; *Soaring* May-June, 1946; *San Diego Union*, March 15, 1946; *Bungee Cord*, Winter 97/98; Ordinance No. 3209, G. Fogel collection; *San Diego Tribune-Sun*, Oct. 29, 1946. **San Diegans at National Competitions in 1946**: *Soaring*, Sept-Oct., 1946; *Flying*, Dec. 39:38-42, 1946. **First Annual Pacific Coast Midwinter Championships**: *San Diego Union*, January, 12, 1947; *San Diego Journal*, Itinerary 23, 1947; *Aviation News Beacon*, February 6, 1947; *San Diego Union*, February 28, 1948; *Wind and Wings*, Mar, 1969; *San Diego Union*, June 1, 1947. **San Diegans at National Competitions in 1947**: *Soaring,* May-June, 1947; *Soaring*, Sept-Oct., 1947; *Soaring*, May-June, 1949; *Soaring*, Jul-Aug, 1947; *Soaring*, Jan-Feb., 1948. **The Second Annual Pacific Coast Midwinter Championships**: *San Diego Union*, February 15, 1948; *San Diego Union*, Feb 28, 1948; *Soaring*, Mar.-Apr., 1948; *San Diego Union*, March 1, 1948; *Soaring*, Jul-Aug., 1948. **San Diegans at National Competitions in 1948**: *Soaring*, Jul.-Aug.,1948; *Air Trails*, November, 1948; *Soaring*, Sept.-Oct., 1948. **El Mirage Dry Lake**: *Soaring*, July-August, 1954; *Soaring*, Nov.-Dec., 1948. **Bishop and the Sierra Wave**: *Flying*, June, 1949. **The Third Annual Pacific Coast Midwinter Championships**: *San Diego Union*, February 20, 1949; *San Diego Union*, Feb 27, 1949; *Soaring*, Nov.-Dec. 1949, *Soaring*, Jul.-Aug., 1949; *San Diego Tribune*, February 28, 1949. **Nation's Youngest Glider Pilot**: San Diego Newsclipping, April 23, 1949; *Soaring,* Jul.-Aug., 1949; *Soaring*, Nov.-Dec., 1949; *Wind and Wings*, Feb, 1961. **The Sierra Mountain Wave Project**: Schweizer, P. *Wings Like Eagles: The Story of Soaring in the United States*, Smithsonian Institution, 1988. **The Fourth Annual Pacific Coast Midwinter Soaring Championship**: "Cliff Hangar," *Soaring*, Feb, 1971. **A Night Flight at Torrey Pines**: *Soaring*, February, 1971. **Montgomery Field**: *San Diego Union*, May 19, 1950; *San Diego Union*, May 21, 1950; *Soaring*, Jan.-Feb., 1949. **John Robinson, First Diamond "C" in the World**: Schweizer, P. *Wings Like Eagles: The Story of Soaring in the United States*, Smithsonian Institution, 1988. **Bill Ivans**: Schweizer, P. *Wings Like Eagles: The Story of Soaring in the United States*, Smithsonian Institution, 1988.

# *Glossary*

**Aerial Train** One or more gliders towed cross-country behind a powered airplane.

**Aerobatic** Acrobatic maneuvers in flight, such as loops, spins, and rolls.

**Aerotow** Launching of a glider or sailplane by means of a cable attached to the rear of a powered aircraft, the powered plane towing the glider to altitude, the cable released by the glider pilot.

**Aileron** A movable surface for lateral control usually found on the outer rear portion of the wing, but occasionally at the very tip of the wing (see Tip-aileron).

**Airfoil** Cross-section design of a wing or lifting surface.

**Airspeed** The speed of an airplane through the air.

**Airspeed indicator** An instrument used for registering the speed of an airplane through the air.

**Altimeter** An instrument used for registering the height of an airplane above the ground from which it took off.

**Anchor men** Members of the launching crew who hold the tail while the shock cord is stretched.

**Aspect ratio** The ratio of wingspan to the mean chord of the wing.

**Auto tow** Launching of a glider or sailplane by means of a cable attached to the rear of an automobile. The automobile is driven forward to provide sufficient airspeed for flight. The cable is released by the pilot upon reaching best altitude on take-off.

**Aviatrix** A woman aviator.

**Ballast** Additional weight added to a sailplane, usually on the center of gravity to increase speed on cross-country flights.

**Biplane** An airplane with two wings set one above the other.

**Blind soaring** Soaring through clouds or mist without visual reference to the horizon.

**Bulkheads** The partitions of the enclosed fuselage of a soaring plane.

**Bungee Cord** See Shock cord.

**Cabane** A structure on the top of a glider fuselage forming support for the wings.

**Cabin fuselage** A fuselage with an enclosed cockpit such as on Frank Hawks' *Eaglet.*

**Canard** An aircraft having an elevator in front of the wing rather than behind.

**Cantilever** A wing having internal supporting structure.

**Center of gravity** The center of weight of an airplane.

**Chord** The width of a wing measured from the leading edge to the trailing edge.

**Cockpit** The open space in which the pilot is accommodated. When the cockpit is completely enclosed, it is sometimes referred to as a cabin.

**Control surface** The surfaces that control the lateral and longitudinal movements of the glider. The ailerons, rudder, and elevators.

**Crewing** see Ground crew.

**Cross-country flight** A flight away from a home airport over generally unfamiliar territory.

**Dihedral** The angle at which the wings rise from the fuselage relative to the wing tips.

**Drag** A retarding force due to aerodynamic resistance.

**Dry lake** A seasonal lake common to desert communities that is filled with water following winter rains and completely dry by late spring through summer. Dry lakes are particularly useful for glider pilots as they represent wide-open spaces suitable for launching and landing as well as providing a surface to generate exceptional thermals.

**D-tube** Structure formed by a combination of spar and curved metal or plywood surfaces of an aircraft.

**Dual control** A double set of controls so that either the pilot or the passenger (co-pilot) can operate the aircraft.

**Duralumin** An aluminum alloy which possesses a combination of lightness and strength.

**Elevator** Hinged, horizontal tail surface for controlling vertical movement.

**Empennage** The tail of the glider, including horizontal and vertical stabilizing and control surfaces.

**Empty weight** Weight of an aircraft without pilot or equipment.

**Fabric** The cloth used to cover the wings of a glider.

**Fin** Fixed, vertical tail surface for longitudinal stability.

**Flaps** Movable surfaces hinged to the trailing edge of the wing to facilitate approaches to landings by increasing lift and drag.

**Flipper** A synonym for elevator.

**Flying wing** An aircraft with no vertical or horizontal tail surfaces.

**Fuselage** The body of the airplane.

**Glide** To maintain flying speed by "coasting downhill" on the air, the pull of gravity furnishing the power.

**Glider** A form of aircraft similar to an airplane but without an engine. In general usage, all motorless planes, whether soaring craft or primary training gliders, are called gliders.

**Gliderport** An airfield or airport used by motorless aircraft.

**Gliding angle** The angle at which the gliding descent is made, usually the flattest angle at which flying speed can be maintained (see Minimum gliding angle).

**Gliding ratio** Ratio of distance covered horizontally to height lost vertically.

**Gross weight** Weight of an aircraft fully loaded with pilot and equipment.

**Ground crew** Persons that aid with the launch and handling of gliders while on the ground, and by following the glider in a chase car to meet the plane following landing.

**Ground loop** A rapid 180° to 360° turn made on the ground following landing.

**Ground speed** The speed of an aircraft relative to the ground. This may be faster or slower than the airspeed of the machine depending upon whether it is flying with a tail wind or into a head wind.

**Hang glider** A flying machine in which the pilot hangs from the wing of the aircraft and maintains balance by shifting his body weight.

**Hop** A short flight.

**Hydroglider** A glider equipped with pontoons for taking off and landing on water.

**Leading edge** The foremost, or entering, edge of a wing.

**Lenticular cloud** A cloud formed by high winds deflected over a mountain range to high altitudes. Lenticular clouds are generally associated with conditions of a "standing wave" in the air, that can be used for extremely high altitude soaring flights.

**Lift** The force exerted by the air on a plane in a direction perpendicular, or nearly so, to the motion.

**Longeron** Principal longitudinal structural members of a fuselage.

**Monoplane** An aircraft with one main supporting surface or wing.

**Motorglider** A glider or sailplane with an engine added for launching or as an aid for maintaining altitude in non-soaring conditions.

**Minimum gliding angle** The flattest angle at which a machine will maintain flying speed in a glide.

**Monocoque** A type of fuselage construction, the strength of which is largely in a metal or plywood shell due to its round or oval design.

**Nacelle** An enclosed body, usually shorter than a fuselage and not carrying the tail unit.

**Overall length** The distance from the farthest point forward to the farthest point back on a glider.

**Pontoons** Floats for supporting an aircraft on water.

**Primary glider** A type of glider common in the late 1920s and early 1930s used generally for instructional purposes. The fuselage is usually of an open framework construction, the pilot sitting exposed at the front of the aircraft.

**Pyralin** A transparent material used for windows in some sailplanes of the 1930s and 1940s.

**Ribs** The members used in a wing to give it strength and shape in a fore-and-aft direction.

**Ridge** An elevation or line of hills long in proportion to its width.

**Ridge soaring** Using the lift generated by wind deflected over a ridge to maintain or gain altitude in a glider or sailplane. Also known as slope soaring.

**Rudder** Vertical, hinged tail surface for directional control in horizontal plane.

**Rudder post** The upright member to which the rudder is hinged.

**Sailplane** A streamlined flying machine capable of sustained free flight without self-propulsion by extracting energy from the atmosphere in the form of lift. Sailplanes can be made to soar more easily than secondary or primary gliders because of attention to design, decreased drag and increased aspect ratio.

**Secondary glider** A glider with an enclosed cockpit used for instruction in gliding and soaring in the 1930s and 1940s. Secondary gliders are generally more streamlined than primary gliders, and under the right conditions can be made to soar.

**Shock cord** A rubber cable which is attached to the nose of a glider for launching it, like a slingshot, into the air. The first cables used were regulation shock cord designed for airplane landing gears, hence the name. Also known as a "bungee cord" or "bungee."

**Single-place** A sailplane made for one pilot and no passengers.

**Skid (noun)** The runner, usually composed of wood or metal and placed under the nose, that a glider slides on during takeoff and landing.

**Skid (verb)** A sideways, slipping maneuver resulting from over-control of the rudder.

**Slope soaring** see Ridge soaring.

**Span** see Wingspan.

**Spar** The beam used as the principal structural unit of the wing.

**Spoiler** A hinged control surface usually on the upper surface of the wing used to decrease lift and increase drag for landing or descent.

**Spot landing** A landing made at a predetermined point.

**Stabilizer** A fixed, horizontal tail surface for vertical stability.

**Stall** A loss of lift due to insufficient airspeed over the wing.

**Standing wave** see Lenticular cloud.

**Stringer** A light, longitudinal structural member to stiffen a fuselage.

**Strut** A bar or rod used as an outside structural member of an aircraft.

**Tandem wing** An aircraft having one wing set directly in front of another.

**Tapering wings** Wings that have more chord at the fuselage than at the tips.

**Tail skid** A small skid under the rear of the fuselage to protect the tail assembly on takeoff and landing.

**Thermals** Rising air currents formed by the sun's heat radiated from the earth.

**Thermal soaring** Soaring by the use of finding thermal lift and avoiding areas of sink.

**Tip-aileron** A type of control system where the entire wingtip can be rotated to provide lateral stability.

**Towline** A rope, cable, or wire used to tow a glider into the air.

**T-tail** A tail configuration where the stabilizer and elevator lie on top of the vertical fin and rudder.

**Trailing edge** The rear edge of a wing.

**Two-place** A sailplane made for one pilot and one passenger.

**V-tail** A tail configuration where the standard horizontal and vertical components are combined in the shape of a "V" configuration.

**Variometer** An instrument used to indicate the rise or descent rate of an aircraft.

**Vee-tail** See V-tail.

**Vertical fin** A fixed surface attached parallel to the longitudinal axis of an aircraft in order to secure stability.

**Wave soaring** see Lenticular cloud.

**Winch launch** Launching of a glider or sailplane by means of a cable attached to a winch, the cable being pulled in by the winch providing sufficient speed for glider flight. The cable is released by the pilot upon reaching best altitude after takeoff.

**Wing** The main supporting surface of an aircraft.

**Wing area** The area of the supporting surfaces of an aircraft, including ailerons, but not the stabilizer or elevator.

**Wing loading** The weight of the glider, fully loaded, divided by the area of the supporting surface. The area used in computing the wing loading should include ailerons but not the stabilizer or elevator.

**Wingspan** The distance between the wing tips of an aircraft.

**Yaw** To turn flatly from side to side.

# *Index*

## C

**D**



**E**

### N



### O



### P

**W**



**Y**

# About the Author

Gary Fogel has been flying radio-controlled model sailplanes since 1975 when his father Larry taught him to fly at the Torrey Pines Gliderport at the age of 7. In 1995, Gary established the current United States declared distance record for class-A hand launched gliders of 4.19 miles. He is currently a contributing editor to Sailplane and Electric Modeler magazine, where he writes a column focusing on the history of soaring. Several of his articles have appeared in other journals. Gary is currently serving as the representative of the Soaring Society of America to the Torrey Pines Soaring Council and is a Leader Member and Contest Director in the Academy of Model Aeronautics. With a Ph.D. in biology, he currently works at Natural Selection, Inc. His research focuses on the application of computational methods for solving problems in biomedicine and biochemistry.